JUMBO BIBLE WORD GAMES

VOL. 1

BARBOUR BOOKS

An Imprint of Barbour Publishing, Inc.

S0-ARV-691

ISBN 1-58660-234-9

All Scripture quotations, unless otherwise noted, are taken from the King James Version of the Bible.

Published by Barbour Books, an imprint of Barbour Publishing, Inc., P.O. Box 719, Uhrichsville, OH 44683 http://www.barbourbooks.com

Member of the
Evangelical Christian
Publishers Association

Printed in the United States of America.

JUMBO
BIBLE
WORD
GAMES

VOL. 1

INTRODUCTION

Welcome to *Jumbo Bible Word Games Volume 1*! Here are more than four hundred pages of challenging and fun word games, all based on the greatest book of all time—the Bible. Featuring traditional crossword puzzles, "Triple Challenge Word Searches," acrostics, "CryptoScriptures," anagrams, and more, you'll have hours of enjoyment and edification.

Eleven types of word games are mingled throughout the pages of this book. Instructions, along with the names of contributors, are at the beginning of each section—please be sure to look them over before you launch into the puzzles. Answers begin on page 413.

Pencils ready? Then put your skills to the test with *Jumbo Bible Word Games Volume 1*!

DROP TWO
PUZZLES

by Dorothy Pryse

Remove two letters from each seven-letter word in the left-hand column to create a new five-letter word (you may need to rearrange the remaining letters). Put the two dropped letters into the spaces to the right of the blanks. Then use these letters to spell out a phrase or sentence from the Bible.

Acts

BLEMISH	Facial move	_____	1. ___ ___
DECEASE	Packaged	_____	2. ___ ___
CHATHAM	Igniter	_____	3. ___ ___
OVERACT	Sketch	_____	4. ___ ___
GENERAL	Stove	_____	5. ___ ___
NIBBLED	Holy book	_____	6. ___ ___
SEABIRD	Facial hair	_____	7. ___ ___
PLUMOSE	Feather	_____	8. ___ ___
PIERCED	Wept	_____	9. ___ ___
ENDWISE	Breezes	_____	10. ___ ___
NESTING	Burn lightly	_____	11. ___ ___
UNHOPED	16 ounces	_____	12. ___ ___
UNYOKED	Northern Territory	_____	13. ___ ___

___ ___ ___ ___ ___ ___ ___ ___ ___ ___ ___ ___ ___

___ ___ ___ ___ ___ ___ ___ ___ ___ ___ ___ ___ ___

1 2 3 4 5 6 7 8 9 10 11 12 13

ISAIAH

LIONESS	Phone wires	_____	1. ___ ___
SULPHUR	Soft	_____	2. ___ ___
LECTERN	Choose	_____	3. ___ ___
EREMITE	Joint	_____	4. ___ ___
FEMORAL	Enclose photo	_____	5. ___ ___
SUAVELY	Ointment	_____	6. ___ ___
SHARPER	Grammar	_____	7. ___ ___
GRANITE	Teach	_____	8. ___ ___
LEATHER	Gladden	_____	9. ___ ___
AMERICA	Cheese or soda	_____	10. ___ ___
TREACLE	Profit	_____	11. ___ ___
SHERIFF	Fast-food	_____	12. ___ ___
BURGESS	Crescendo	_____	13. ___ ___

— — — — — — — — — — — — —

— — — — — — — — — — — — —

1 2 3 4 5 6 7 8 9 10 11 12 13

ZECHARIAH

ISHMAEL	Eating times	_____	1. ___ ___
OVERSAW	Relish	_____	2. ___ ___
ALIFORM	Plants	_____	3. ___ ___
BOILING	Game	_____	4. ___ ___
PEDICLE	Music score	_____	5. ___ ___
MADNESS	Titles	_____	6. ___ ___
FITCHEW	Leader	_____	7. ___ ___
POACHER	To dry	_____	8. ___ ___
HERSELF	Transparent	_____	9. ___ ___
SHALLOT	Sandbar	_____	10. ___ ___
ETHICAL	Shoe grip	_____	11. ___ ___
REAGENT	Large	_____	12. ___ ___
DEEPEST	Hasten	_____	13. ___ ___

__ __ __ __ __ __ __ __ __ __ __ __ __

__ __ __ __ __ __ __ __ __ __ __ __ __

1   2   3   4   5   6   7   8   9   10   11   12   13

COLOSSIANS

ADAPTER	Bandaged	____	1. __ __
NASTIER	Step	____	2. __ __
DISTAFF	Unyielding	____	3. __ __
LEGHORN	Hopeless person	____	4. __ __
MENTHOL	1/12 year	____	5. __ __
PLICATE	Put	____	6. __ __
SCATHED	Performed	____	7. __ __
BRAIDED	Anxiety	____	8. __ __
ENABLED	Knife part	____	9. __ __
FLAGGED	Woods opening	____	10. __ __
STETSON	Encampment	____	11. __ __

__ __ __ __ __ __ __ __ __ __ __

__ __ __ __ __ __ __ __ __ __ __

1   2   3   4   5   6   7   8   9   10   11

1 PETER

STEALTH	Warms	_____	1. ___ ___
HAPLOID	Checked	_____	2. ___ ___
ERODENT	Softened sound	_____	3. ___ ___
WRAPPED	Document	_____	4. ___ ___
OPERATE	Candle	_____	5. ___ ___
RAMPANT	Florida city	_____	6. ___ ___
DRAFTED	Not before	_____	7. ___ ___
OEDIPUS	Caught sight of	_____	8. ___ ___
FRESHET	Bed cover	_____	9. ___ ___
TRAIPSE	Mates	_____	10. ___ ___
NIGHTLY	Fibbing	_____	11. ___ ___
STROPHE	Harbor towns	_____	12. ___ ___

__ __ __ __ __ __ __ __ __ __ __ __

__ __ __ __ __ __ __ __ __ __ __ __

| 1 | 2 | 3 | 4 | 5 | 6 | 7 | 8 | 9 | 10 | 11 | 12 |

MICAH

SAWBILL	Herb	_____	1. ___ ___
HOLIDAY	Circadian	_____	2. ___ ___
ROASTER	Put away	_____	3. ___ ___
TRIPLED	Danger	_____	4. ___ ___
DRESDEN	Thick-headed	_____	5. ___ ___
EPISODE	Caught sight of	_____	6. ___ ___
QUENTIN	Boredom	_____	7. ___ ___
HUMERUS	Body fluid	_____	8. ___ ___
ASEPTIC	Room	_____	9. ___ ___
HARDEST	Advantage	_____	10. ___ ___
ENABLED	Dull	_____	11. ___ ___

— — — — — — — — — —

— — — — — — — — — — —

1 2 3 4 5 6 7 8 9 10 11

DANIEL

LANTERN	Memorize	_____	1. ___ ___
HOLIEST	Shoulder covering	_____	2. ___ ___
ENDWISE	Weaves	_____	3. ___ ___
KESTREL	Oak and maple	_____	4. ___ ___
AMIABLE	Easy walk	_____	5. ___ ___
GRANTED	Scored	_____	6. ___ ___
GURGLED	Stuck	_____	7. ___ ___
MENACED	Beat	_____	8. ___ ___
ABALONE	Aristocrat	_____	9. ___ ___
BLASTED	Apathetic	_____	10. ___ ___
MACHINE	Dishes	_____	11. ___ ___
INVADES	Grape plants	_____	12. ___ ___
AVENGER	Brink	_____	13. ___ ___

___ ___ ___ ___ ___ ___ ___ ___ ___ ___ ___ ___ ___

___ ___ ___ ___ ___ ___ ___ ___ ___ ___ ___ ___ ___

1　2　3　4　5　6　7　8　9　10　11　12　13

1 SAMUEL

HABITAT	Tropical grass	_____	1. ___ ___
PHARAOH	TV hostess	_____	2. ___ ___
SKILLET	Cultivates	_____	3. ___ ___
LARDING	Wonderful	_____	4. ___ ___
TONGUES	Visitor	_____	5. ___ ___
MONGREL	Citrus fruit	_____	6. ___ ___
THORIDE	Plural pronoun	_____	7. ___ ___
SHRIVEL	Angers	_____	8. ___ ___
CRUSADE	Whey	_____	9. ___ ___
RECEIPT	Portion	_____	10. ___ ___
DEATHLY	Doled out	_____	11. ___ ___
ONWARDS	Sketched	_____	12. ___ ___
PASTEUR	Fastener	_____	13. ___ ___

— — — — — — — — — — — — —

— — — — — — — — — — — — —

1 2 3 4 5 6 7 8 9 10 11 12 13

2 Chronicles

SOMEHOW	Elk	_____	1. ___ ___
HOSPICE	Range	_____	2. ___ ___
SEAPORT	Meaningless talk	_____	3. ___ ___
RICHEST	English county	_____	4. ___ ___
HATEFUL	Musical instrument	_____	5. ___ ___
COUNTRY	Woo	_____	6. ___ ___
JUNIPER	Accustom	_____	7. ___ ___
STATURE	Begin	_____	8. ___ ___
DECODED	Granted	_____	9. ___ ___
GRAPHIC	Dept. head	_____	10. ___ ___
ELLIPSE	Heaps	_____	11. ___ ___
CLIMATE	Assert	_____	12. ___ ___

__ __ __ __ __ __ __ __ __ __ __

__ __ __ __ __ __ __ __ __ __ __ __

1   2   3   4   5   6   7   8   9   10   11   12

Nehemiah

WIDOWER	Eerie	_____	1. ___ ___
FRIGHTS	Hominy	_____	2. ___ ___
GRAVELY	Bolero composer	_____	3. ___ ___
RAVIOLI	Competitor	_____	4. ___ ___
SMASHED	Disgrace	_____	5. ___ ___
TRIFLED	Angry	_____	6. ___ ___
HEROISM	Skinflint	_____	7. ___ ___
READILY	Regularly	_____	8. ___ ___
HIGHEST	Octave	_____	9. ___ ___
ADENOSE	Stupid	_____	10. ___ ___
DUSKIER	Removes wet	_____	11. ___ ___
SLACKEN	Ringing sound	_____	12. ___ ___
ENDLESS	Sleighs	_____	13. ___ ___

___ ___ ___ ___ ___ ___ ___ ___ ___ ___ ___ ___ ___

___ ___ ___ ___ ___ ___ ___ ___ ___ ___ ___ ___ ___

1   2   3   4   5   6   7   8   9   10   11   12   13

PHILEMON

NEITHER	Triad	____	1. __ __
ASTRIDE	Soils	____	2. __ __
VARSITY	Wander	____	3. __ __
ETHANOL	Reluctant	____	4. __ __
JACINTH	Links	____	5. __ __
HEIRDOM	Entangled	____	6. __ __
EYELASH	Restraint	____	7. __ __
OBELISK	2-wheelers	____	8. __ __
FLOTSAM	Shakes	____	9. __ __
GREATER	Avid	____	10. __ __
DELIGHT	Legal	____	11. __ __

— — — — — — — — — — —

— — — — — — — — — — —

1　2　3　4　5　6　7　8　9　10　11

DEUTERONOMY

LEFTIST	Records	_____	1. __ __
UNHITCH	Overskirt	_____	2. __ __
OPERATE	Chatter	_____	3. __ __
BALEFUL	Legend	_____	4. __ __
EARSHOT	World	_____	5. __ __
COWHERD	Frightened	_____	6. __ __
DETAILS	Floor cover	_____	7. __ __
INSTALL	Killed	_____	8. __ __
SEVENTH	Not odds	_____	9. __ __
BEASTLY	Sew temporarily	_____	10. __ __
BACKLOG	Ebony	_____	11. __ __
APPROVE	Document	_____	12. __ __
PLEASED	Jumps	_____	13. __ __

__ __ __ __ __ __ __ __ __ __ __ __ __

__ __ __ __ __ __ __ __ __ __ __ __ __

1 2 3 4 5 6 7 8 9 10 11 12 13

2 CORINTHIANS

MEDICAL	Sticker	_____	1. ___ ___
CLARIFY	Fragile	_____	2. ___ ___
GLACIER	Understandable	_____	3. ___ ___
PREMIER	Highest grade	_____	4. ___ ___
ANGERED	Avarice	_____	5. ___ ___
CHATTED	Abhorred	_____	6. ___ ___
FEASTED	Help	_____	7. ___ ___
SCORPIO	Marines	_____	8. ___ ___
RESTFUL	Recorder	_____	9. ___ ___
THERMOS	4-base hit	_____	10. ___ ___
UNCOUTH	Nobleman	_____	11. ___ ___
FEARING	Oats	_____	12. ___ ___
FRAGILE	Holy cup	_____	13. ___ ___

— — — — — — — — — — — — —

— — — — — — — — — — — — —

1 2 3 4 5 6 7 8 9 10 11 12 13

PHILIPPIANS

ALBANIA	Veranda	_____	1. ___ ___
POINTER	Trash	_____	2. ___ ___
AVENGER	Novice	_____	3. ___ ___
MACHETE	Instruct	_____	4. ___ ___
RESPITE	Stumbles	_____	5. ___ ___
WHARVES	Apportion	_____	6. ___ ___
HAIRNET	Railroad cars	_____	7. ___ ___
INDOORS	Fabric bag	_____	8. ___ ___
CLARIFY	Style	_____	9. ___ ___
HANGING	Ripening	_____	10. ___ ___
MALARIA	Warning	_____	11. ___ ___
FLOTSAM	Parade exhibit	_____	12. ___ ___
ASCRIBE	Baby beds	_____	13. ___ ___

—— —— —— —— —— —— —— —— —— —— —— —— ——

—— —— —— —— —— —— —— —— —— —— —— —— ——

1   2   3   4   5   6   7   8   9   10   11   12   13

2 THESSALONIANS

HURTLED	Attracted	_____	1. ___ ___
HEARTEN	Devoured	_____	2. ___ ___
GREASED	Pulls	_____	3. ___ ___
RESPOND	Modeled	_____	4. ___ ___
ENDLESS	Lets borrow	_____	5. ___ ___
FEASTED	Alleviated	_____	6. ___ ___
BEGONIA	Commence	_____	7. ___ ___
FLANKER	Chip	_____	8. ___ ___
EPISODE	Bearing	_____	9. ___ ___
FIBSTER	Sacraments	_____	10. ___ ___
BARRING	Carry	_____	11. ___ ___
REVISED	Operate vehicle	_____	12. ___ ___
FLATTER	Signal light	_____	13. ___ ___

__ __ __ __ __ __ __ __ __ __ __ __ __

__ __ __ __ __ __ __ __ __ __ __ __ __

1   2   3   4   5   6   7   8   9   10   11   12   13

PROVERBS

GARFISH	Expositions	_____	1. ___ ___
ORATION	Educate	_____	2. ___ ___
TROUPER	Cowboy	_____	3. ___ ___
SUCROSE	Oath	_____	4. ___ ___
MANTLES	Resources	_____	5. ___ ___
HUMERAL	Kingdom	_____	6. ___ ___
GRAINED	Outflow	_____	7. ___ ___
GOADING	Acting	_____	8. ___ ___
ALCORAN	Pink	_____	9. ___ ___
GREATER	Concur	_____	10. ___ ___
DRAFTED	Succeeded	_____	11. ___ ___

__ __ __ __ __ __ __ __ __ __ __

__ __ __ __ __ __ __ __ __ __ __

1   2   3   4   5   6   7   8   9   10   11

ECCLESIASTES

CLOTHES	Nearby	_____	1. ___ ___
OPALINE	Not fancy	_____	2. ___ ___
DECLARE	Tied shoes	_____	3. ___ ___
REVOLVE	Sweetheart	_____	4. ___ ___
CEILING	Adhere	_____	5. ___ ___
DESSERT	Horse	_____	6. ___ ___
ANALYST	Diagonal	_____	7. ___ ___
STALEST	Slightest	_____	8. ___ ___
INSHORE	Found in varnish	_____	9. ___ ___
ALGERIA	Royal	_____	10. ___ ___
SINGLED	Move smoothly	_____	11. ___ ___
GUNSHOT	Shift	_____	12. ___ ___
INSTANT	Discolor	_____	13. ___ ___

__ __ __ __ __ __ __ __ __ __ __ __ __ __ __ __ __

__ __ __ __ __ __ __ __ __ __ __ __ __ __ __

1   2   3   4   5   6   7   8   9   10   11   12   13

PSALMS

FITMENT	Pretense	_____	1. ___ ___
HONESTY	Rock	_____	2. ___ ___
HOSTILE	Panel part	_____	3. ___ ___
USHERED	Tear into strips	_____	4. ___ ___
AGAINST	Bite	_____	5. ___ ___
FINLAND	Last	_____	6. ___ ___
COWERED	Doctrine	_____	7. ___ ___
INITIAL	Dead language	_____	8. ___ ___
CHASTEN	Pursue	_____	9. ___ ___
FREIGHT	Sorrow	_____	10. ___ ___
TROUBLE	Speak out	_____	11. ___ ___
CESSION	Breakfast roll	_____	12. ___ ___
SCARLET	Frighten	_____	13. ___ ___

— — — — — — — — — — — — —

— — — — — — — — — — — — —

1 2 3 4 5 6 7 8 9 10 11 12 13

EPHESIANS

CHARITY	Dept. head	_____	1. ___ ___
HEADMAN	Titled	_____	2. ___ ___
SMARTEN	Streetcars	_____	3. ___ ___
BLADDER	Leaf of grass	_____	4. ___ ___
ELEANOR	Find out	_____	5. ___ ___
GENTIAN	Representative	_____	6. ___ ___
RICKETS	Magic	_____	7. ___ ___
OVERSAW	Vacillate	_____	8. ___ ___
PARSNIP	French capital	_____	9. ___ ___
EROSIVE	Left-hand page	_____	10. ___ ___
GRABBER	Flat-bottom boat	_____	11. ___ ___
OPALINE	Woodworking tool	_____	12. ___ ___
REDDEST	Woodwinds	_____	13. ___ ___

__ __ __ __ __ __ __ __ __ __ __ __ __

__ __ __ __ __ __ __ __ __ __ __ __ __

1 2 3 4 5 6 7 8 9 10 11 12 13

JAMES

BLOTCHY	Angrily	____	1. ___ ___
ARCUATE	Wood case	____	2. ___ ___
NASCENT	Weaves	____	3. ___ ___
NATURAL	Related to hearing	____	4. ___ ___
HOODING	Performing	____	5. ___ ___
MARKETS	Bare	____	6. ___ ___
ASEPTIC	Paprika	____	7. ___ ___
ORATION	Proportion	____	8. ___ ___
NOBLEST	Tree trunks	____	9. ___ ___
AGAINST	Color	____	10. ___ ___
UMPIRED	Self-esteem	____	11. ___ ___
ESCAPEE	Cloaks	____	12. ___ ___

— — — — — — — — — — — —

— — — — — — — — — — — —

1   2   3   4   5   6   7   8   9   10   11   12

DECODER PUZZLES

by Christy Barritt

Using the decoder grid, uncover a Bible verse for each puzzle. For each two-digit number in the puzzle, find a corresponding letter by matching the first number with the vertical column and the second number with the horizontal row. Place all letters in the puzzle blanks, and the verse will appear.

PSALM 27:14

	1	2	3	4	5
1	A	K	E	L	T
2	N	H	F	J	U
3	I	Y	B	X	G
4	O	S	M	D	W
5	R	C	Q	V	P

45-11-31-15   41-21   15-22-13   14-41-51-44   33-13

41-23   35-41-41-44   52-41-25-51-11-35-13

11-21-44   22-13   42-22-11-14-14

42-15-51-13-21-35-15-22-13-21   15-22-31-21-13

22-13-11-51-15   45-11-31-15   31   42-11-32   41-21

15-22-13   14-41-51-44

1 CORINTHIANS 3:16

	1	2	3	4	5
1	A	K	E	L	T
2	N	H	F	J	U
3	I	Y	B	X	G
4	O	S	M	D	W
5	R	C	Q	V	P

12-21-41-45   32-13   21-41-15   15-22-11-15

32-13   11-51-13   15-22-13   15-13-43-55-14-13

41-23   35-41-44   11-21-44   15-22-11-15   15-22-13

42-55-31-51-31-15   41-23   35-41-44

44-45-13-14-14-13-15-22   31-21   32-41-25

1 Corinthians 13:11

	1	2	3	4	5
1	A	K	E	L	T
2	N	H	F	J	U
3	I	Y	B	X	G
4	O	S	M	D	W
5	R	C	Q	V	P

33-25-15   45-22-13-21   31   33-13-52-11-43-13   11

43-11-21   31   55-25-15   11-45-11-32

52-22-31-14-44-31-42-22   15-22-31-21-35-42

ECCLESIASTES 12:13

	1	2	3	4	5
1	A	K	E	L	T
2	N	H	F	J	U
3	I	Y	B	X	G
4	O	S	M	D	W
5	R	C	Q	V	P

14-13-15   25-42   22-13-11-51   15-22-13

52-41-21-52-14-25-42-31-41-21   41-23   15-22-13

45-22-41-14-13   43-11-15-15-13-51   23-13-11-51

35-41-44   11-21-44   12-13-13-55   22-31-42

52-41-43-43-11-21-44-43-13-21-15-42   23-41-51

15-22-31-42   31-42   15-22-13   45-22-41-14-13

44-25-15-32   41-23   43-11-21

1 Thessalonians 5:9

	1	2	3	4	5
1	A	K	E	L	T
2	N	H	F	J	U
3	I	Y	B	X	G
4	O	S	M	D	W
5	R	C	Q	V	P

23-41-51   35-41-44   22-11-15-22   21-41-15

11-55-55-41-31-21-15-13-44   25-42   15-41

45-51-11-15-22   33-25-15   15-41   41-33-15-11-31-21

42-11-14-54-11-15-31-41-21   33-32   41-25-51

14-41-51-44   24-13-42-25-42   52-22-51-31-42-15

1 Timothy 4:12

	1	2	3	4	5
1	A	K	E	L	T
2	N	H	F	J	U
3	I	Y	B	X	G
4	O	S	M	D	W
5	R	C	Q	V	P

14-13-15   21-41   43-11-21   44-13-42-55-31-42-13

15-22-32   32-41-25-15-22   33-25-15   33-13   15-22-41-25

11-21   13-34-11-43-55-14-13   41-23   15-22-13

33-13-14-31-13-54-13-51-42   31-21   45-41-51-44

31-21   52-41-21-54-13-51-42-11-15-31-41-21   31-21

42-55-31-51-31-15   31-21   23-11-31-15-22   31-21

55-25-51-31-15-32

COLOSSIANS 3:23

	1	2	3	4	5
1	A	K	E	L	T
2	N	H	F	J	U
3	I	Y	B	P	G
4	O	S	M	D	W
5	R	C	Q	V	P

11-21-44   45-22-11-15-42-41-13-54-13-51   32-13

44-41   44-41   31-15   22-13-11-51-15-31-14-32

11-42   15-41   15-22-13   14-41-51-44   11-21-44

21-41-15   25-21-15-41   43-13-21

Romans 12:19

	1	2	3	4	5
1	A	K	E	L	T
2	N	H	F	J	U
3	I	Y	B	P	G
4	O	S	M	D	W
5	R	C	Q	V	P

44-13-11-51-14-32   33-13-14-41-54-13-44

11-54-13-21-35-13   21-41-15

32-41-25-51-42-13-14-54-13-42   33-25-15

51-11-15-22-13-51   35-31-54-13   55-14-11-52-13

25-21-15-41   45-51-11-15-22   23-41-51   31-15   31-42

45-51-31-15-15-13-21   54-13-21-35-13-11-21-52-13

31-42   43-31-21-13   31   45-31-14-14   51-13-34-11-32

42-11-31-15-22   15-22-13   14-41-51-44

PSALM 27:1

	1	2	3	4	5
1	T	L	E	K	A
2	U	J	F	H	N
3	G	Z	B	Y	I
4	W	D	M	S	O
5	P	V	Q	C	R

11-24-13   12-45-55-42   35-44   43-34   12-35-31-24-11

15-25-42   43-34   44-15-12-52-15-11-35-45-25

41-24-45-43   44-24-15-12-12   35   23-13-15-55

11-24-13   12-45-55-42   35-44   11-24-13

44-11-55-13-25-31-11-24   45-23   43-34   12-35-23-13

45-23   41-24-45-43   44-24-15-12-12   35   33-13

15-23-55-15-35-42

ROMANS 14:8

	1	2	3	4	5
1	T	L	E	K	A
2	U	J	F	H	N
3	G	Z	B	Y	I
4	W	D	M	S	O
5	P	V	Q	C	R

23-45-55　41-24-13-11-24-13-55　41-13　12-35-52-13

41-13　12-35-52-13　21-25-11-45　11-24-13

12-45-55-42　15-25-42　41-24-13-11-24-13-55　41-13

42-35-13　41-13　42-35-13　21-25-11-45　11-24-13

12-45-55-42　41-24-13-11-24-13-55　41-13

12-35-52-13　11-24-13-55-13-23-45-55-13　45-55

42-35-13　41-13　15-55-13　11-24-13　12-45-55-42-44

EPHESIANS 4:31

	1	2	3	4	5
1	T	L	E	K	A
2	U	J	F	H	N
3	G	Z	B	Y	I
4	W	D	M	S	O
5	P	V	Q	C	R

12-13-11   15-12-12   33-35-11-11-13-55-25-13-44-44

15-25-42   41-55-15-11-24   15-25-42   15-25-31-13-55

15-25-42   54-12-15-43-45-21-55   15-25-42

13-52-35-12   44-51-13-15-14-35-25-31   33-13

51-21-11   15-41-15-34   23-55-45-43   34-45-21

41-35-11-24   15-12-12   43-15-12-35-54-13

MATTHEW 7:8

	1	2	3	4	5
1	T	L	E	K	A
2	U	J	F	H	N
3	G	Z	B	Y	I
4	W	D	M	S	O
5	P	V	Q	C	R

23-45-55   13-52-13-55-34   45-25-13   11-24-15-11

15-44-14-13-11-24   55-13-54-13-35-52-13-11-24

15-25-42   24-13   11-24-15-11   44-13-13-14-13-11-24

23-35-25-42-13-11-24   15-25-42   11-45   24-35-43

11-24-15-11   14-25-45-54-14-13-11-24   35-11

44-24-15-12-12   33-13   45-51-13-25-13-42

JAMES 1:2

	1	2	3	4	5
1	T	L	E	K	A
2	U	J	F	H	N
3	G	Z	B	Y	I
4	W	D	M	S	O
5	P	V	Q	C	R

43-34   33-55-13-11-24-55-13-25   54-45-21-25-11

35-11   15-12-12   22-45-34   41-24-13-25   34-13

23-15-12-12   35-25-11-45   42-35-52-13-55-44

11-13-43-51-11-15-11-35-45-25-44

EPHESIANS 6:11

	1	2	3	4	5
1	T	L	E	K	A
2	U	J	F	H	N
3	G	Z	B	Y	I
4	W	D	M	S	O
5	P	V	Q	C	R

51-21-11   45-25   11-24-13   41-24-45-12-13

15-55-43-45-21-55   45-23   31-45-42   11-24-15-11

34-13   43-15-34   33-13   15-33-12-13   11-45

44-11-15-25-42   15-31-15-35-25-44-11   11-24-13

41-35-12-13-44   45-23   11-24-13   42-13-52-35-12

PSALM 4:2

	1	2	3	4	5
1	T	L	E	K	A
2	U	J	F	H	N
3	G	Z	B	Y	I
4	W	D	M	S	O
5	P	V	Q	C	R

45   34-13   44-45-25-44   45-23   43-13-25

24-45-41   12-45-25-31   41-35-12-12   34-13

11-21-55-25   43-34   31-12-45-55-34   35-25-11-45

44-24-15-43-13   24-45-41   12-45-25-31   41-35-12-12

34-13   12-45-52-13   52-15-25-35-11-34   15-25-42

44-13-13-14   15-23-11-13-55   12-13-15-44-35-25-31

1 CORINTHIANS 10:14

	1	2	3	4	5
1	T	L	E	K	A
2	U	J	F	H	N
3	G	Z	B	Y	I
4	W	D	M	S	O
5	P	V	Q	C	R

41-24-13-55-13-23-45-55-13   43-34

42-13-15-55-12-34   33-13-12-45-52-13-42

23-12-13-13   23-55-45-43   35-42-45-12-15-11-55-34

PSALM 24:9

	1	2	3	4	5
1	T	U	G	W	P
2	L	J	Z	D	V
3	E	F	B	M	Q
4	K	H	Y	S	C
5	A	N	I	O	R

21-53-32-11   12-15   43-54-12-55   42-31-51-24-44

54   43-31   13-51-11-31-44   31-25-31-52

21-53-32-11   11-42-31-34   12-15   43-31

31-25-31-55-21-51-44-11-53-52-13   24-54-54-55-44

51-52-24   11-42-31   41-53-52-13   54-32

13-21-54-55-43   44-42-51-21-21   45-54-34-31

53-52

1 Corinthians 9:22

	1	2	3	4	5
1	T	U	G	W	P
2	L	J	Z	D	V
3	E	F	B	M	Q
4	K	H	Y	S	C
5	A	N	I	O	R

11-54   11-42-31   14-31-51-41   33-31-45-51-34-31

53   51-44   14-31-51-41   11-42-51-11   53

34-53-13-42-11   13-51-53-52   11-42-31   14-31-51-41

53   51-34   34-51-24-31   51-21-21   11-42-53-52-13-44

11-54   51-21-21   34-31-52   11-42-51-11   53

34-53-13-42-11   33-43   51-21-21   34-31-51-52-44

44-51-25-31   44-54-34-31

PSALM 18:3

	1	2	3	4	5
1	T	U	G	W	P
2	L	J	Z	D	V
3	E	F	B	M	Q
4	K	H	Y	S	C
5	A	N	I	O	R

53   14-53-21-21   45-51-21-21   12-15-54-52

11-42-31   21-54-55-24   14-42-54   53-44

14-54-55-11-42-43   11-54   33-31

15-55-51-53-44-31-24   44-54

44-42-51-21-21   53   33-31   44-51-25-31-24

32-55-54-34   34-53-52-31   31-52-31-34-53-31-44

Proverbs 27:1

	1	2	3	4	5
1	T	U	G	W	P
2	L	J	Z	D	V
3	E	F	B	M	Q
4	K	H	Y	S	C
5	A	N	I	O	R

33-54-51-44-11   52-54-11   11-42-43-44-31-21-32

54-32   11-54-34-54-55-55-54-14   32-54-55

11-42-54-12   41-52-54-14-31-44-11   52-54-11

14-42-51-11   51   24-51-43   34-51-43

33-55-53-52-13   32-54-55-11-42

ACROSTIC PUZZLES

by Christy Barritt

Read the definition in the left-hand column and write the word it describes in the right-hand column. Then place the coded letters from the right-hand column in the puzzle form following to spell out the Bible verse indicated.

ROMANS 14:19

A sign, symbol, or indication

$$\overline{30}\ \overline{36}\ \overline{23}\ \overline{14}$$

Fabric that represents one's country

$$\overline{7}\ \overline{26}\ \overline{1}\ \overline{20}$$

Exhibiting much weight

$$\overline{16}\ \overline{32}\ \overline{6}\ \overline{11}\ \overline{39}$$

An auxiliary form of the verb will

$$\overline{8}\ \overline{24}\ \overline{2}\ \overline{18}\ \overline{13}$$

To type out something in full

$$\overline{33}\ \overline{3}\ \overline{29}\ \overline{17}\ \overline{9}\ \overline{4}\ \overline{25}\ \overline{21}\ \overline{12}\ \overline{28}$$

Stubborn continuance

$$\overline{22}\ \overline{35}\ \overline{10}\ \overline{38}\ \overline{27}\ \overline{19}\ \overline{37}\ \overline{5}\ \overline{15}\ \overline{31}\ \overline{34}$$

26-32-33   2-38   33-16-28-25-5-7-24-10-5

7-24-26-18-24-8   1-7-33-28-10   33-16-32

37-16-21-17-20-19   8-16-21-4-16   30-36-14-28

7-24-25   22-35-29-31-35,   1-17-13

33-16-21-17-20-9   8-16-34-3-28-8-27-37-16

24-15-28   30-1-39   28-13-27-7-39

6-17-24-33-16-28-23.

1 CORINTHIANS 15:58

A metal object worn over the finger while sewing

$\overline{}$ $\overline{}$ $\overline{}$ $\overline{}$ $\overline{}$ $\overline{}$ $\overline{}$
10 33 18 5 1 28 24

Time spent on the job

$\overline{}$ $\overline{}$ $\overline{}$ $\overline{}$ $\overline{}$ $\overline{}$ $\overline{}$
29 34 9 25 4 21 17

A feeling that leads to scratching

$\overline{}$ $\overline{}$ $\overline{}$ $\overline{}$ $\overline{}$
38 42 2 13 44

To work more hours than you've been scheduled

$\overline{}$ $\overline{}$ $\overline{}$ $\overline{}$ $\overline{}$ $\overline{}$ $\overline{}$ $\overline{}$
11 41 20 32 15 27 6 12

Moved from one location to another

$\overline{}$ $\overline{}$ $\overline{}$ $\overline{}$ $\overline{}$ $\overline{}$ $\overline{}$ $\overline{}$ $\overline{}$ $\overline{}$ $\overline{}$
36 39 3 22 14 19 31 8 37 45 23

Lacking worth

$\overline{}$ $\overline{}$ $\overline{}$ $\overline{}$ $\overline{}$ $\overline{}$ $\overline{}$
26 43 35 7 30 16 40

15-13-20-8-24-19-11-32-12,   6-44

1-35-7-11-41-31-23   1-9-30-10-33-32-35-22,   1-35

44-20   16-36-30-23-19-3-43-15,

26-21-6-34-41-24-3-1-28-45,   3-28-29-3-44-14

3-1-11-26-22-23-27-22-17   38-22

42-13-20   29-34-37-25   11-19   42-13-24

28-34-39-23.

MATTHEW 6:24

To put something over something else

$\overline{21}$ $\overline{11}$ $\overline{34}$ $\overline{5}$ $\overline{27}$

The place where one lives

$\overline{33}$ $\overline{12}$ $\overline{4}$ $\overline{28}$

Making no noise

$\overline{6}$ $\overline{32}$ $\overline{17}$ $\overline{30}$ $\overline{22}$ $\overline{15}$

Microscopic plants and animals that fish feed off of

$\overline{23}$ $\overline{7}$ $\overline{20}$ $\overline{1}$ $\overline{29}$ $\overline{16}$ $\overline{26}$ $\overline{10}$

Having lots of money

$\overline{13}$ $\overline{35}$ $\overline{8}$ $\overline{31}$ $\overline{3}$ $\overline{24}$ $\overline{19}$

Melted cheese used as a dip

$\overline{2}$ $\overline{25}$ $\overline{14}$ $\overline{18}$ $\overline{9}$ $\overline{39}$

1-12   4-20-10   21-20-10   6-35-27-34-28   15-13-26

4-8-6-16-30-27-6:   2-25-27   35-32-3-24-5-27

24-35   13-32-17-31   33-20-15-28   15-24-35

12-1-39,   8-22-18   17-11-34-28   16-24-28

25-3-24-5-27;   12-27   28-17-6-30   24-35

13-32-7-31   33-26-31-18   3-11   16-24-35

12-1-28,   8-14-18   18-30-6-23-32-6-30   16-24-28

26-16-24-35-27.

ISAIAH 1:18

A personal wardrobe

$$\overline{34}\ \overline{7}\ \overline{21}\ \overline{16}\ \overline{1}\ \overline{30}\ \overline{12}$$

The location of something

$$\overline{26}\ \overline{5}\ \overline{31}\ \overline{17}\ \overline{13}\ \overline{35}\ \overline{4}\ \overline{42}\ \overline{25}\ \overline{9}\ \overline{20}$$

A place suitable to the person in it

$$\overline{38}\ \overline{6}\ \overline{43}\ \overline{32}\ \overline{44}$$

A wide variety of food

$$\overline{33}\ \overline{8}\ \overline{36}\ \overline{14}\ \overline{27}\ \overline{18}\ \overline{3}\ \overline{41}\ \overline{11}\ \overline{29}\ \overline{23}$$

Full of spices

$$\overline{10}\ \overline{40}\ \overline{2}\ \overline{22}\ \overline{19}$$

A fictitious tale

$$\overline{37}\ \overline{24}\ \overline{39}\ \overline{15}\ \overline{28}$$

34-21-8-30   38-21-26,   35-38-23   7-31-9   25-37

14-44-18-20-39-38   9-21-27-31-9-1-31-15,

3-18-2-24-5   16-32-44   7-36-15-23:

16-32-21-25-27-5   19-11-25-17   20-2-38-37

41-30   35-20   10-22-18-17-7-30-9,   24-5-30-28

12-5-35-7-7   4-31   35-10   26-1-6-16-13   35-20

33-38-42-26.

Psalm 1:3

Charmed by an irresistable appeal

$\overline{32}$ $\overline{5}$ $\overline{40}$ $\overline{27}$ $\overline{16}$ $\overline{20}$ $\overline{1}$ $\overline{38}$ $\overline{10}$ $\overline{42}$

The projects a child does outside school

$\overline{36}$ $\overline{4}$ $\overline{17}$ $\overline{30}$ $\overline{41}$ $\overline{24}$ $\overline{39}$ $\overline{23}$

Full of fog

$\overline{43}$ $\overline{18}$ $\overline{22}$ $\overline{6}$ $\overline{33}$

Clear, transparent quartz

$\overline{7}$ $\overline{11}$ $\overline{29}$ $\overline{31}$ $\overline{15}$ $\overline{21}$ $\overline{3}$

Looking on the bright side

$\overline{44}$ $\overline{12}$ $\overline{37}$ $\overline{2}$ $\overline{14}$ $\overline{28}$ $\overline{8}$ $\overline{34}$ $\overline{19}$ $\overline{25}$

A baby rabbit

$\overline{45}$ $\overline{26}$ $\overline{13}$ $\overline{9}$ $\overline{35}$

5-13-42   36-30   31-36-5-3-3   45-30

3-16-23-10   21   27-11-10-30

40-3-5-9-37-10-42   45-33   27-36-30

39-28-20-10-39-8   44-43   41-21-27-30-11,

27-36-5-27   45-39-16-13-22-10-34-36

43-4-39-38-36   36-2-8   43-11-26-19-15   16-13

36-28-31   8-30-1-31-18-9.

1 CORINTHIANS 14:10

The parts of a garment that cover the arm

$$\overline{38}\ \overline{20}\ \overline{26}\ \overline{8}\ \overline{1}\ \overline{37}\ \overline{14}$$

Not a definite yes or no

$$\overline{25}\ \overline{30}\ \overline{9}\ \overline{4}\ \overline{21}$$

Blood relatives

$$\overline{36}\ \overline{5}\ \overline{15}\ \overline{32}\ \overline{10}\ \overline{24}$$

Injured unjustly

$$\overline{35}\ \overline{13}\ \overline{22}\ \overline{18}\ \overline{3}\ \overline{34}\ \overline{28}$$

To have great depth from side to side

$$\overline{2}\ \overline{17}\ \overline{12}\ \overline{7}\ \overline{29}$$

Made a coherent whole

$$\overline{31}\ \overline{16}\ \overline{6}\ \overline{27}\ \overline{23}\ \overline{11}\ \overline{19}$$

2-17-26-13-21   5-13-8,   12-2   25-5-9   4-11,   14-22

15-5-18-24   29-32-16-19-14

22-36   1-22-12-7-34-14   32-16   2-17-21

35-22-13-10-28,   30-18-28   16-22-18-37

22-36   2-17-34-25   12-38   35-32-2-17-22-31-2

14-6-3-16-32-36-12-7-30-2-32-22-16.

1 CORINTHIANS 6:20

A tongue of fire

$\overline{31}$ $\overline{38}$ $\overline{5}$ $\overline{17}$ $\overline{9}$

Not old

$\overline{39}$ $\overline{18}$ $\overline{12}$ $\overline{3}$ $\overline{33}$

The state whose capital is Madison

$\overline{24}$ $\overline{28}$ $\overline{8}$ $\overline{32}$ $\overline{21}$ $\overline{37}$ $\overline{13}$ $\overline{35}$ $\overline{29}$

An account of a person's life written by another

$\overline{20}$ $\overline{34}$ $\overline{2}$ $\overline{26}$ $\overline{23}$ $\overline{42}$ $\overline{11}$ $\overline{16}$ $\overline{7}$

An exaggerated picture of a person

$\overline{10}$ $\overline{30}$ $\overline{1}$ $\overline{22}$ $\overline{14}$ $\overline{6}$ $\overline{36}$ $\overline{27}$ $\overline{19}$ $\overline{41}$

What a person eats and drinks

$\overline{15}$ $\overline{40}$ $\overline{4}$ $\overline{25}$

31-18-23   39-41   6-1-41   20-21-12-33-16-36

24-40-25-16   5   11-23-28-32-9:

25-16-41-23-4-31-2-1-4   33-38-2-23-40-31-7

26-2-15   35-29   7-18-27-23   20-2-15-39,

42-3-15   28-37   39-2-12-19   13-11-34-23-22-36,

24-16-34-10-16   5-19-41   26-2-15'-8.

1 CORINTHIANS 3:17

A set of stairs between floors

$$\overline{14}\ \overline{25}\ \overline{37}\ \overline{3}\ \overline{20}\ \overline{7}$$

Sunrise to sunset

$$\overline{24}\ \overline{8}\ \overline{30}\ \overline{26}\ \overline{19}\ \overline{2}\ \overline{13}$$

To see something beforehand

$$\overline{34}\ \overline{23}\ \overline{43}\ \overline{31}\ \overline{39}\ \overline{4}\ \overline{18}$$

An alternate name

$$\overline{38}\ \overline{27}\ \overline{40}\ \overline{10}\ \overline{33}\ \overline{28}\ \overline{16}\ \overline{5}\ \overline{22}$$

A critical study or examination

$$\overline{9}\ \overline{35}\ \overline{1}\ \overline{29}\ \overline{15}\ \overline{41}\ \overline{21}\ \overline{11}$$

A male chicken

$$\overline{44}\ \overline{12}\ \overline{32}\ \overline{42}\ \overline{6}\ \overline{17}\ \overline{36}$$

37-14   8-16-5   22-8-16   24-43-14-41-25-13

15-20-40   7-4-2-34-25-17   12-14   3-32-33,

20-19-22   9-20-8-25-25   3-12-33

24-13-27-15-23-28-11;   14-28-36

6-20-43   26-40-22-34-25-43   28-14   3-12-24

39-27   20-32-25-30   18-20-41-35-20,

7-40-22-38-25-40   30-13   8-1-13.

PHILIPPIANS 2:14

Continuance of time

$$\overline{7}\ \overline{18}\ \overline{13}\ \overline{34}\ \overline{4}\ \overline{39}\ \overline{27}\ \overline{20}$$

Another word for trash

$$\overline{31}\ \overline{5}\ \overline{40}\ \overline{23}\ \overline{19}\ \overline{11}\ \overline{17}$$

Unruly and illegal

$$\overline{37}\ \overline{12}\ \overline{35}\ \overline{30}\ \overline{42}\ \overline{24}\ \overline{6}$$

Something to be imitated or modeled

$$\overline{21}\ \overline{43}\ \overline{32}\ \overline{14}\ \overline{28}\ \overline{1}\ \overline{9}$$

To prove the truth of something

$$\overline{8}\ \overline{38}\ \overline{3}\ \overline{2}\ \overline{15}\ \overline{33}\ \overline{26}$$

Agreeable musical sounds

$$\overline{2}\ \overline{36}\ \overline{25}\ \overline{41}\ \overline{29}\ \overline{16}\ \overline{10}$$

7-38   12-37-1   4-2-15-3-31-24   35-39-4-2-29-18-4

41-18-40-14-18-13-15-16-31-6   32-20-7

7-15-24-28-18-4-39-20-11-6.

PSALM 23:6

Fear of being in a confined place

$\overline{}$ $\overline{}$ $\overline{}$ $\overline{}$ $\overline{}$ $\overline{}$ $\overline{}$ $\overline{}$ $\overline{}$ $\overline{}$ $\overline{}$ $\overline{}$ $\overline{}$ $\overline{}$
6 45 13 28 21 47 26 7 43 34 11 39 20 4

Faulty

$\overline{}$ $\overline{}$ $\overline{}$ $\overline{}$ $\overline{}$ $\overline{}$ $\overline{}$ $\overline{}$ $\overline{}$
14 46 35 5 44 22 42 12 27

The month after April

$\overline{}$ $\overline{}$ $\overline{}$
15 41 29

A person who indulges in too much food

$\overline{}$ $\overline{}$ $\overline{}$ $\overline{}$ $\overline{}$ $\overline{}$ $\overline{}$
16 30 9 37 19 33 3

To go over something

$\overline{}$ $\overline{}$ $\overline{}$ $\overline{}$ $\overline{}$ $\overline{}$
8 31 24 36 1 17

The second story

$\overline{}$ $\overline{}$ $\overline{}$ $\overline{}$ $\overline{}$ $\overline{}$ $\overline{}$ $\overline{}$
2 38 10 23 32 40 25 18

21-28-26-46-30-29   16-33-11-14-3-31-18-10

13-3-14   15-46-25-44-29   21-34-13-45-30

35-33-30-45-11-17   15-46   32-30-45   22-34-46

14-4-29-21   11-35   15-29   30-20-35-27:

41-3-14   42   17-40-45-30   14-17-5-45-30   36-3

19-34-27   34-11-9-21-27   11-35

23-34-27   30-33-25-14   35-11-26   1-24-31-8.

PROVERBS 22:1

Covered with wet dirt

$\overline{12}\ \overline{20}\ \overline{5}\ \overline{17}\ \overline{11}$

A small green plant with usually three but sometimes four leaflets

$\overline{6}\ \overline{25}\ \overline{21}\ \overline{33}\ \overline{30}\ \overline{8}$

A male parent

$\overline{22}\ \overline{29}\ \overline{7}\ \overline{16}\ \overline{26}\ \overline{15}$

The supposed disembodied spirit of a dead person

$\overline{9}\ \overline{31}\ \overline{35}\ \overline{19}\ \overline{2}$

Not nice

$\overline{10}\ \overline{18}\ \overline{1}\ \overline{13}\ \overline{27}\ \overline{3}\ \overline{24}$

A person named to receive benefits

$\overline{14}\ \overline{28}\ \overline{38}\ \overline{4}\ \overline{37}\ \overline{39}\ \overline{23}\ \overline{40}\ \overline{34}\ \overline{36}\ \overline{32}$

18   9-35-21-5   10-29-12-26   39-19

36-18-3-27-30-8   3-35   14-4   6-16-21-19-26-38

3-16-29-10   9-36-4-18-3   8-40-23-31-4-19,

18-38-17   25-21-33-40-10-13   22-29-33-21-20-15

36-18-2-27-4-36   7-16-34-10   19-39-25-33-28-36

18-38-17   13-35-25-5.

PROVERBS 17:28

To disguise for the purpose of blending into the background

<u> </u> <u> </u> <u> </u> <u> </u> <u> </u> <u> </u> <u> </u> <u> </u> <u> </u> <u> </u>
15 33 8 41 13 36 1 25 20 3

The season that comes after autumn

<u> </u> <u> </u> <u> </u> <u> </u> <u> </u> <u> </u>
7 21 14 35 17 2

Number of sides in a pentagon

<u> </u> <u> </u> <u> </u> <u> </u>
39 22 42 29

Joyful

<u> </u> <u> </u> <u> </u> <u> </u> <u> </u>
4 16 9 19 12

Worship

<u> </u> <u> </u> <u> </u> <u> </u> <u> </u> <u> </u> <u> </u> <u> </u> <u> </u>
10 26 31 18 38 6 27 34 23

Lacking energy

<u> </u> <u> </u> <u> </u> <u> </u> <u> </u> <u> </u> <u> </u> <u> </u>
5 32 40 28 11 37 30 24

29-42-37-14   38   39-34-41-1,   7-4-37-23   4-37

4-34-5-26-37-6-4   4-22-24   19-3-10-15-29,   21-30

15-41-13-14-35-29-26   7-32-40-37:   10-14-26   4-17

35-4-33-28   30-4-13-35-6-29-28-4   4-32-40

11-27-9-30   27-24   3-30-35-3-17-8-37-26   33

8-16-23   31-39   13-14-26-3-2-40-6-25-14-26-32-14-20.

Psalm 1:2

To make something beautiful

$$\overline{}\ \overline{}\ \overline{}\ \overline{}\ \overline{}\ \overline{}\ \overline{}\ \overline{}$$
17 40 45 27 7 21 16 37

To repair

$$\overline{}\ \overline{}\ \overline{}\ \overline{}$$
39 38 5 12

Soaked with fluid

$$\overline{}\ \overline{}\ \overline{}\ \overline{}\ \overline{}\ \overline{}\ \overline{}\ \overline{}\ \overline{}\ \overline{}\ \overline{}$$
9 30 2 24 43 20 34 15 44 42 14

Funeral director

$$\overline{}\ \overline{}\ \overline{}\ \overline{}\ \overline{}\ \overline{}\ \overline{}\ \overline{}\ \overline{}\ \overline{}$$
46 32 11 41 49 23 50 8 4 25

A 100th anniversary

$$\overline{}\ \overline{}\ \overline{}\ \overline{}\ \overline{}\ \overline{}\ \overline{}\ \overline{}\ \overline{}\ \overline{}$$
47 22 48 28 51 10 19 31 1 6

Undecided or doubtful

$$\overline{}\ \overline{}\ \overline{}\ \overline{}\ \overline{}\ \overline{}\ \overline{}\ \overline{}$$
3 26 35 29 13 18 33 36

17-27-7   3-21-35   11-26-20-29-15-3-2   21-35

31-19   28-3-38   6-50-9   34-16   7-3-22

6-34-25-14;   1-32-11   29-33   3-29-35   20-30-9

12-34-13-3   3-24   39-4-11-21-23-45-13-40

11-18-37   18-48-12   10-29-44-3-36.

MATTHEW 6:6

Confused

$\overline{}$ $\overline{}$ $\overline{}$ $\overline{}$ $\overline{}$ $\overline{}$ $\overline{}$ $\overline{}$ $\overline{}$ $\overline{}$
42 6 23 35 15 30 1 25 19 31

An impediment

$\overline{}$ $\overline{}$ $\overline{}$ $\overline{}$ $\overline{}$ $\overline{}$ $\overline{}$ $\overline{}$ $\overline{}$
33 24 14 40 22 4 12 36 9

A dentifrice

$\overline{}$ $\overline{}$ $\overline{}$ $\overline{}$ $\overline{}$ $\overline{}$ $\overline{}$ $\overline{}$ $\overline{}$ $\overline{}$
46 10 27 44 34 5 38 26 17 32

A soft, plastic mixture used to hold things together

$\overline{}$ $\overline{}$ $\overline{}$ $\overline{}$ $\overline{}$
11 3 20 29 37

A sudden, brief light

$\overline{}$ $\overline{}$ $\overline{}$ $\overline{}$ $\overline{}$
13 2 21 7 41

The soul

$\overline{}$ $\overline{}$ $\overline{}$ $\overline{}$ $\overline{}$ $\overline{}$
45 28 43 8 39 16

42-3-20   44-34-10-3,   23-33-1-14   46-34-27-3

28-8-21-37-1-45-20,   6-12-46-19-25   39-14-16-10

46-34-37   36-15-27-45-1-29,   21-14-40

23-34-32-14   46-34-10-3   41-21-26-17   26-34-3-16

16-41-37   31-27-10-22,   11-22-4-37   17-27

29-41-37   13-38-20-41-9-8   23-33-43-36-34

24-26   35-14   7-6-36-22-19-29.

PROVERBS 25:11

A close acquaintance

$$\overline{26} \ \overline{3} \ \overline{20} \ \overline{13} \ \overline{33} \ \overline{6}$$

Existing only in one's head

$$\overline{12} \ \overline{21} \ \overline{1} \ \overline{34} \ \overline{31} \ \overline{17} \ \overline{28} \ \overline{22} \ \overline{7}$$

An abbreviation for the state of which Salt Lake City is the capital

$$\overline{5} \ \overline{8}$$

A clasp for fastening a strap or belt

$$\overline{27} \ \overline{14} \ \overline{29} \ \overline{9} \ \overline{23} \ \overline{32}$$

Wet, marshy land

$$\overline{10} \ \overline{24} \ \overline{15} \ \overline{2} \ \overline{19}$$

One who makes or sells gloves

$$\overline{4} \ \overline{16} \ \overline{18} \ \overline{30} \ \overline{11} \ \overline{25}$$

15   24-18-22-6   26-12-8-23-7   10-19-18-9-11-33

31-10   23-20-9-11   1-19-19-23-13-10   18-26

4-18-23-6   31-17   19-12-29-8-14-25-32-10   18-26

10-12-16-30-13-3.

PSALM 12:6

To be involved in

$\overline{16}$ $\overline{38}$ $\overline{26}$ $\overline{17}$ $\overline{36}$ $\overline{48}$ $\overline{1}$ $\overline{43}$ $\overline{9}$ $\overline{34}$ $\overline{24}$

An exciting undertaking

$\overline{47}$ $\overline{3}$ $\overline{37}$ $\overline{44}$ $\overline{18}$ $\overline{25}$ $\overline{2}$ $\overline{49}$ $\overline{12}$

Perfect

$\overline{19}$ $\overline{46}$ $\overline{27}$ $\overline{13}$ $\overline{42}$ $\overline{8}$ $\overline{40}$ $\overline{33}$

To grumble

$\overline{29}$ $\overline{35}$ $\overline{10}$ $\overline{28}$ $\overline{5}$ $\overline{20}$

The real thing

$\overline{4}$ $\overline{22}$ $\overline{31}$ $\overline{11}$ $\overline{45}$ $\overline{14}$ $\overline{7}$ $\overline{21}$ $\overline{39}$

Directed forward

$\overline{15}$ $\overline{30}$ $\overline{32}$ $\overline{41}$ $\overline{23}$ $\overline{6}$

17-11-8   13-15-26-3-40   15-19   7-11-44

42-15-49-3   41-20-5   43-35-20-8   32-15-49-3-33:

9-40   40-1-46-37-12-49   25-23-21-45-6   36-14   27

19-2-49-30-4-39-45   15-19   24-38-20-31-11,

16-22-26-21-19-36-8-6   33-5-37-8-18

10-21-29-8-40.

COLOSSIANS 3:16

An elected official

$\overline{6}$ $\overline{29}$ $\overline{11}$ $\overline{37}$ $\overline{27}$ $\overline{40}$ $\overline{34}$ $\overline{3}$ $\overline{17}$ $\overline{22}$

To twist and whirl

$\overline{18}$ $\overline{4}$ $\overline{15}$ $\overline{10}$ $\overline{36}$

Word endings that sound alike

$\overline{30}$ $\overline{16}$ $\overline{26}$ $\overline{5}$ $\overline{38}$

A container for restaurant leftovers

$\overline{12}$ $\overline{28}$ $\overline{7}$ $\overline{21}$ $\overline{32}$ $\overline{2}$ $\overline{13}$ $\overline{23}$ $\overline{35}$

To rotate

$\overline{1}$ $\overline{8}$ $\overline{14}$ $\overline{24}$

To fail to remember

$\overline{25}$ $\overline{9}$ $\overline{33}$ $\overline{20}$ $\overline{39}$ $\overline{31}$

36-38-27   1-16-39   4-28-30-12   9-25

34-16-30-37-18-31   12-4-2-11-36   32-24   26-29-8

10-15-34-16-11-26   40-22   17-36-11

4-40-18-12-9-5;   27-39-17-34-16-32-24-7   23-22-12

17-12-5-29-22-15-18-16-3-24-20   29-24-39

17-24-9-1-16-2-33   32-24   6-18-17-36-5-18

17-22-12   16-26-5-24-18   23-22-12

18-6-37-14-15-31-8-17-11   18-28-24-35-18.

PSALM 13:6

Jekyll and. . .

$\overline{}$ $\overline{}$ $\overline{}$ $\overline{}$
30 4 18 9

To struggle with something

$\overline{}$ $\overline{}$ $\overline{}$ $\overline{}$ $\overline{}$ $\overline{}$ $\overline{}$
17 8 24 3 32 15 11

A bison

$\overline{}$ $\overline{}$ $\overline{}$ $\overline{}$ $\overline{}$ $\overline{}$ $\overline{}$
25 16 26 5 35 23 31

Humid

$\overline{}$ $\overline{}$ $\overline{}$ $\overline{}$ $\overline{}$
28 2 10 36 19

Relating to times long past

$\overline{}$ $\overline{}$ $\overline{}$ $\overline{}$ $\overline{}$ $\overline{}$ $\overline{}$
14 1 20 12 33 7 27

Of herbs

$\overline{}$ $\overline{}$ $\overline{}$ $\overline{}$ $\overline{}$ $\overline{}$
6 29 22 13 21 34

12   17-12-23-15   3-12-1-10   2-1-27-31   27-6-29

34-31-8-18,   13-11-20-35-16-3-11   30-33

6-14-32-30   18-9-21-23-27

25-31-16-7-27-12-5-16-15-34-4   17-12-27-6   28-24.

PSALM 8:1

Costly

$\overline{10}$ $\overline{44}$ $\overline{34}$ $\overline{13}$ $\overline{26}$ $\overline{2}$ $\overline{42}$ $\overline{20}$ $\overline{7}$

Using correct reasoning

$\overline{24}$ $\overline{39}$ $\overline{8}$ $\overline{35}$ $\overline{30}$ $\overline{14}$ $\overline{18}$

An onlooker

$\overline{21}$ $\overline{25}$ $\overline{17}$ $\overline{43}$ $\overline{36}$ $\overline{6}$ $\overline{40}$ $\overline{19}$ $\overline{38}$

To beg in a childish, undignified way

$\overline{31}$ $\overline{3}$ $\overline{15}$ $\overline{9}$ $\overline{27}$

A signature

$\overline{4}$ $\overline{28}$ $\overline{47}$ $\overline{1}$ $\overline{22}$ $\overline{45}$ $\overline{16}$ $\overline{37}$ $\overline{11}$

To hug

$\overline{23}$ $\overline{46}$ $\overline{5}$ $\overline{41}$ $\overline{29}$ $\overline{12}$ $\overline{32}$

39   24-1-41-40,   39-28-38   18-39-45-40,

11-39-31   7-44-30-10-24-18-19-6-43   42-2

43-11-25   26-14-46-23   35-26   29-24-18

47-3-7   19-14-38-43-3!   31-3-1   11-4-17-43

2-23-43   43-3-25   22-24-1-41-25   36-5-1-20-10

43-11-27   3-13-16-20-32-9-2.

PROVERBS 16:32

Finicky

$\overline{16}\ \overline{36}\ \overline{30}\ \overline{1}\ \overline{9}$

Took into the stomach

$\overline{39}\ \overline{10}\ \overline{31}\ \overline{15}\ \overline{25}\ \overline{4}\ \overline{21}\ \overline{8}\ \overline{42}$

A raised area

$\overline{5}\ \overline{26}\ \overline{22}\ \overline{35}$

To rinse the throat with a liquid, using air from the lungs to make bubbles

$\overline{12}\ \overline{38}\ \overline{17}\ \overline{2}\ \overline{32}\ \overline{43}$

A person hired as a driver

$\overline{33}\ \overline{3}\ \overline{11}\ \overline{24}\ \overline{37}\ \overline{7}\ \overline{28}\ \overline{14}\ \overline{18}$

Nourishing

$\overline{6}\ \overline{20}\ \overline{29}\ \overline{40}\ \overline{19}\ \overline{41}\ \overline{27}\ \overline{34}\ \overline{13}\ \overline{23}$

3-28   29-3-31-29   36-39   23-32-4-10   29-34

31-6-12-43-17   19-23   5-8-29-41-8-18   29-3-31-6

29-3-8   22-19-2-3-41-9;   31-6-42   3-28

29-3-31-41   17-24-15-8-29-3   3-36-23

39-16-36-40-19-41   29-3-31-6   3-28   41-3-31-29

41-11-1-8-29-3   38   30-27-41-9.

WORD SEARCH
PUZZLES

by John Hudson Tiner

Find and circle the search words in the puzzle grid. Spell out the hidden phrase with the leftover letters.

MONUMENT TO
A RIVER CROSSING

JOSHUA 3:14—4:10

BARE

CHILDREN

CLEAN

COVENANT

FIRM

FOREVER

GROUND

ISRAEL

JORDAN

LORD

MEMORIAL

MIDST

NUMBER

OVER

PASSED

PEOPLE

PRIESTS

STONES

STOOD

TOOK

TRIBES

TWELVE

M	E	L	P	O	E	P	W	C	A	M
I	T	C	A	D	E	R	F	H	R	S
D	O	F	O	I	J	O	O	I	R	S
S	R	O	S	V	R	L	F	L	D	E
T	T	E	A	E	E	O	O	D	N	N
S	W	L	V	W	B	N	M	R	E	O
R	G	E	C	O	E	I	A	E	D	T
C	R	A	L	U	T	O	R	N	M	S
F	O	R	E	V	K	O	O	T	T	B
F	U	S	A	B	E	E	F	S	A	O
R	N	I	N	U	M	B	E	R	E	T
H	D	E	A	R	K	I	E	O	F	T
H	E	N	A	D	R	O	J	C	O	V
E	N	A	N	P	A	S	S	E	D	T

Hidden Phrase: __ __ __ __ __ __   __ __

__ __ __ __ __ __   __ __ __ __   __ __ __   __ __ __

__ __ __ __ __ __   __ __ __   __ __ __   __ __

__ __ __   __ __ __ __ __ __ __ __

DEFEAT AND VICTORY AT AI

JOSHUA 7:1–8:29

ACCURSED	FLED	SILVER
ACHAN	GARMENT	SINNED
AGAINST	GOLD	SMOTE
AMBUSH	HEARTS	SPOILS
ANGER	INDEED	STONED
ANSWERED	ISRAEL	THOUSAND
BEATEN	JOSHUA	TOOK
CHASED	KINDLED	TRESPASS
CITY	KING	VALLEY
COMMITTED	LORD	WATER
ENTERED	MELTED	WEDGE
FIRE	PEOPLE	WILDERNESS
FIVE	SHEKELS	

```
T F T N E M R A G R H S V E
L L E L O R C O E D T E A T
R E G N A C L V S R A V L O
A D A C U D L B A I D I L M
W N U R H I N E T U N F E S
I A S O S A H A J D H L Y O
L E T W S I S T E H T S D U
D P A E E N T E R E D R O F
E E E E R R D N D A O D R J
R O T G S H E K E L S E D N
N P R T D E L D N I K N S O
E L E S I E R I F H A O L T
S E S N I M W N E S Y T I C
S I P I T N M G U U T S O H
E R A A O B N O E B T H P O
U D S G O I H E C M I S S M
A Y S A K T E D D A C H A N
```

Hidden Phrase: ___ ____ ____

____ _____, ____

___, _____ __ ____

_____

LAND FOR JOSHUA AND CALEB

JOSHUA 14:1–15; 19:49–51

ALIVE	HALF	MOUNT
BLESSED	HEADS	NINE
BUILT	HEBRON	NOTHING
CALEB	INHERITED	OTHER
CANAAN	ISRAEL	SAVE
CITIES	JORDAN	SIDE
CITY	JOSHUA	STRONG
DIVIDING	KEPT	SWARE
DWELT	LAND	THEREIN
EPHRAIM	LEVITES	TRIBES
FEET	LORD	TRODDEN
GAVE	MOSES	

```
T F D O D E T I R E H N I
R R T R N I H L P E V A G
I T N U O M V H I R E A Y
B K E P T L R I E U H N S
E A V C H A S H D A B A W
S E I T I C T E J I D C A
V T L M N O S O T N N S R
Y J A S G S S E G I W G E
N O R B E H H N O E V B L
L R Y L U S O I S R A E L
F D B A T R O D D E N L L
O A L E T L O M W H I A E
D N E S T D W E L T N C H
E F L A H L O S I D E R D
```

Hidden Phrase: _ _ _   _ _ _ _   _ _ _ _

_ _ _ _ _ _ _   _ _ _ _ _ _ _ _

_ _ _   _ _ _ _ _

Gideon's Special Army

Judges 7:1–25

BLEW	HAND	REMAINED
BOWED	HOST	REST
BRAKE	HUNDRED	SAVE
CAMP	LAPPED	SWORD
COMPANIES	MANY	THEIR
CRIED	MIDIANITES	THEMSELVES
DELIVER	MOUTH	THOUSAND
DEPART	OUTSIDE	THREE
DIVIDED	PEOPLE	TRUMPETS
FEARFUL	PITCHED	VAULT
FELLOW	PITCHERS	WHOSOEVER
GIDEON	PUTTING	

```
T R U M P E T S D B Y T D
H L H E T H R E V I L E D
E A R P E O P L E E I N W
M P E H U A L U F R A E F
S P N T R E S T C S L E C
E E G T S R R D U B L O V
L D T N R O E O E L M D A
V D E I I D H M O P M N U
E R R W N T C W A E N A L
S O T E O A T N R I E H T
H W U C V B I U A T N D G
L S A T A E P D P P E E I
P M B E S D O W I R V D D
P I O R L I Y S D M A I E
L I S U A A D N O V S V O
E E R H T K U E A H E I N
Y P I T C H E D O M W D U
```

Hidden Phrase: __ __   __ __ __   __ __ __ __ __

__ __ __ __ __ __ __   __ __ __   __ __ __ __

__ __ __ __ __ __   __ __ __ __ __   __   __ __ __ __

__ __ __

A Strong Man

Judges 13:1–25

ALTAR	DRINK	OFFERING
ANGEL	ENTREATED	PLEASED
APPEARED	FLAME	RAZOR
BARREN	GREW	SAMSON
BEGAN	HEAD	SECRET
BEWARE	HEARKENED	SHALL
BLESSED	HEAVEN	SPIRIT
CALLED	LORD	STRONG
CAMP	MEAT	TEACH
CHILD	NAME	TIMES
CONCEIVE	NAZARITE	TOWARD

```
S A M S O N L O R D T N O R
M W F A F Z D O R E D A E H
S E L H F S H E A L E A L L
E R A W E B G C R L T C P O
M G M T R A H N M A A E M O
I N E H I I R S O C E H A E
T D R I N K A K D R R P C H
D F O A G T R E T T O P E
H E G E E S O T S N N S S A
C E M R P W I L S C E H H V
B A C I A R I A E L H D A E
N E R R A B D I L G S I L N
S I D Z H A V L B T N L L B
T E A P L E A S E D A A A D
N N A Z A R I R O Z A R T E
```

Hidden Phrase: __ __   __ __ __ __ __ __   __ __ __ __ __ __

__ __ __ __   __ __   __ __ __   __ __ __ __ : __ __ __

__ __ __   __ __ __ __ __   __ __ __ __ __   __ __

__   __ __ __ __ __ __ __ __

Samson
and the Lion

Judges 14:5–14

BEES	PLEASED
CAME	RENT
CARCASE	RIDDLE
COMPANION	ROARED
EATER	SAMSON
FEAST	SPIRIT
HAND	STRONG
HONEY	SWARM
LINE	SWEETNESS
LION	TALKED
MEAT	VINEYARDS
MIGHTILY	WOMAN
NOTHING	YOUNG

```
S  A  B  M  S  O  N  S  A  C  T  I  L
D  U  N  E  Y  T  O  T  M  E  A  T  I
V  H  T  O  E  L  D  D  I  R  L  M  N
E  I  U  S  M  S  E  I  C  M  K  W  E
Y  N  N  W  A  S  R  O  A  R  E  D  I
G  L  L  E  A  E  M  L  C  A  D  N  O
N  W  I  E  Y  P  F  A  T  W  L  T  P
I  U  L  T  A  A  R  E  T  S  I  F  O
H  P  Y  N  H  C  R  S  T  R  O  N  G
T  R  I  E  A  G  R  D  I  T  N  A  H
O  O  A  S  N  E  I  P  S  R  I  M  D
N  D  E  S  N  O  S  M  A  S  L  O  E
U  N  T  T  O  Y  H  A  N  D  O  W  U
```

Hidden Phrase: _ _ _ _ _ _   _ _ _ _

_ _ _ _   _ _ _ _ , _   _ _ _ _

_ _ _   _ _ _   _ _ _ _ _   _

_ _ _ _ _ _   _ _ _ _   _ _ _

RUTH AND BOAZ

RUTH 2:1–17

AFTER	HUSBANDS
ANSWERED	KINSMAN
BLESS	LORD
BOAZ	MIGHTY
DAMSEL	MOABITESS
FAMILY	NAME
FAVOUR	NAOMI
FIELD	REAPERS
FIND	RUTH
FRIENDLY	SHEAVES
GLEANED	SPOKEN
HANDMAID	WEALTH

B F L E S M A D G O A A
S S R E P A E R L Z F T
S O H I O R K Z E H T R
E D U T E S H E A V E S
T T N W L N H N N O R P
I D S A A A D N E D B O
B N D Y B M E L D S I K
A I H L A S I W Y R M E
O F E I E N U G E R O N
M S D M W I A H H U A L
S S A A H K F I S T N W
I N F F A V O U R H Y E

Hidden Phrase: _ _ _ _ _ _ _ _ _ _ _ _ ,
_ _ _ _ _ _ _ _ _ _ _ _
_ _ _ _

WHERE WERE YOU?

JOB 38

ANSWERED	LIONS	SNOW
BIND	LOOSE	SONS
CAUSE	LORD	STARS
CLOUDS	MORNING	THOU
DECLARE	ORION	THUNDER
DEMAND	PLEIADES	TOGETHER
EARTH	PROVIDETH	TREASURES
FOOD	RAIN	WAST
FOUNDATIONS	RAVEN	WHERE
LAID	SANG	WHIRLWIND
LIGHTNINGS	SHOUTED	WISDOM

```
H A T F U O H T H T H S C E
R F O O D R A S I W N A N A
F A N U T I N S H O U T E D
G N I N R O M I I S L A I D
S H A D W N R L E H D N I B
W G R A E L E R T C R S O R
A P N T W M D R O L E W S S
S W R I L I A H O O D E E A
T N N O N E S N H U N R D N
E D O N V T S D D D U E A G
R S A S N I H R O S H D I T
E R A L C E D G A M T H E B
H E G O T T V E I T E N L T
W H E D R O R A T L S P P S
O T O G E T H E R H F D E W
```

Hidden Phrase: __ __ __ __   __ __ __   __ __ __ __ __   __ __ __ __ __ __ __ __?   __ __   __ __ __   __ __ __ __   __ __ __ __ __ __ __ __   __ __ __   __ __ __ __ __ __   __ __   __ __ __?

How Excellent is the Lord

Psalm 8

ABOVE

AVENGER

BABES

BEASTS

BECAUSE

CONSIDER

CROWNED

DOMINION

EARTH

ENEMIES

EXCELLENT

FINGERS

FOWL

GLORY

HEAVENS

HONOUR

LORD

MINDFUL

MOON

MOUTH

NAME

ORDAINED

OVER

OXEN

SHEEP

STARS

STRENGTH

SUCKLINGS

THINE

VISITEST

WORK

```
F O O E S U A C E B R S T H
O U R H Y U S X T H I N E A
S O D B T R C R O W N E D M
A V A D E E O K E H H V I M
A E I G L A L L S T A R S S
I R N L M W S D G I G E T T
L I E E L O O T L O N H W T
F N D D M M O F S O E G S E
T H S E I M E N E A R E S P
R O T N N S H V R A T D E N
T N I H D E N T O I S E B N
A O N G F E H O S B H L A E
N U H T U O M I C S A M B X
K R O W L A V E N G E R S O
```

Hidden Phrase: _ _ _ _ _ _ _ _ _ _ _

_ _ _ _ _ _ _ _ _ _ _ _ _ _

_ _ _ _ _ _ _ _ _ _ _ _

_ _ _ _ _ _

RASH WORDS

PSALM 14

ABOMINABLE

ASIDE

CORRUPT

COUNSEL

DONE

FEAR

FILTHY

FOOL

GENERATION

GLAD

GONE

GOOD

GREAT

HEART

INIQUITY

KNOWLEDGE

LOOKED

NONE

PEOPLE

POOR

REFUGE

REJOICE

RIGHTEOUS

SAID

SALVATION

SEEK

SHAMED

THEY

TOGETHER

UNDERSTAND

WORKERS

WORKS

```
T U H E E T O G E T H E R E
E L N N L E S N U O C L K O
R D O D D P G O O D N B E G
S D I L E R O D O O O A E K
K H T S E R E E E D N N S D
R O A W A N S F P L E I F S
O R V M H O M T U R W M U W
W H L E E N O G A G E O I O
Y D A L G D A T V N E B N R
H R S E N U I P D T D A I K
T P U R R O C E H O G N Q E
L R T H N E K G F R D C U R
I O R E J O I C E I H I I S
F O O L O R L A A D R E T N
O P F L M E T S R T H E Y N
```

Hidden Phrase: __ __ __   __ __ __ __

__ __ __ __ __ __   __ __ __ __   __ __ __ __

__ __ __ __ __ __   __ __ __ __   __ __ __

__ __ __ __ __ __ __ __   __ __   __ __ __

THE GLORY OF GOD

PSALM 19

BRIDEGROOM

CHAMBER

DECLARE

EARTH

FIRMAMENT

GLORY

GONE

HANDIWORK

HEARD

HEAVENS

KNOWLEDGE

LANGUAGE

LINE

MAKING

NIGHT

PURE

RACE

SHEWETH

SIMPLE

STATUTES

STRONG

SURE

TABERNACLE

TESTIMONY

THROUGH

VOICE

WISE

WORDS

WORLD

```
M T W I S E H V E L A W O Y
F O T W L H W O R D S H N T
F E O P O E N I L L E O S H
O I M R R R T C H A M B E R
D I R E G H L E R I I H T O
S S P M G E E D T R F A U U
N E G I A D D S E C B N T G
E R N N T M E I S E C D A H
V U E O I T E L R T O I T N
A P C V G K G N W B R W S E
E G A U G N A L T O E O A R
H E R U S C T M O I N R N N
G D E C L A R E T R T K H G
E H T E W E H S S H Y O U L
```

Hidden Phrase: __ __ __ __ __ __ __ __ __ __ __ __

__ __ __ __ __ __ __ __ __ __ __ __ __ __,

__ __ __ __ __ __ __ __ __ __ __ __ __ __

__ __ __ __

A Cry
of Anguish

Psalm 22

BRETHREN	HELPING	SEASON
CONGREGATION	HOLY	SILENT
DAYTIME	LAUGH	STRENGTH
DECLARE	LORD	SWORD
DELIVER	MIDST	THEM
DESPISED	NAME	TRUSTED
DRIED	NIGHT	WORDS
FATHERS	PRAISE	WORLD
FORSAKEN	REMEMBER	WORM
GLORY	ROARING	WORSHIP
HASTE	SCORN	

```
G S W O R D B T H E Y P A R
N O I T A G E R G N O C N T
I S D R O W M S E M Y G R F
P M A U R M I E I T N T O S
L I W S S T T P A P H R C T
E D O T H M Y O R G S R S R
H S R E H T A F L A E E E E
N T M D M G D O K B I T D N
P D E C L A R E M H H S O G
N I G H T Y N E E M G S E T
A L H D N D M C A S A U N H
T O L S R E V I L E D E A Y
O R O A R I N G S T L S S L
U D P O N O E M Y I T V E O
S T D L R O W D S E U R E H
```

Hidden Phrase: __ __ __ __   __ __ __ __ __   __ __

__ __ __ __ __ __ __ __   __ __ __ __ __

__ __ __ __ ,   __ __ __   __ __ __ __   __ __ __ __

__ __ __ __   __ __   __ __ __ __ __ __ __

THE GOOD SHEPHERD

PSALM 23

BESIDE	LEADETH	SHALL
COMFORT	LORD	SHEPHERD
DEATH	MAKETH	SOUL
DOWN	NAME	STAFF
DWELL	PASTURES	STILL
ENEMIES	PATHS	SURELY
EVIL	PRESENCE	TABLE
FEAR	RESTORETH	VALLEY
FOREVER	RIGHTEOUSNESS	WALK
GREEN	SAKE	WANT
HOUSE	SHADOW	WATERS

```
S U R W A N T E L Y G O S O
L I V E A H N W O D D S D N
E L S M S F O R E V E R S S
H T E D A E L U A N O A H A
N T Y W D M R L S L E E T E
R R L C D Y L U S E P E H H
A O E L L E O F T H K L R O
L F R S Y E L P E S L L S G
W M U S T O W R M I A E A E
A O S H P O D E T H I P K W
T C G A R E R S T M A L E L
E I T L A L T E E H L E D A
R H Y L E B K N T S O U F M
S T A F F A E C S H A D O W
Y L I F M T E E D I S E B S
```

Hidden Phrase: __ __ __ __ __ __

__ __ __ __ __ __ __ __ __ __ __ __ __ __ __ __ __

__ __ __ __ __ __ __ __ __ __ __ __ __ __ __ __

__ __ __ __ __ __ __ __ __ __ __ __ __ __ __ __

A Prayer
for Protection

Psalm 25

ACCORDING	MINE	TENDER
ASHAMED	NONE	THEE
CAUSE	PATHS	TRANSGRESS
ENEMIES	REMEMBER	TRIUMPH
GOODNESS	SAKE	TRUST
KINDNESSES	SALVATION	TRUTH
LEAD	SHEW	WAIT
LIFT	SINS	WAYS
LORD	SOUL	WITHOUT
LOVING	TEACH	YOUTH
MERCIES		

```
A L E T Y O U T H M E N O
T C A U S E F B E A W S H
K W C G N I V O L A A S M
E I D O L O S E I C R E M
S T N F R T I T O E T I G
R H I D R D P T D R T M O
H O T U N U I N A R T E O
P U S A M E E N U V Y N D
M T T M P T S T G E L E N
U S N I S G H S E K M A E
I R L N R U D S E A T E S
R E M E M B E R H S C E S
T I S W A Y S S O W E H S
N S O U L D A T H L E T E
```

Hidden Phrase: __ __ __ __ __ __ __ __ __ __

__ __ __ __ __ __ __; __ __ __ __ __ __ __

__ __ __ __ __ __ __ __ __ __ __ __ __

WICKED AND UPRIGHT

PSALM 37

AGAINST	GIVE	PEACE
BECAUSE	GOOD	RIGHTEOUSNESS
BRING	HEART	SHALL
COMMIT	INHERIT	THEE
DELIGHT	INIQUITY	THEMSELVES
DESIRES	JUDGMENT	THINE
DWELL	LAND	THYSELF
EARTH	LORD	TRUST
ENVIOUS	MEEK	WAIT
EVILDOERS	NEITHER	WORKERS
FRET	NOONDAY	

```
T T S E R I S E D H A E L S
T H S U O I V N E R G L E P
S D E L I G H T E E A I O T
F A N M L K G C T H I O V H
E W S A S E A O S T N D M E
S O U A L E W N U I S A R E
U R O N P M L D R E T I F E
A K E O O R D V T N N L E B
C E T O T H I N E I E R E R
E R H N D H D M Q S M E D I
B S G D E L G U Y B A M R N
Y T I A W D I H T R D O O G
H E R Y U T T V T E R F L C
L T O J Y I N H E R I T R D
```

Hidden Phrase: _ _ _   _ _ _ _ _ _   _ _   _

_ _ _ _   _ _ _   _ _ _

_ _ _ _ _ _ _ _   _ _   _ _ _   _ _ _ _

Rejoice!

Psalm 46

CARRIED	MELTED	SWELLING
CITY	MIDST	TABERNACLES
EARTH	MOUNTAINS	THEREFORE
FEAR	PRESENT	THEREOF
GLAD	REFUGE	THOUGH
HELP	REMOVED	TROUBLE
HIGH	RIVER	UTTERED
HOLY	ROAR	VERY
HOSTS	SHAKE	VOICE
LORD	STRENGTH	WATERS

```
P C T H E R E O F O R S M
V L H A E B D H G I H R E
H E E T B O D E V O M E R
S L R H N E D E T O D T G
H T E Y C E R T U L F A N
A H F I I S S N D E E W I
K E O R W D T E A O D M L
E V R R I A R R R C A K L
H A E M I E A O E P L S E
C O R N T O O F L N G E W
I T S T H E R E F U G E S
T L U T H E L B U O R T O
Y L O H S R D T H O U G H
```

Hidden Phrase: __ __ __ __, __ __ __ __ __ __ __

__ __ __ __ __ __ __ __ __ __ __ __ __ __

__ __ __ __

Dwell in God's House

Psalm 84

AMIABLE

ANOINTED

BLESSED

COURTS

CRIETH

DOORKEEPER

DWELL

FACE

FLESH

FOUND

HEART

HERSELF

HOSTS

HOUSE

LIVING

LONGETH

LORD

NEST

PRAISING

RATHER

SHIELD

SOUL

SPARROW

STRENGTH

SWALLOW

TABERNACLES

TENTS

THEY

UPRIGHTLY

WALK

WICKEDNESS

YOUNG

```
I E W S T N E T F L E S H
H L Y O H A D L F A C E R
S B A L R I O T H S T L P
W A E S T R E N G T H C R
A I R B D H A L E S E A A
L M C A R C G P D O Y N I
L A H K R A D I S H O R S
O O T I E F T G R I E E I
W O E W O D N H N P L B N
R T G U A I N T E K U A G
H E N E V L E E S R O T P
E D O I L D K S S E S E R
A F L E S R E H U S N I N
R T W H O E G N U O Y H O
T D C O U R T S U S H E O
F M D E S S E L B Y G O D
```

Hidden Phrase: __ __ __ __ __ __ __ __ __ __

__ __ __ __ __ __ __ __ __ __ __ __ __ __

__ __ __ __ __ __ __ __ __ __ __ __ __ __ __

GOD WILL
PROTECT HIS PEOPLE

PSALM 91

ABIDE	DWELLETH	PLACE
AFRAID	EYES	REFUSE
AGAINST	FOOT	REWARD
ALMIGHTY	FORTRESS	SECRET
ARROW	HANDS	SHADOW
BEAR	HIGH	SHIELD
BEHOLD	LORD	SNARE
COVER	MOST	STONE
DASH	NIGHT	TERROR
DELIVER	NOONDAY	TRUST
DESTRUCTION	PESTILENCE	WICKED

```
E C A L P T S U R T F O R H
R E B H S H E A W I C K E D
A S I P T L L R E F U S E G
N T D C E E H I C V H L E A
S H E N O S L E I E I G R S
A N A R A V T L Y V S R I S
T E L D R H E I E E O S H H
S N M T S O M R L W S A D I
N O I T C U R T S E D G R E
I T G E L A H S R O N C A L
A S H H E G A T W T L C W D
G R T B I G R E D L O H E B
A O Y N O O N D A Y R O R V
D I A R F A E R T H D E F E
```

Hidden Phrase: _ _ _ _ _ _ _ _ _ _

_ _ _ _ _ _ _ _ _ _ _ _ _

_ _ _ _ _ _ _ _ _ _ _ _ _ _

GOD
THE CREATOR

PSALM 95

ABOVE	JOYFUL	PSALMS
BEFORE	KING	ROCK
COME	KNEEL	SALVATION
DEEP	LORD	SHEEP
EARTH	MAKE	SING
GENERATION	NOISE	STRENGTH
GREAT	PASTURE	TEMPTED
GRIEVED	PEOPLE	THANKSGIVING
HANDS	PLACES	VOICE
HEAR	PRESENCE	WORSHIP
HILLS	PROVED	

```
T H E S S L L I H D T E A I
S G S T E M P T E D H G H G
I H E E I S G V A N A R N P
N D E N A N O L H E N I R I
G M R E E R O F E B K E A H
D E U R P R T I I T S V A S
N D T H D I A H T E G E S R
H S S A L N G T N A I D D O
P L A C E S R C I J V S F W
E L P O E P E H O O I L M R
S V R M N M A E I Y N D A T
I R O C K N T C H F G E K S
O C E B D P E E D U H D E R
N Y L S A A P S A L M S N D
```

Hidden Phrase: _ _ _ _ _ _ _ _ _ _ _,
_ _ _ _ _ _ _ _ _ _ _: _ _ _
_ _ _ _ _ _ _ _ _ _ _ _ _ _ _
_ _ _ _ _ _ _ _ _ _

THE GOODNESS OF GOD

PSALM 104

ANGELS	FLAMING	MOUNTAINS
BEAST	FOUNDATIONS	SATISFIED
BLESS	FOUNDED	SOUL
CHARIOT	FRUIT	SPIRITS
CLOTHED	GARMENT	THUNDER
CLOUDS	GIVE	VALLEYS
CURTAIN	GREAT	VOICE
DOWN	HEAVENS	WATERS
DRINK	HONOUR	WIND
EARTH	LIGHT	WINGS
FIELD	LORD	WORK
FIRE	MAJESTY	

```
M A J E S T Y S R E T A W
F O U N D E D B H N E D V
S D U O L C C E S A O U
S E D N I W H M P A I W T
G R E A T A R I H C S N T
T D H E R A R R E A R T H
K G E I G I I R U E V I G
S N O I T A D N U O F A I
S T I S F E G C S A N L L
S G S R H S N U T N V O O
G R N T D N I R O G A R H
W F O I L E M T B E L D F
F L I U W V A A A L L I O
C W O R K A L I R S E T H
E S C F E E F N A L Y S T
R E D N U H T T D L S E S
```

Hidden Phrase: __ __   __ __ __ __ __ __ __ __   __ __ __

__ __ __ __ __   __ __   __ __ __ __   __ __ __

__ __ __   __ __ __ __ __ __

Joy in Zion's Return

Psalm 126

AGAIN	HEATHEN	SINGING
AMONG	LAUGHTER	SOUTH
BEARING	LIKE	STREAMS
BRINGING	LORD	THEM
CAPTIVITY	MOUTH	THEY
COME	PRECIOUS	THINGS
DOUBTLESS	REAP	TONGUE
DREAM	REJOICING	TURNED
FILLED	SAID	WEEPETH
FORTH	SEED	WHEN
GLAD	SHEAVES	ZION
GREAT		

```
S T R E A M S T C S W H
E E O E N E H T A E H Y
E F K N J D C H P V E T
D I A S G O H E T A N A
L L D T M U I Y I E T H
S L R E O B E C V H A T
W E E P E T H P I S E U
S D A W R L R I T N R O
N G M G G E T E Y M G S
A R N N C S T Z E N I S
S H O I D S A H I N A H
L M O R H E T G G O T L
A U E A L T N I A U N D
S A R E O I N R O I A A
P E A B R G P M U I N L
N J O B D Y F O R T H G
```

Hidden Phrase: __ __ __ __   __ __ __ __   __ __ __ __

__ __   __ __ __ __ __   __ __ __ __ __   __ __ __ __

__ __   __ __ __

THE ROAD
TO WISDOM

PROVERBS 3

ABOUT

ACKNOWLEDGE

BIND

COMMANDMENTS

DAYS

DEPART

EVIL

FAVOUR

FIND

FORGET

HEART

KEEP

LENGTH

LIFE

LONG

MERCY

NECK

PATHS

PEACE

TABLE

THEM

TRUST

TRUTH

UNDERSTANDING

UPON

WRITE

E	G	D	E	L	W	O	N	K	C	A
T	N	T	H	E	M	H	G	N	O	L
E	I	R	L	S	Y	A	D	E	M	O
R	D	U	H	D	B	P	Y	C	M	W
N	N	T	P	E	E	K	I	K	A	S
O	A	H	Y	A	F	L	D	W	N	O
P	T	M	C	O	I	H	A	R	D	T
U	S	E	R	F	T	H	T	I	M	R
D	R	G	E	T	R	U	S	T	E	A
F	E	U	M	E	O	D	O	E	N	E
T	D	P	O	B	L	E	N	G	T	H
U	N	N	A	V	I	B	V	I	S	D
E	U	D	T	R	A	N	A	I	F	H
E	E	A	R	T	T	F	D	T	L	H

Hidden Phrase: _ _ _   _ _ _ _   _ _

_ _ _ _ _ _   _ _ _ _

_ _ _ _ _ _ _   _ _ _   _ _ _ _ _

Wisdom and Folly

Proverbs 10

BLESSINGS	HAND	RECEIVE
COMMANDMENTS	HEAD	RICH
DEATH	HEAVINESS	RIGHTEOUSNESS
DELIVERETH	JUST	SLACK
DILIGENT	LORD	SOLOMON
FALL	MAKETH	SOUL
FAMISH	MOTHER	SUFFER
FATHER	NOTHING	TREASURES
FOOLISH	POOR	WICKEDNESS
FROM	PROFIT	WILL
GLAD	PROVERBS	WISE

```
S B R E V O R P T S K H W R
T S N O T H I N G C O D I O
N M E E Y E D N A H R U L O
E O N N H S I L O O F W L P
M T O S S S R L A I R R S
D H M O S U H E H C M O F T
N E O E H E O C K S F O T E
A R L W M I N E I I I R R C
M B O I K A D I T R E M E F
M H S E V N K V V H G L A D
O T D U E E S E T A G H S F
C A E S F F R A T A E I U L
L E S S A F F E B H E H R S
H D I L I G E N T O D A E H
R T L E N W E R D H J U S T
```

Hidden Phrase: _ _ _ _ _ _ _ _ _ _ _

_ _ _ _ _ _ _ _ _ _ _ _ _ _ _ _

_ _ _ _ _ _ _ _ _ _

Rich and Poor

Proverbs 14

BELIEVETH

BUILDETH

CROWNED

DEATH

DESPISETH

DOWN

EVERY

FALSE

FLOURISH

FOOLISH

GOING

HOUSE

KNOWLEDGE

LORD

OVERTHROWN

PERVERSE

PLUCKETH

PRIDE

PRUDENT

SEEMETH

SIMPLE

TABERNACLE

THEREOF

UPRIGHT

WAYS

WELL

WICKED

WISE

WITNESS

WOMAN

WORD

```
L L E W H S I R U O L F W G
E I S V E T T E L P M I S D
S T R T B O E H T E T H E E
U P E N U S T V E N S S O O
O R V E I E A H E R P L N D
H V R D L E T S G I E E A H
K O E U D M S H S I L O O F
U N P R E E S E D C R E F H
A L O P T T E A T S P B H
S Y A W H H K N G I A E U V
W E E T L C R O W N E D W L
O V A T I E I O R E A I O S
R E U W B N D O W N R R M E
D R I A G N H G E N D P A A
V Y T P L U C K E T H E N N
```

Hidden Phrase: _ _ _ _   _ _   _ _ _ _

_ _ _ _, _ _ _ _ _ _ _ _ _ _ _ _ _

_ _ _ _ _ _ _ _ _ _ _ _ _ _

_ _ _ _ _ _

Proper Training

Proverbs 22

BORROWER	LENDER	RICHES
CHOSEN	LIFE	SERVANT
EVIL	LION	SILVER
FAVOUR	LORD	SIMPLE
FORESEETH	LOVING	SLAIN
GOLD	MAKER	SLOTHFUL
GOOD	NAME	SNARES
GREAT	PRUDENT	STREETS
HONOUR	PUNISHED	THEM
HUMILITY	RATHER	THORNS
INIQUITY	REAP	VANITY

```
B T R A I N U P A C H T I
D O O G N S N R O H T A L
E D R I E Y R N M A K E R
E M T R S U T N E D U R P
H F A V O U R I H P E G S
M N I N H W G T U E V I L
S E O L C R E N M Q M W L
I H H S A E I R I P I U A
L Y H T S S P V L V F N R
V E H E H S A E I H O D I
E E R E D N E L T H L L C
R O D R I O R O Y U I O H
F L O T D S L A I N O G E
G L Y S O S E R V A N T S
```

Hidden Phrase: __ __ __ __ __ __   __ __   __

__ __ __ __ __   __ __   __ __ __   __ __ __   __ __

__ __ __ __ __ __   __ __

Proper Conduct

Proverbs 23

APPETITE

CAUSE

CHILD

CONSIDER

CORRECTION

DAINTIES

DECEITFUL

DELIVER

DESIROUS

DESPISE

DILIGENTLY

EARS

FOOL

FROM

GIVEN

GUIDE

HEART

KNIFE

LANDMARK

MEAT

MIGHTY

PLEAD

REDEEMER

RULER

SOUL

SPEAK

THROAT

WHEN

WISDOM

```
B U A Y W D E S P I S E
T S P W H I E E C T M E A R S
R S P H U I S O S T I R S
G O E E T H N D U N G S
Y U T N A S T A O R H T
A L I D I K N I R M T D
S A T D E H T E I O Y K
D E E N E C M A S R L R
A R L A E E E I E F T R A
E N R R E G S I D M R M
L T R D I O I U T T E D
P O E V F O O L A F L N
C R E V I L E D I C U A
K N I F E C H I L D R L
```

Hidden Phrase: __ __ __   __ __ __   __ __ __ __ __ __,

__ __ __   __ __ __ __ __   __ __   __ __ __

In Defense
of Wisdom

Ecclesiastes 7

BETTER

BIRTH

CONSIDER

COUNTENANCE

CROOKED

DEATH

EARTH

FEASTING

FOOLS

GOOD

HEAR

HOUSE

JUST

LAUGHTER

MAKE

MOURNING

NAME

OINTMENT

PATIENT

PRECIOUS

PROFIT

PROUD

REBUKE

SADNESS

SINNETH

SONG

SORROW

SPIRIT

STRAIGHT

WISDOM

WORK

E T G H T A E D B I R T H H

E C P N A M E K R A E H A T

I T N E I T A P U E T N P T

I T S A D N E S S B T N R W

F N I S N C R O O K E D O P

I E L R H E D U M C B R F W

R M A F I O T S O A K I I H

T T U S O P U N I M K S T S

B N G G T O S S U E D E T S

D I H T I I L E E O N A O O

U O T C D R N S M N C R T N

O T E E H T H G I A R T S G

R R R A N T H S E O P H U R

P O U D I N S P W I R I J T

Hidden Phrase: __ __ __   __ __ __ __ __ __ __ __ __   __ __

__ __ __ __ __ __ __   __ __   __ __ __ __ __ __

__ __ __ __ __   __ __ __   __ __ __ __ __ __   __ __

__ __ __ __ __ __ __

ADVICE
TO YOUTH

ECCLESIASTES 11

AWAY	FIND	SHALL
BEHOLD	FLESH	SIGHT
BREAD	HEART	SORROW
BRING	JUDGMENT	SWEET
CAST	LIGHT	TRULY
CHILDHOOD	MORNING	UPON
DAYS	PLEASANT	VANITY
EVENING	PROSPER	WATERS
EVIL	REMOVE	YOUTH
EYES	SEED	

```
R E M E D M R E M O V E B
U P O N E A R N C O V M W
T H I Y S C Y H T E R O Y
D F J W E A I S N R T R T
O L E U L L A I Y E R N I
I E O L D C N G A P A I N
T S A H I G N H W S D N A
W H O L E V M T A O E G V
S O T H I B E E E R E Y H
D B R I N G L D N P S E E
D A E R B P H A Y T A S O
F H T U O Y T T T R U L Y
H Y Y O U S R E T A W T H
```

Hidden Phrase: __ __ __ __ __ __ __ __ __ __ __

__ __ __ __ __ __ __ __ __ __ __ __ __ __

__ __ __ __ __ __ __ __ __ __ __ __ __ __

Isaiah Tells about Jesus

Isaiah 53:1–8

ACQUAINTED

AFFLICTED

BEAUTY

BORNE

BROUGHT

BRUISED

CARRIED

COMELINESS

DESIRE

DESPISED

DUMB

ESTEEMED

GRIEF

HEALED

INIQUITIES

LAMB

MOUTH

OPENED

OPPRESSED

PEACE

REJECTED

REVEALED

ROOT

SHEARERS

SHEEP

SLAUGHTER

SMITTEN

SORROW

STRICKEN

STRIPES

SURELY

TENDER

TRANSGRESSIONS

TURNED

WOUNDED

```
P P H I L D I S T R I P E S P B
D E L A E V E R E G A N N U S N
F A A S H E A R E R S O R R O E
T E I C T D H E S J I A O E R K
M R I D E M E E T S E S B L R C
E E S R C R D I S D E C A Y O I
S L A U G H T E R I U M T M W R
A D I D E N R U T R B M E E S T
F E E P T G T I D N A L B U D S
F S R S S E U E E A I C R N W D
L S Y N P Q S T N N P A O O R E
I E A T I I T A E D M O U T H R
C R C N U I S S P H E N G Q O E
T P I R M A S E O D D R H O C U
E P B S H E E P D E N T T O H A
D O I M J E S B D E L A E H U S
```

Hidden Phrase: __ __ __ __ __ __ ... __ __ __ __ __

__ __ __ __ __ __ __ __ __

__ __ __ __ __ __ __ __ __ , __ __ __

__ __ __ __ __ __ __ __ __ __ __ __ __ __ __

__ __ __ __ __

Sower, Seeds, and Soils

Matthew 13:3–23

ABUNDANCE	GROUND	SEEDS
CARE	HEARING	SIXTY
CHOKE	HEART	SOWER
CLOSED	HEAVEN	SPAKE
DEVOURED	HUNDREDFOLD	SPRUNG
DISCIPLES	KINGDOM	STONY
DULL	KNOW	TAKEN
EARS	MYSTERIES	THIRTY
EARTH	PARABLES	THORNS
EYES	PLACES	UNDERSTAND
FOWLS	RECEIVED	WICKED
FRUIT	RICHES	WITHERED
GIVEN	ROOT	WORLD
GOOD	SCORCHED	

```
S I X T Y D E R E H T I W H E
T R A E H L O A D M R M S T H
N U C Y N O T S Y O G O O E W
E O N A T F R S E R O D W R Y
V C D D R D T N O H S G E T A
I N N U E E D U S D C N R S R
G E I A R R N R E C E I V E D
C T R I D D S E L E H K R Y I
V T E E I N S T B T D I C E T
H S P D S U U P A E A R S I D
A H L L C H N B R N D B R E W
H E A R I N G U A U D I S K O
N A C O P G O F P O N O P O N
R V E W L V T D U L L G A H K
H E S D E H C R O C S F K C R
U N I D S L W O F T A K E N T
```

Hidden Phrase: __ __ __ __   __ __ __   __ __ __ __,

__ __ __   __ __ __ __ __ __ __ __   __ __,   __ __ __

__ __ __ __ __ __   __ __ __ __ __   __ __ __ __ __

SCRAMBLED CIRCLE PUZZLES

by Ken Save

Unscramble the words from the list provided, placing the corrected words in the numbered blanks. Then use the circled letters to answer the question following.

1. SJUSE
2. ERPOTHPS
3. DHWSASO
4. SLDNAA
5. ZATPBEI
6. APALHNIT

7. REAABPL
8. PIRSTI
9. RESHSEIAP
10. UEDETBSATI
11. LSTA

He really lost his head over Jesus. Who was he?

1. ◯ __ __ __ __
2. __ __ ◯ __ __ __ __ __
3. __ ◯ __ __ __ __ __
4. __ __ ◯ __ __ __
5. ◯ __ __ __ __ __
6. __ ◯ __ __ __ __ __
7. ◯ __ __ __ __ __ __
8. __ __ __ __ __ ◯
9. __ __ __ __ ◯ __ __ __
10. __ __ __ __ __ __ __ __ ◯
11. __ __ __ ◯

Answer: __ __ __ __ the __ __ __ __ __ __ __

1. VERSEREPE

2. NGPASA

3. REHTRBO

4. TVERILENOA

5. NSIS

6. ELUSFSNL

7. LSPIEWFHLO

This church had a golden lampstand named after it.

1. _ ◯ _ _ _ _ _ _
2. ◯ _ _ _ _ _
3. _ _ _ _ ◯ _ _
4. _ _ _ ◯ _ _ _ _ _
5. ◯ _ _ _
6. _ ◯ _ _ _ _ _
7. _ _ _ _ _ ◯ _ _

Answer: _ _ _ _ _ _ _

1. OPLEEP
2. IOGNRANG
3. NDSRCOEI
4. ROVGSEIEN
5. YRECM
6. FLINSU
7. GTESLURG
8. NTOLCOR
9. IPNSAOSS

She may have had the same name, but she was *not* the wife of the famous singer. Who was she?

1. _ _ _ O _ _
2. _ O _ _ _ _ _ _
3. _ _ _ _ O _ _ _
4. O _ _ _ _ _ _ _ _
5. _ _ _ O _
6. _ O _ _ _ _
7. _ _ _ _ _ _ O _
8. _ _ _ _ _ _ O
9. _ O _ _ _ _ _ _

Answer: _ _ _ _ _ _ _ _ _

1. ZAEBITP   6. RNESKTIC

2. NWEDOR   7. LUYMPTIL

3. RCYESRO   8. RAHTE

4. TYHUO   9. DHNSA

5. RDCEEAL

This prophet was the son of Berekiah.

1. _ _ _ _ _ ◯ _

2. _ _ _ _ ◯ _

3. _ _ _ ◯ _ _ _

4. _ _ _ ◯

5. _ _ _ _ ◯ _ _

6. _ _ ◯ _ _ _ _

7. _ _ _ _ ◯ _ _ _

8. _ ◯ _ _ _

9. ◯ _ _ _ _

Answer: _ _ _ _ _ _ _ _ _

1. EPLEOP   6. TOSUATC

2. ETARG   7. ODBLEH

3. EISNAREC   8. SAPS

4. ERERTOS   9. TMSEI

5. REUDVO

Such a wind was worth the wait.

1. Ⓞ＿ ＿ ＿ ＿ ＿

2. ＿ ＿ Ⓞ＿ ＿

3. ＿ Ⓞ＿ ＿ ＿ ＿ ＿ ＿

4. ＿ ＿ ＿ Ⓞ＿ ＿ ＿

5. ＿ Ⓞ＿ ＿ ＿ ＿

6. ＿ ＿ ＿ Ⓞ＿ ＿ ＿

7. ＿ ＿ ＿ Ⓞ＿ ＿

8. ＿ ＿ Ⓞ＿

9. ＿ ＿ ＿ Ⓞ＿

Answer: ＿ ＿ ＿ ＿ ＿ ＿ ＿ ＿ ＿

1. ANRE

2. EGNER

3. EIGES

4. SRRUEL

5. SGERLID

6. ESRITS

7. NDOEIRSI

8. NCOIANT

9. RSECATT

10. TPIY

11. UHSOE

12. NAEHEHT

What is it that all believers will experience?

1. — — — ◯

2. — — ◯ — —

3. ◯ — — — — —

4. — ◯ — — — — —

5. — — ◯ — — — —

6. — — — — — ◯

7. — ◯ — — — — — —

8. ◯ — — — — — —

9. — — — — ◯ — —

10. — ◯ — — —

11. — ◯ — — —

12. — — — — — ◯

Answer: __ __ __ __ __ __ __ __ __ __ __ __

1. DLEBSES

2. RIPSIT

3. UNORM

4. DFAOBRE

5. LPEINCAN

He threw a party for Jesus but was not prepared for the woman with the perfume.

1. _ _ _ ⭕ _ _ _

2. _ _ ⭕ _ _ _

3. ⭕ _ _ _ _

4. _ ⭕ _ _ _ _ _

5. _ _ _ ⭕ _ _ _ _

Answer: _ _ _ _ _

1. LREEVI

2. EGAELIL

3. ETLEPM

4. YCROTUN

5. ELNGA

6. DEHRA

7. ERCOJIE

8. DROHE

9. NROPSI

10. ELRPA

11. DBEAL

Who is like the greatest in heaven?

1. _ _ _ _ O _
2. _ _ _ O _ _ _
3. O _ _ _ _ _
4. _ _ _ _ O _ _
5. _ _ _ _ O
6. _ O _ _ _
7. _ _ _ _ _ O _
8. O _ _ _ _
9. _ _ O _ _ _
10. _ _ _ _ O
11. _ _ _ O _

Answer: _ _ _ _ _ _   _ _ _ _ _

1. SJEUS

2. SDLEMA

3. RDPEAT

4. MITE

5. ECVIEER

6. HRONO

7. MKOIDNG

Many feet meant a dramatic change for this place.

1. ◯ __ __ __ __

2. __ __ __ __ ◯ __

3. __ __ __ __ ◯ __

4. __ ◯ __ __

5. __ __ ◯ __ __ __ __

6. ◯ __ __ __ __ __

7. __ __ __ __ __ ◯ __

Answer: __ __ __ __ __ __ __

1. EPHES

2. CANGNDI

3. EWMNO

4. NNETUIODC

5. PRTUEAC

6. HTENIPSLII

With a little oil, he made David king. Who was he?

1. ◯ _ _ _ _

2. _ ◯ _ _ _ _ _ _

3. _ _ ◯ _ _ _

4. _ _ _ _ _ _ _ ◯ _ _

5. _ _ _ _ _ _ ◯

6. _ _ _ ◯ _ _ _ _ _ _

Answer: _ _ _ _ _ _ _

1. DZINO

2. TBATEL

3. SRINIG

4. BSTERI

5. SPILNA

6. STHTRNEG

7. TCSHOAIR

8. WTODRA

9. EHTDA

This town was home to a widow and her son who were very glad to have Elijah stay with them.

1. ◯ __ __ __ __

2. __ ◯ __ __ __ __

3. ◯ __ __ __ __ __

4. __ __ __ __ ◯ __

5. ◯ __ __ __ __ __

6. __ __ __ __ __ __ __ ◯

7. __ __ ◯ __ __ __ __ __

8. ◯ __ __ __ __ __

9. __ __ __ __ ◯

Answer: __ __ __ __ __ __ __

1. VAEBO

2. CZRACU

3. TUJNEDGM

4. AWONMRK

5. NIWGILL

6. CEESRIV

7. LBOSW

Wheels and scrolls—a vision for this prophet. Who was he?

1. _ _ _ _ ○

2. ○ _ _ _ _ _

3. _ _ _ _ _ ○ _ _

4. _ _ _ ○ _ _ _

5. _ ○ _ _ _ _ _

6. _ _ _ _ _ ○

7. _ _ _ ○ _

Answer: _ _ _ _ _ _ _

1. OBJ

2. EADPPTNOI

3. PRSTOO

4. SRERTOR

5. RISPLAL

6. EBDZEEE

7. TEDXAEL

In the old days, a little water would clean one right up!

1. _ _ ◯

2. ◯ _ _ _ _ _ _ _ _

3. _ _ _ _ ◯ _

4. ◯ _ _ _ _ _ _

5. _ ◯ _ _ _ _ _

6. ◯ _ _ _ _ _ _

7. _ _ _ _ _ ◯ _

Answer: _ _ _ _ _ _ _

1. SOECMNU

2. LEXTA

3. AEPELRUS

4. NSTERAV

5. EANRWS

6. RHIOPWS

7. RAUPETS

In the beginning, there was nothing to separate the water, until God created it. What was it?

1. _ _ _ _ _ _ ◯

2. _ ◯ _ _ _

3. ◯ _ _ _ _ _ _ _

4. _ _ _ _ ◯ _ _

5. _ ◯ _ _ _ _

6. _ _ _ ◯ _ _ _

7. _ _ _ _ _ ◯

Answer: _ _ _ _ _ _ _

1. NAEET

2. EBSON

3. ETLEBRIR

4. RHTHAE

5. SRUIOGEHT

6. EOCRNDAIN

7. YEMEN

This righteous man had a difficult time with fear.

1. __ ◯ __ __ __

2. ◯ __ __ __ __

3. __ __ ◯ __ __ __ __ __

4. __ __ ◯ __ __ __

5. __ __ __ ◯ __ __ __ __ __

6. __ __ __ __ ◯ __ __ __

7. __ __ __ ◯ __

Answer: __ __ __ __ __ __ __

1. HJAEIRME

2. OTERULB

3. KSAPE

4. RNHEEIT

5. DBLUI

6. HTSAIRSH

This son of Nun took control of a nation.

1. ◯ _ _ _ _ _ _ _

2. _ _ ◯ _ _ _ _

3. ◯ _ _ _ _

4. _ _ _ _ ◯ _ _

5. _ ◯ _ _ _

6. _ ◯ _ _ _ _ _ _

Answer: _ _ _ _ _ _

1. SWSIELNDRE

2. YCROTUN

3. TWHAE

4. TWHEGI

5. RMEREMEB

6. RLDO

7. EBTRALEC

8. OZNI

This couple fell in love on a threshing floor.

1. _ _ _ _ _ ◯ _ _ _ _

2. _ _ ◯ _ _ _ _ _

3. _ _ _ _ ◯

4. _ _ _ _ ◯ _

5. _ _ _ _ _ ◯ _ _

6. _ ◯ _ _

7. _ _ ◯ _ _ _ _ _

8. ◯ _ _ _

Answer: _ _ _ _ and _ _ _ _

1. AGTRE

2. EHOSSR

3. SLJUEOA

4. DTIMS

5. MJEELRAUS

6. TPELMUM

7. SHTOS

He should have ducked. Who was he?

1. ⃝ __ __ __ __

2. __ ⃝ __ __ __ __

3. __ __ __ ⃝ __ __ __

4. __ ⃝ __ __ __

5. __ __ __ __ __ ⃝ __ __ __

6. __ __ __ __ __ __ ⃝

7. ⃝ __ __ __ __

Answer: __ __ __ __ __ __ __

1. LSUIFN

2. RFEAHT

3. EALSBSEM

4. NVOISI

5. SGSLEAND

6. NBERHETR

7. HFTAI

8. DOEPEN

9. DFNOU

Whom shall we fear when the Lord is our light and our...?

1. ◯ _ _ _ _ _

2. _ ◯ _ _ _ _

3. _ _ _ _ _ _ ◯ _

4. ◯ _ _ _ _ _

5. _ _ ◯ _ _ _ _ _

6. _ _ _ ◯ _ _ _ _

7. _ _ ◯ _ _

8. ◯ _ _ _ _ _

9. _ _ _ ◯ _

Answer: _ _ _ _ _ _ _ _ _

1. ASIMAAR

2. ERVEMO

3. ESEPRHUCL

4. DAENTION

5. MBETEHLHE

6. TCNOAVNE

7. NCIAATP

He made the right choice and was blessed more than any other man.

1. ◯ _ _ _ _ _ _

2. _ _ _ ◯ _ _ _

3. _ _ _ _ ◯ _ _ _ _

4. _ _ ◯ _ _ _ _ _

5. _ _ _ _ _ _ _ _ ◯

6. _ ◯ _ _ _ _ _ _

7. _ _ _ _ _ _ ◯

Answer: _ _ _ _ _ _ _

1. RDEEVLI

2. EPCRENES

3. NCIEART

4. NHEEVA

5. SFDIEL

6. EPSRIA

She became queen and saved Israel. Who was she?

1. __ ◯ __ __ __ __ __

2. __ __ __ ◯ __ __ __ __

3. __ __ __ ◯ __ __ __

4. ◯ __ __ __ __ __

5. __ __ ◯ __ __ __

6. __ ◯ __ __ __ __

Answer: __ __ __ __ __ __

1. TLNAEM
2. ESCEIRV
3. ECMO
4. DBLEOH
5. YTTWNE
6. EFKOARS

7. DBLIU
8. TDREPA
9. LSUO
10. EHATS
11. EVYALL
12. SESTRNVA

This book of the Bible is good for learning.

1. ___ ___ ___ ⭕ ___ ___
2. ___ ___ ___ ___ ___ ⭕ ___
3. ⭕ ___ ___ ___
4. ___ ___ ___ ___ ⭕ ___
5. ___ ___ ⭕ ___ ___ ___
6. ___ ___ ___ ⭕ ___ ___ ___
7. ___ ___ ⭕ ___ ___
8. ___ ___ ___ ⭕ ___ ___
9. ⭕ ___ ___ ___
10. ___ ___ ___ ⭕ ___
11. ___ ___ ___ ⭕ ___
12. ___ ___ ___ ___ ___ ___ ⭕

Answer: ___ ___ ___ ___ ___ ___ ___ ___ ___ ___ ___

1. RPEOTR

2. SWSIETN

3. EDLIPSIC

4. DSEAV

5. RFEAHT

6. RSETGRNA

He asked Jesus if He was the King of the Jews.

1. Ⓞ— — — — —

2. —Ⓞ— — — — —

3. — — — — — — Ⓞ—

4. —Ⓞ— — — —

5. — —Ⓞ— — —

6. — — — — — Ⓞ—

Answer: — — — — — —

1. EGSELNIT
2. YMFAIGN
3. TRNEEP
4. HFTAI
5. TFIRU
6. FUENBEIL
7. DSONU

8. SMOES
9. LGOEPS
10. SREIHC
11. RSULEMB
12. SJEYUAOL
13. TOBAS

This will lead to an abundance of grief. What is it?

1. _ _ _ _ _ _ _◯
2. _ _ _ _◯_ _ _
3. _ _ _ _◯_
4. ◯_ _ _ _ _
5. _◯_ _ _ _
6. _ _ _ _◯_ _ _
7. _ _ _ _◯
8. _ _ _◯_
9. _ _◯_ _ _
10. _◯_ _ _ _
11. _ _ _ _ _◯
12. _◯_ _ _ _ _ _
13. _ _ _◯_

Answer: _ _ _ _ _ _   _ _ _ _ _ _ _

1. KTNHI
2. SNANOTI
3. WRGO
4. SPSWAORR
5. SLIELI

6. SRNAEV
7. YEDLA
8. SGERVA
9. SCSERBI

Charity edifies, but this puffs up. What is it?

1. _ _ _ _ ◯
2. ◯ _ _ _ _ _ _
3. _ _ ◯ _
4. _ _ _ _ _ _ ◯ _
5. _ _ ◯ _ _ _
6. _ _ _ ◯ _ _
7. ◯ _ _ _ _
8. ◯ _ _ _ _ _
9. _ _ _ _ _ ◯ _

Answer: _ _ _ _ _ _ _ _ _

1. YGLRO

2. RMEANN

3. KWLA

4. EALNG

5. TPERAIV

6. ERSPIOM

7. YGIRANP

8. TANCUCO

9. EPSLAE

Who were these people who were bewitched?

1. ◯ _ _ _ _

2. _ ◯ _ _ _ _

3. _ _ ◯ _

4. ◯ _ _ _ _

5. _ _ _ _ _ ◯ _

6. _ _ _ _ ◯ _ _

7. _ _ ◯ _ _ _ _

8. _ _ _ _ _ ◯ _

9. _ _ _ _ ◯ _

Answer: _ _ _ _ _ _ _ _ _

1. RTNEE

2. HISTTE

3. TINFSIRMIEI

4. RCDNIETO

5. EOTMRH

6. LHYO

7. RFTOY

Who was Paul's own son in the faith?

1. __ __ ◯ __ __

2. __ ◯ __ __ __ __

3. __ __ __ __ ◯ __ __ __ __ __

4. __ ◯ __ __ __ __ __ __

5. __ __ ◯ __ __ __

6. ◯ __ __ __

7. __ __ __ __ ◯

Answer: __ __ __ __ __ __ __

1. EHLFS
2. RLBIYTE
3. NIRTTWE
4. RNEUD
5. AECRG
6. TBDWSEOE

7. LARGYLOE
8. AINSI
9. AOGDNBE
10. VLAENE
11. RTHSIC
12. SOANSE

Satan comes with all power, signs, and what else?

1. __ ◯ __ __ __
2. __ __ __ __ __ __ ◯
3. __ __ ◯ __ __ __ __
4. __ ◯ __ __ __
5. ◯ __ __ __ __
6. __ __ __ __ ◯ __ __ __
7. __ __ __ __ __ ◯ __ __
8. __ __ ◯ __ __ __
9. __ __ ◯ __ __ __
10. __ ◯ __ __ __ __
11. __ __ ◯ __ __ __
12. ◯ __ __ __ __ __

Answer: __ __ __ __ __   __ __ __ __ __ __

1. ETGHNSRT
2. NIONOMDI
3. TASSNI
4. TRABHED
5. WROEP

6. USWHLIF
7. HARETG
8. TWRHA
9. NURPCDEE

What is a laborer worthy of?

1. _ _ _ _ _ _ _ ◯
2. _ _ _ _ ◯ _ _ _
3. ◯ _ _ _ _ _
4. _ ◯ _ _ _ _ _
5. _ _ _ ◯ _
6. ◯ _ _ _ _ _ _
7. _ ◯ _ _ _ _
8. _ ◯ _ _ _
9. _ _ _ ◯ _ _ _ _

Answer: _ _ _   _ _ _ _ _ _

1. REINTCA
2. RSXEEPS
3. ELPEPO
4. SREOA
5. NCETAGIH
6. SSEEDSAI
7. NISERDF
8. TLDETMUIU
9. SYLRHA

The Spirit speaks in what way regarding the latter times?

1. _ ◯ _ _ _ _ _
2. _ ◯ _ _ _ _ _
3. _ _ _ ◯ _ _
4. _ ◯ _ _ _
5. _ ◯ _ _ _ _ _ _
6. _ _ ◯ _ _ _ _
7. _ _ _ _ _ _ ◯
8. _ _ ◯ _ _ _ _ _ _
9. _ _ _ _ _ ◯

Answer: _ _ _ _ _ _ _ _ _

1. HRNETBER

2. SEILWEIK

3. EARTGSG

4. MHASADE

5. ANECIPET

6. TNLAEER

7. KESNILES

8. REFDE

9. TFUYISJ

10. QTINYUII

Jesus is considered the Apostle and what of our profession?

1. _ _ _ _ ◯ _ _ _

2. _ ◯ _ _ _ _ _ _

3. _ _ _ _ ◯ _ _ _

4. _ _ ◯ _ _ _ _

5. ◯ _ _ _ _ _ _

6. _ _ _ ◯ _ _ _

7. _ ◯ _ _ _ _ _ _

8. _ _ _ ◯ _

9. _ _ ◯ _ _ _ _

10. _ _ _ _ _ _ ◯ _

Answer: _ _ _ _   _ _ _ _ _ _

1. ENGSUOT   6. EAPHSC

2. UEIDRB   7. BREON

3. LLEYVO   8. GMEAI

4. ATLYREH   9. IIWNGTLKN

5. EAFTMSIN   10. UTBSEJC

Only the Lamb is worthy to open these. What are they?

1. _ _ _ _ _ _ ◯

2. _ _ _ _ ◯ _

3. _ _ ◯ _ _ _

4. ◯ _ _ _ _ _ _

5. _ _ ◯ _ _ _ _ _

6. _ _ _ _ _ ◯

7. _ _ _ _ ◯

8. _ _ ◯ _ _

9. _ _ _ _ _ ◯ _ _ _

10. ◯ _ _ _ _ _ _

Answer: _ _ _ _ _   _ _ _ _ _

1. RVSEEPRE
2. WRSOSRO
3. OLSEUCN
4. RTTFNOOGE
5. URSFEF
6. SCTVUEOO

7. XDLETAE
8. RDPUO
9. HLMEBU
10. TNNSAOI
11. ITERNIH

This book is the only one of its kind in the Bible.

1. _ _ _ ◯ _ _ _ _
2. _ ◯ _ _ _ _ _
3. _ _ _ ◯ _ _ _
4. _ _ _ ◯ _ _ _ _ _
5. ◯ _ _ _ _ _
6. _ _ _ _ _ ◯ _ _
7. _ _ _ ◯ _ _ _
8. _ _ ◯ _ _
9. _ _ ◯ _ _ _
10. _ _ _ _ ◯ _ _
11. _ ◯ _ _ _ _

Answer: The _ _ _ _ of _ _ _ _ _ _ _ _

1. SUSJE

2. RWOSD

3. HNREET

4. ELTNMA

5. AHHPROA

6. TWDLE

7. TTLHWFE

8. NLAIS

9. EANLFL

10. TUDETMLIU

Jesus made reference to this slimy story.

1. ◯ _ _ _ _

2. _ _ ◯ _ _

3. ◯ _ _ _ _ _

4. _ ◯ _ _ _ _

5. _ _ _ _ _ ◯

6. _ ◯ _ _ _

7. _ _ _ _ _ ◯

8. _ _ ◯ _ _

9. _ _ _ ◯ _ _

10. _ _ _ _ _ _ _ ◯

Answer: _ _ _ _ _ and the _ _ _ _ _

1. DUEDHRN

2. SREET

3. UHECIBMR

4. SHUEO

5. NRDGUO

6. RESMSAUE

7. AHRCSE

She was a female judge who ruled Israel.

1. _ _ _ _ _ _ ◯

2. _ _ ◯ _ _

3. _ _ _ _ ◯ _ _

4. _ ◯ _ _ _

5. _ ◯ _ _ _ _

6. _ _ ◯ _ _ _ _ _

7. _ _ _ ◯ _ _

Answer: _ _ _ _ _ _ _

1. RSFFIGNEO

2. ANTSUYRCA

3. EOERVM

4. ISOPL

5. TMNHO

6. TOOPRIN

Missing part of his hair, he couldn't do much.

1. _ _ _ _ _ _ _ _ (O)
2. _ (O) _ _ _ _ _ _ _
3. _ _ (O) _ _ _
4. (O) _ _ _ _
5. _ (O) _ _ _
6. _ _ _ _ _ (O)

Answer: _ _ _ _ _ _

1. DRHETBA

2. MSYABELS

3. AESSGRTRN

4. MAEN

5. NDARK

She had Abraham's first son. Who was she?

1. __ __ __ __ __ __ ⭘
2. ⭘ __ __ __ __ __ __ __
3. __ __ __ __ __ ⭘ __ __ __
4. __ ⭘ __ __
5. __ ⭘ __ __ __

Answer: __ __ __ __ __

1. EDNALI

2. RSASB

3. TCUBI

4. OANBLBY

5. LUSRCELONO

It took seven years of his life for Jacob to wed this girl. Who made him wait so long?

1. _ _ _ _ _ ◯

2. _ _ ◯ _ _

3. _ _ ◯ _ _

4. _ ◯ _ _ _ _ _

5. _ _ _ ◯ _ _ _ _ _ _

Answer: _ _ _ _ _

1. SMREAT

2. TBASES

3. ESNVE

4. NOKMDIG

5. TOSOR

6. COAOSNIC

7. EPKSA

8. IRNGE

What plant with purple or white flowers is used for medicines?

1. ◯ _ _ _ _ _

2. _ _ ◯ _ _ _

3. _ _ _ _ ◯

4. _ _ _ _ _ ◯ _ _

5. ◯ _ _ _ _

6. _ _ _ ◯ _ _ _ _

7. _ _ _ _ ◯

8. _ ◯ _ _ _

Answer: _ _ _ _ _ _ _ _

1. LOEUBTR

2. ESRTSNAGE

3. EOTPTNII

4. HENEVA

5. RBETLEM

6. ELSVI

It means "the house of God."

1. _ _ _ _ ◯ _ _

2. _ _ ◯ _ _ _ _ _ _

3. _ _ _ _ ◯ _ _ _

4. ◯ _ _ _ _ _

5. _ _ _ _ _ ◯

6. ◯ _ _ _ _

Answer: _ _ _ _ _ _

1. RNMIOF

2. SIHFNI

3. TDYSEOR

4. LBTIU

5. TSLDEEAO

6. NONOATMBIIA

7. TIYMGH

8. IATAGSN

9. ESEAL

10. NVSOII

Who sold Joseph to Potiphar in Egypt?

1. _ _ _ _ _ ◯

2. _ ◯ _ _ _ _

3. ◯ _ _ _ _ _ _

4. _ _ ◯ _ _

5. _ _ _ _ _ ◯ _ _

6. _ _ _ _ _ ◯ _ _ _ _ _

7. _ ◯ _ _ _ _

8. _ _ _ _ _ _ ◯

9. _ _ _ _ ◯

10. _ _ ◯ _ _ _

Answer: the _ _ _ _ _ _ _ _ _ _

1. CSEIDENWKS
2. HAMIPER
3. NBDIL
4. RTCNOE
5. VHTRSAE

6. ERSDEI
7. LLVYOE
8. RDAEEP
9. TEISRS

It's one of the longest waterways in the world.

1. _ _ _ _ _ _ ◯ _ _ _
2. _ _ _ _ _ ◯ _
3. _ ◯ _ _ _ _
4. _ _ _ _ ◯ _
5. _ _ ◯ _ _ _ _
6. _ _ _ ◯ _ _ _
7. _ _ ◯ _ _ _ _
8. _ _ _ _ ◯ _
9. _ _ _ _ _ ◯

Answer: the _ _ _ _ _ _ _ _ _ _

1. EUDBNR

2. TYRULET

3. SEAIR

4. EACHSTSI

5. DNLWKEEOG

6. MOESCNU

"I'm up to my elbows in mud and straw. What am I making?"

1. ◯ _ _ _ _ _

2. _ _ _ _ ◯ _ _

3. _ _ ◯ _ _

4. ◯ _ _ _ _ _ _ _

5. ◯ _ _ _ _ _ _ _

6. _ _ _ ◯ _ _ _

Answer: _ _ _ _ _ _

1. EPESMTL

2. AETRSPU

3. MSAGNRTE

4. NNHTROER

5. LVYLAE

This was found on the ground, but it was good for eating.

1. __ __ ◯ __ __ __ __
2. __ ◯ __ __ __ __ __
3. __ __ __ __ __ ◯ __ __
4. ◯ __ __ __ __ __ __ __
5. __ ◯ __ __ __ __

Answer: __ __ __ __ __

1. PNURTDE

2. LRTAA

3. NSRAGRE

4. ETLOEDSA

5. TNOTER

6. RVEYLI

7. DHRSE

8. WWDHTARI

This meal helps Jewish families remember that God saved them when they were slaves in Egypt.

1. ⭘ _ _ _ _ _ _

2. _ _ _ ⭘ _

3. _ _ _ _ _ _ ⭘

4. _ _ ⭘ _ _ _ _ _

5. _ ⭘ _ _ _ _

6. ⭘ _ _ _ _ _

7. _ ⭘ _ _ _

8. _ _ _ _ _ ⭘ _ _

Answer: the _ _ _ _ _ _ _ _

1. ELBDOH

2. RKNDI

3. UNTNFAOI

4. LSACEEN

5. LDGEWNIL

6. TNGRNEAEOI

This is known as a message from God.

1. _ _ _ ◯ _ _

2. _ ◯ _ _ _

3. _ _ _ _ _ ◯ _ _

4. ◯ _ _ _ _ _ _

5. _ _ _ ◯ _ _ _

6. _ _ _ ◯ _ _ _ _ _ _

Answer: _ _ _ _ _ _ _

1. CLEAP
2. WDRENA
3. DGNRSAE
4. OIMLPACR
5. YRSVDINAE
6. EWTIRH
7. SVDYARERA
8. VRYOI
9. LYIMULTP
10. VTRHESA

These were made of wood, straw, or metal and were worshiped by many.

1. ◯ _ _ _ _
2. _ ◯ _ _ _ _
3. ◯ _ _ _ _ _ _
4. _ _ _ _ _ ◯ _ _
5. _ _ ◯ _ _ _ _ _ _
6. _ ◯ _ _ _ _
7. _ ◯ _ _ _ _ _ _
8. _ _ ◯ _ _
9. _ _ _ _ _ _ ◯ _
10. _ _ _ _ _ ◯ _

Answer: _ _ _ _ _ _ _ _ _ _

1. NRGHIEOB

2. QIYITNIU

3. RHNBCA

4. NERITAM

5. IENV

6. TTSRECA

7. TTEALC

It smells sweet, but it is not for wearing.

1. __ __ ◯ __ __ __ __ __ __

2. __ ◯ __ __ __ __ __ __

3. __ __ __ __ ◯ __

4. __ __ __ __ ◯ __ __

5. __ __ ◯ __

6. ◯ __ __ __ __ __ __

7. __ __ __ __ ◯

Answer: __ __ __ __ __ __ __

1. NTSTE

2. UHDAJ

3. NBRGI

4. APLRE

5. NDKRIED

6. RHYITT

7. YRSAAIS

These were made of stone, with a whole new way of living chiseled on them.

1. ◯ _ _ _ _

2. _ _ _ ◯ _

3. ◯ _ _ _ _

4. _ _ _ _ ◯

5. _ _ _ _ _ ◯ _

6. ◯ _ _ _ _ _

7. _ _ ◯ _ _ _ _

Answer: _ _ _ _ _ _ _

1. RMNOU

2. WJLEE

3. EWSI

4. YGUON

5. PBEZAIT

6. TAVNIY

7. HTAER

As Jewish people left their homes, they would touch these boxes that hung on their door frames.

1. ◯ _ _ _ _

2. _ _ _ ◯ _

3. _ _ ◯ _

4. _ _ ◯ _ _

5. _ _ _ _ _ ◯ _

6. _ ◯ _ _ _ _

7. ◯ _ _ _ _

Answer: _ _ _ _ _ _ _

1. RGTAERE

2. HLYMBAEPS

3. ARHET

4. REMESAU

5. BBHSTAA

She was a woman with a "worldly profession."

1. __ Ⓞ __ __ __ __ __

2. __ __ Ⓞ __ __ __ __ __ __

3. __ __ __ __ Ⓞ

4. __ __ Ⓞ __ __ __ __

5. __ __ __ Ⓞ __ __ __

Answer: __ __ __ __ __

1. NDSUMCEO
2. CKDMEO
3. MTNOU
4. LOEGRLAY
5. TRSTUO
6. EAFITMSN
7. EYAWR
8. FSLHE

A pile of stones would serve as a way to remember a special event.

1. _ _ _ _ _ ○ _ _

2. _ _ _ _ ○ _

3. ○ _ _ _ _

4. _ _ _ _ _ ○ _ _

5. _ _ _ _ ○ _

6. _ _ _ ○ _ _ _ _

7. _ _ ○ _ _ _

8. _ ○ _ _ _

Answer: _ _ _ _ _ _ _ _

1. RVCDEOE
2. AWHTLE
3. FAUWLL
4. NSRDIOHO
5. DYEIF
6. SDPSDIEO
7. EPATKRA
8. HMESA

These were the tanks of ancient armies. What were they?

1. ◯ _ _ _ _ _ _
2. _ _ _ _ _ ◯
3. _ ◯ _ _ _ _
4. _ _ _ _ _ _ _ ◯
5. _ _ ◯ _ _
6. _ _ _ _ ◯ _ _ _
7. _ _ _ ◯ _ _ _
8. ◯ _ _ _ _

Answer: _ _ _ _ _ _ _ _

1. SRGLOUOI
2. PEORW
3. ERSBARLW
4. ITELYFDI
5. SVRAOI

6. NMSESEKE
7. EEISPDS
8. ENCSARTI
9. IHSRE

They didn't have plastic bottles back then, but they did carry liquid with them. What did they use?

1. ◯ _ _ _ _ _ _ _
2. _ ◯ _ _ _ _
3. _ _ ◯ _ _ _ _ _
4. _ _ _ _ _ _ ◯ _
5. ◯ _ _ _ _ _
6. _ _ _ ◯ _ _ _ _ _
7. _ _ _ _ ◯ _ _
8. _ _ _ _ _ _ ◯ _
9. _ _ _ _ ◯

Answer: _ _ _ _   _ _ _ _ _

1. UEPRSCOI   6. BEIDLR

2. TNFAIONU   7. RNDFEI

3. UNYRLU   8. ATWNON

4. TSUECRPRI   9. MBSMERE

5. IDUPMET

In the Old Testament times, some men had one or more of these.

1. _ _ _ ◯ _ _ _ _

2. _ ◯ _ _ _ _ _

3. _ ◯ _ _ _ _

4. _ ◯ _ _ _ _ _ _ _

5. _ _ _ ◯ _ _ _

6. ◯ _ _ _ _ _

7. _ _ ◯ _ _ _

8. _ _ ◯ _ _ _

9. _ _ _ _ ◯ _ _

Answer: _ _ _ _ _ _ _ _ _

1. NTROYCU
2. AHLE
3. MTIES
4. MTRSNEII
5. ZRATHANE
6. HPNASICYI

7. BCPNAULI
8. KELNI
9. DDCNEA
10. LCSONUE
11. UHETOCD
12. TBTPASI

This amount came to be equated with betrayal.

1. _ _ _ _ ◯ _ _
2. ◯ _ _ _
3. _ _ ◯ _ _
4. _ _ _ _ _ _ _ ◯
5. _ _ _ _ _ _ ◯ _
6. _ _ ◯ _ _ _ _ _ _
7. ◯ _ _ _ _ _ _ _
8. _ ◯ _ _ _
9. _ _ _ ◯ _ _
10. ◯ _ _ _ _ _ _
11. _ _ _ _ _ ◯ _
12. _ _ _ _ _ ◯ _

Answer: _ _ _ _ _ _   _ _ _ _ _ _

1. LADISE
2. RNTAUE
3. HSTLO
4. GNVEI
5. ASRNE

6. ENCTOMPT
7. ENITATR
8. RCIPEN
9. AGSRS

Many who had an important job to do for the Lord received this first. What was it?

1. _ Ⓐ _ _ _ _
2. Ⓝ _ _ _ _ _
3. _ _ Ⓞ _ _
4. _ Ⓘ _ _ _
5. _ Ⓝ _ _ _
6. _ _ _ Ⓣ _ _ _ _
7. Ⓘ _ _ _ _ _ _
8. _ _ _ Ⓝ _ _
9. Ⓖ _ _ _ _

Answer: _ _ _ _ _ _ _ _ _

1. FMAEL

2. LTMUESB

3. DRSTSSIE

4. TGRASGE

5. LWVVAOLS

6. RNWOC

7. TMORS

He led a rebellion against his father. Who was he?

1. __ __ ◯ __ __

2. __ __ __ __ ◯ __ __

3. __ __ ◯ __ __ __ __ __

4. __ __ ◯ __ __ __

5. __ __ __ __ ◯ __ __

6. __ __ ◯ __ __

7. __ __ __ __ ◯

Answer: __ __ __ __ __ __ __

1. NPKSOE

2. GAHLU

3. HDBELO

4. FBEROE

5. WTSAE

6. GDERTUAH

7. HORASCIT

To the Jews, this was the most important day of the week.

1. ◯ _ _ _ _ _

2. _ ◯ _ _ _

3. ◯ _ _ _ _ _

4. ◯ _ _ _ _ _

5. _ ◯ _ _ _

6. _ _ _ _ _ ◯ _ _

7. _ ◯ _ _ _ _ _

Answer: _ _ _ _ _ _ _ _

CROSSWORD PUZZLES

by Evelyn Boyington

Place answers from numbered clues in the appropriately numbered puzzle grid spaces, making sure to match the clues "across" or "down." When completed correctly, all answers should interlock in the puzzle grid.

ACROSS

1 "Filled with the fruits of righteousness, which _____ by Jesus Christ." Phil. 1:11
4 "(I) will _____ thee with my hand." Exod. 33:22
9 Opal or ruby.
12 They departed from _____. Num. 33:45
13 "When I _____ with thy likeness." Ps. 17:15
14 Highway: abbr.
15 "_____ me not in thine anger." Ps. 6:1
17 "The _____ of righteousness quietness." Isa. 32:17
19 "The swallow (hath found) _____ _____ for herself." Ps. 84:3
21 Mythical bird.
22 "Cottages for shepherds, and _____ for flocks." Zeph. 2:6
24 "Neither shall the _____ pitch tent there." Isa. 13:20
28 Weapon: French
29 "_____ the Ahohite." 1 Chron. 11:29
30 "Him that fashioned it long _____." Isa. 22:11
31 "_____, and let us be going." Judg. 19:28
32 Venturing.
35 _____ , _____, C , D.
36 "Forsake not the _____ of thy mother." Prov. 1:8
38 "_____ ye fasted and mourned in the fifth and seventh month." Zech. 7:5
39 Seed covering.
41 "To every thing _____ _____ a season." Eccles. 3:1
43 "His face did _____ as the sun." Matt. 17:2
44 "From Shepham to Riblah, on the east side of _____." Num. 34:11
45 "Every place whereon the soles of your feet shall _____." Deut. 11:24

47 "All the _____ of the children of Israel." Acts 5:21
50 "The _____ which were in heaven followed him." Rev. 19:14
53 "Adam called his wife's name _____." Gen. 3:20
54 "Be strong, ye that hear in _____ days." Zech. 8:9
56 Depression Agency.
57 Assist.
58 "One cake of _____ bread." Exod. 29:23
59 "_____ you hence, walk to and fro." Zech. 6:7

DOWN

1 "The way of an eagle in the _____." Prov. 30:19
2 "The wheat and the _____ were not smitten." Exod. 9:32
3 "Joseph commanded his servants and physicians to _____ his father." Gen. 50:2
4 "Bake twelve _____ thereof." Lev. 24:5
5 "If he _____ you anything." Phile. 18 NKJV
6 Veterans Administration: abbr.
7 Piece out.
8 "Let him _____ his tongue from evil." 1 Peter 3:10
9 "The rough goat is the king of _____." Dan. 8:21
10 And so forth.
11 "Much people _____ him." Luke 9:37
16 "The Lord God. . ._____ whose wings thou art." Ruth 2:12
18 Watch chain.
20 "Why _____ thou with her?" John 4:27
22 "I have found no _____ in him." 1 Sam. 29:3
23 "_____ kissed her mother-in-law." Ruth 1:14

25 "Thou, O God, didst send a plen-
tiful _____." Ps. 68:9

26 "I will not _____ pass by."
Amos 7:8

27 "One of the king's most _____
princes." Esther 6:9

29 "Thou shalt call me _____."
Hos. 2:16

33 "_____ _____ _____ Damascus
with authority." Acts 26:12

34 "Reumah. . .bare also Tebah, and
_____." Gen. 22:24

37 "Them that are _____ from milk."
Isa. 28:9

40 "Behold a man _____ upon a red
horse." Zech. 1:8

42 Creek.

43 "Of _____, the family of the
Sardites" Num. 26:26

46 "_____ it, even to the foundation."
Ps. 137:7

47 "Before it shall ye encamp by the
_____." Exod. 14:2

48 "The rest of them that were slain;
namely, _____." Num. 31:8

49 A son of Benjamin. Gen. 46:21

51 "How long will it be _____ ye
make an end?" Job 18:2

52 "He that _____ was to look upon
like a jasper." Rev. 4:3

55 "He. . .called the place _____-
bethel." Gen. 35:7

ACROSS

1 "Seek. . .unto wizards that __."
Isa. 8:19
5 "_____ the son of Omri reigned
over Israel in Samaria."
1 Kings 16:29
9 Noe's son. Luke 3:36
12 "Repent; or _____ I will come
unto thee quickly." Rev. 2:16
13 " _____ thou in God: for I shall
yet praise Him." Ps. 42:5
14 "The king of Assyria brought men
from Babylon. . .and from _____."
2 Kings 17:24
15 "As vinegar upon _____, so is he
that singeth songs to a heavy
heart." Prov. 25:20
17 "Intending after _____ to bring
him forth." Acts 12:4
19 "The labourer is worthy of his
_____." Luke 10:7
21 "The shadow of a great rock in a
_____ land." Isa. 32:2
22 "An high priest which cannot be
touched with the _____ of our
infirmities." Heb. 4:15
25 "There was no room for them in
the _____." Luke 2:7
26 "First the blade, then the _____."
Mark 4:28
27 "The Almighty hath _____ very
bitterly with me." Ruth 1:20
29 "Potipherah priest of _____."
Gen. 41:45
31 "Ye shall be _____ gods." Gen. 3:5
32 "_____ to God ye could bear
with me." 2 Cor. 11:1
33 Greek letter.
34 Last book in the NT.
35 "Wash the disciples' feet, and to
wipe them with the _____."
John 13:5
36 "The king. . .went in haste unto
the _____ of lions." Dan. 6:19
37 "The water _____ round about
the altar." 1 Kings 18:35
38 "For, _____, _____ enemies. . .shall

perish." Ps. 92:9
41 "And a little _____ shall lead
them." Isa. 11:6
43 Jonah said he had some of this
thing wrapped around his head.
44 "That he might _____ us from all
iniquity." Titus 2:14
46 One of the people who sent
Timothy greetings. 2 Tim. 4:21
49 Compass point.
50 "Whosoever shall _____ this
writing." Dan. 5:7
53 "I am the _____ of Sharon."
Song of Sol. 2:1
54 "They continued three years without _____." 1 Kings 22:1
55 "_____ up the gift of God."
2 Tim. 1:6
56 In Gen. 25:29, pottage was like a
_____.

DOWN

1 "I will not with ink and _____
write unto thee." 3 John 13
2 "They. . .brought the child to
_____." 1 Sam. 1:25
3 "_____ arose, and stood before
the king." Esther 8:4
4 "Who shall separate us from the
love of Christ? shall tribulation. . .
or _____, or sword?" Rom. 8:35
5 "Then said I, _____, Lord GOD."
Jer. 4:10
6 "_____, every one that thirsteth."
Isa. 55:1
7 The king's navy brought things like
gold, silver, ivory, _____, and pea-
cock. 1 Kings 10:22
8 "He will _____ _____ _____
man." Gen. 16:12
9 "Get thee hence, ___." Matt. 4:10
10 "I will praise Thee for _____."
Ps. 52:9
11 "The virgin's name was _____."
Luke 1:27
16 "_____, the family of the Erites."

Num. 26:16

18 "He _____ forth a raven." Gen. 8:7

20 "He shall surely _____ her to be his wife." Exod. 22:16

22 "_____ God and keep his commandments." Eccles. 12:13

23 "Take thine _____, eat, drink, and be merry." Luke 12:19

24 _____ was the son of Machi of the tribe of Gad. Num. 13:15

28 "That which I do I _____ not." Rom. 7:15

29 "A fool layeth _____ his folly." Prov. 13:16

30 "But where are the _____?" Luke 17:17

32 "Tomorrow the LORD will do _____ among you." Josh. 3:5

35 "We spend our years as a _____ that is told." Ps. 90:9

36 "And he _____ _____ many mighty works there." Matt. 13:58

37 "The horse and his _____ hath he thrown into the sea." Exod. 15:1

39 "I came to them of the captivity at _____-abib." Ezek. 3:15

40 "The Gentiles should be fellow _____." Eph. 3:6

41 "Immediately the cock _____." Matt. 26:74

42 "Where is the king of. . .the city of Sepharvaim, _____, and Ivah?" Isa. 37:13

45 "He went, and _____ him in the mount of God." Exod. 4:27

47 "When ye pray, _____ not vain repetitions." Matt. 6:7

48 "A time to rend, and a time to _____." Eccles. 3:7

51 "King of Jerusalem had heard how Joshua had taken _____." Josh. 10:1

52 M.D.

ACROSS

1 "It is vain. . .to sit up _____." Ps. 127:2

5 "Carry down the man a present, a little _____." Gen. 43:11

9 "_____, even the ancient high places are ours." Ezek. 36:2

12 "Cut off the inhabitant from the plain of _____." Amos 1:5

13 Solomon's grandson. 1 Chron. 3:10

14 "I shook my _____, and said, So God shake out." Neh. 5:13

15 "They put him in _____ in chains." Ezek. 19:9

16 "They had _____ with Jesus." Acts 4:13

17 "I _____ no pleasant bread." Dan. 10:3

18 "Only _____ not ye against the LORD." Num. 14:9

20 "_____ have they, but they smell not." Ps. 115:6

22 "After this manner will I mar the _____ of Judah." Jer. 13:9

24 "There stood before the river a _____." Dan. 8:3

25 "_____ not the poor." Prov. 22:22

26 "They stood still in the prison _____." Neh. 12:39

29 "Toward the coast of Edom southward were Kabzeel and _____." Josh. 15:21

33 "The inhabitant of this _____ shall say." Isa. 20:6

35 Command to horse.

36 "Let us _____ up and build." Neh. 2:18

37 "Therefore came I forth to _____ thee." Prov. 7:15

38 "Is not this the fast. . .to _____ the heavy burdens." Isa. 58:6

40 Animal Dr.

41 "What _____ we, that ye murmur against us?" Exod. 16:7

43 "He fashioneth their hearts _____." Ps. 33:15

45 "Thy neighbor hath put thee to _____." Prov. 25:8

48 "And the _____ of this world." Mark 4:19

50 "Then I came to them of the captivity at _____-abib." Ezek. 3:15

51 "They came to the threshing floor of _____." Gen. 50:10

53 Military assistant.

56 "He hath showed strength with his _____." Luke 1:51

57 "These men shall _____ with me at noon." Gen. 43:16

58 "It was without form, and _____." Jer. 4:23

59 Legal action.

60 "Thou crownest the _____ with thy goodness." Ps. 65:11

61 "All the _____ of the earth have seen the salvation of our God." Ps. 98:3

DOWN

1 "Have ye not read in the _____?" Matt. 12:5

2 "The king of Assyria brought men from Babylon. . .and from _____." 2 Kings 17:24

3 "Thy right hand shall teach thee _____ things." Ps. 45:4

4 "On the seventh day God _____ his work." Gen. 2:2

5 "Ye shall find the _____ wrapped in swaddling clothes." Luke 2:12

6 "_____ was a keeper of sheep." Gen. 4:2

7 "Ye shall not. . ._____ one to another." Lev. 19:11

8 "He humbled thee. . .and fed thee with _____." Deut. 8:3

9 "_____! for that day is great." Jer. 30:7

10 "Who _____ the good, and love the evil." Micah 3:2

11 "The navy of Tharshish, bringing gold. . .ivory, and _____." 1 Kings 10:22

19 "Therefore shall he _____ in harvest." Prov. 20:4

21 "An _____ for every man." Exod. 16:16

22 _____ and proper.

23 "Cain _____ up against Abel." Gen. 4:8

24 "They smote him on the head with a _____." Mark 15:19

27 "I will even appoint over you terror. . .and the burning _____." Lev. 26:16

28 "Abram had dwelt _____ years in the land of Canaan." Gen. 16:3

30 "I tell you, nay, but rather _____." Luke 12:51

31 "He called the name of the well _____." Gen 26:20

32 Network.

34 "He. . .dwelt in the top of the rock _____." Judg. 15:8

39 "All that handle the _____, the mariners." Ezek. 27:29

42 "Be ye also _____." Matt. 24:44

44 "Thou wilt not _____ my soul in hell." Ps. 16:10

45 "There fell a great _____ from heaven." Rev. 8:10

46 "Set it _____ before my brethren." Gen. 31:37

47 "They laid daily. . .to ask _____." Acts 3:2

48 "There was a marriage in _____ of Galilee." John 2:1

49 "The inhabitants of Aijalon, who drove away the inhabitants of. . .Arad, and _____." 1 Chron. 8:13, 15

52 "_____ them about thy neck." Prov. 6:21

54 "The rulers knew not. . .what I _____." Neh. 2:16

55 Correctors of books: abbr.

ACROSS

1 "_____shall judge his people."
Gen. 49:16
4 After being healed, the demoniac
was in his right mind, or _____.
8 "There is but a _____ between
me and death." 1 Sam. 20:3
12 A son of Jether. 1 Chron. 7:38
13 Isaiah the prophet's father.
2 Kings 19:2
14 Sea eagle.
15 "_____ do I not forget thy
statutes." Ps. 119:83
16 "Thou hast taught _____ against
the Lord." Jer. 28:16
18 "A land whose stones are _____."
Deut. 8:9
20 "Ten women shall bake your
bread in one _____." Lev. 26:26
21 "Because the children. . ._____ in
the streets of the city." Lam. 2:11
23 "Ye have _____ in pleasure on the
earth." James 5:5
25 "Thoughts of the diligent _____
only to plenteousness." Prov. 21:5
26 "The law of the _____ and
Persians, which altereth not."
Dan. 6:8
27 Compass point.
29 Curved letter.
30 "A book. . .sealed with seven
_____." Rev. 5:1
31 "Whom do _____say that I the
Son of man am?" Matt. 16:13
32 Liquid measure: abbr.
33 "Cause these men to _____."
Ezra 4:21
34 "The good _____ are the children
of the kingdom." Matt. 13:38
35 "Sippai, that was of the children of
the _____." 1 Chron. 20:4
36 Jesus' coat was without _____
woven from the top. John 19:23
37 Composition for two.

38 "Praise Him for his mighty
_____." Ps. 150:2
39 Ezek. 13:11,13 tells us that the
Lord would even use a large
_____ for His purpose.
42 One of Bani's sons. Ezra 10:34
45 French female.
46 "_____ knew that the seed should
not be his." Gen. 38:9
47 "Let her be as the loving hind and
pleasant _____." Prov. 5:19
48 "They _____ not depart."
Matt. 14:16
49 "He _____ his way." Luke 8:39
50 "Sing. . .praise from the _____of
the earth." Isa. 42:10

DOWN

1 "A _____ in thy courts is better."
Ps. 84:10
2 "Whose names _____ not written
in the book of life." Rev. 13:8
3 "He increaseth the _____."
Job 12:23
4 "All that dwell at Lydda and
_____ saw him." Acts 9:35
5 "Let all the people say, _____."
Ps. 106:48
6 "_____, the city of the priests."
1 Sam. 22:19
7 Compass point.
8 "Know ye not your own _____?"
2 Cor. 13:5
9 "Silver _____ in a furnace of
earth." Ps. 12:6
10 "John also was baptizing in
_____." John 3:23
11 "The _____ of the scribes is in
vain." Jer. 8:8
17 "Let us solace ourselves with
_____." Prov. 7:18
19 "Thy _____ and thy staff they
comfort me." Ps. 23:4

21 "If my _____ hath turned out of the way." Job 31:7

22 "I will save my people from the... _____ country." Zech. 8:7

23 "Mustard seed...is the _____ of all seeds." Matt. 13:31–32

24 "An _____ soul shall suffer hunger." Prov. 19:15

26 "Peter doubted...what this vision ...should _____." Acts 10:17

27 "If any man among you _____ to be." James 1:26

28 "Dominion...to the _____of the earth." Zech. 9:10

30 "And love...the chief _____ in the synagogues." Matt. 23:6

31 "It shall be given unto you; good _____, pressed down." Luke 6:38

33 "Is it time for you...to dwell in your _____ houses?" Haggai 1:4

34 "I have _____ before thee an open door." Rev. 3:8

35 "An Israelite indeed, in whom is no _____!" John 1:47

36 "The _____ thereof shall be as the wine of Lebanon." Hosea 14:7

37 "A pillar, which is in the king's _____." 2 Sam. 18:18

38 One of those who sealed the covenant. Neh. 10:26

39 "As a _____ doth gather her brood." Luke 13:34

40 "A thread of _____ is broken when it toucheth the fire." Judg. 16:9

41 "There was not _____ of them left." Ps. 106:11

43 Division of geological time.

44 "He was _____ as a sheep to the slaughter." Acts 8:32

ACROSS

1 "The poison of _____ is under their lips." Rom. 3:13
5 "His mother's name also was _____." 2 Kings 18:2
8 "He walked with me in _____." Mal. 2:6
10 "_____ up the gift of God, which is in thee." 2 Tim. 1:6
11 "Except ye repent, ye shall all likewise _____." Luke 13:3
13 "All the presidents. . .have consulted together to establish a royal _____." Dan. 6:7
15 Greek letter.
16 "Bless the _____; and let my name be named." Gen. 48:16
17 Apiece: abbr.
18 "Blind guides, which strain at a _____." Matt. 23:24
19 "Their lies caused them to _____." Amos 2:4
20 "Praise him for his mighty _____." Ps. 150:2
21 "_____ took all the silver and the gold." 1 Kings 15:18
24 "Thy counsels of old _____ faithfulness and truth." Isa. 25:1
25 Golf mound.
26 "He beheld the city, and _____ over it." Luke 19:41
27 "Affliction by the _____ of his wrath." Lam. 3:1
28 City of Judah in the mountains. Josh. 15:50
29 Railway: abbr.
30 "We came with a straight course unto _____." Acts 21:1
34 Steep flax.
35 "The remnant of his people. . . from Assyria. . .and from the _____ of the sea." Isa. 11:11
37 "The Lord sent _____ unto David." 2 Sam. 12:1
40 "I. . .being such an one as Paul the _____." Phile. 9

41 "I will _____ out the inhabitants of the land." Jer. 10:18
42 "_____ verily, their sound went into all the earth." Rom. 10:18
43 "Upon whom the _____ of the world are come." 1 Cor. 10:11

DOWN

1 "There _____ unto them cloven tongues." Acts 2:3
2 "To _____ thy power and thy glory." Ps. 63:2
3 Average.
4 "Avoiding. . .oppositions of _____." 1 Tim. 6:20
5 "They came to the threshing floor of _____." Gen. 50:10
6 "We put _____ in the horses' mouths." James 3:3
7 Caleb's son. 1 Chron. 4:15
9 "Condescend to men of low _____." Rom. 12:16
10 As it stands: music.
12 These men were bound in their coats. . .and their _____." Dan. 3:21
13 Straight line: abbr.
14 "_____ are turned upon me." Job 30:15
18 "Moses. . ._____ him up into the mount." Exod. 24:18
19 "I put. . ._____ in thine ears." Ezek. 16:12
21 "_____, which had kept his bed eight years." Acts 9:33
22 "He. . .made clay of the _____." John 9:6
23 Place for banking: abbr.
26 "As my beloved sons I _____ you." 1 Cor. 4:14
30 "A _____ is full of birds." Jer. 5:27
31 "It came up four notable _____." Dan. 8:8
32 "The _____ number. . .is to be redeemed." Num. 3:48
33 Baseball position: abbr.

36 "_____ up for yourselves treasures in heaven." Matt. 6:20

38 "An _____ of oil for an ephah." Ezek. 45:24

39 "Jesus the author _____ finisher of our faith." Heb. 12:2

ACROSS

1 "He saith among the trumpets, _____ _____." Job 39:25

5 "Ye have heard of the patience of _____." James 5:11

8 "Joshua built an altar. . .in mount _____." Josh. 8:30

12 Son of Eliphaz. Gen. 36:11

13 "Why make ye this _____, and weep?" Mark 5:39

14 The length of King Og's bedstead was _____ cubits. Deut. 3:11

15 "He shall be surely _____." Exod. 21:20

17 Male deer.

18 "Jabin. . .which perished at _____." Ps. 83:9–10

19 "I discerned among the _____, a young man." Prov. 7:7

21 Army rank: abbr.

24 _____ Haw.

25 "I _____ above all things that thou mayest prosper." 3 John 2

28 "The children of Benjamin. . .dwelt at Michmash, and _____." Neh. 11:31

30 Greek letter R.

33 "_____ not thou he, O LORD our God?" Jer. 14:22

34 "When they had _____, Jesus saith." John 21:15

35 "They of Persia and of _____. . . were in thine army." Ezek. 27:10

36 "They did so at the going up to _____." 2 Kings 9:27

37 Part of a foot.

38 "Who. . .cometh from Edom, with _____ garments?" Isa. 63:1

39 "Stand in _____, and sin not." Ps. 4:4

41 "Were not the Ethiopians and the Lubim a _____ host?" 2 Chron. 16:8

43 "Ointment. . .that went down to the _____ of his garments." Ps. 133:2

46 "_____ also, the seventh from Adam." Jude 14

50 "My fellowprisoners, who are of _____." Rom. 16:7

51 Minute part.

54 Unrefined metals.

55 "Thine asses that were lost three days _____." 1 Sam. 9:20

56 "Dwelt in the top of the rock _____." Judg.15:8

57 "And Cain _____ out from the presence of the LORD." Gen. 4:16

58 "As a wild bull in a _____." Isa. 51:20

59 "_____, a man of Issachar." Judg.10:1

DOWN

1 "The eye of the LORD is upon them. . .that _____ in his mercy." Ps. 33:18

2 Egyptian king of gods.

3 "O God, lift up thine _____." Ps. 10:12

4 "Then _____ brought in Daniel before the king." Dan. 2:25

5 "Extol him. . .by his name _____." Ps. 68:4

6 Poem such as a psalm.

7 "Now ye are the _____ of Christ." 1 Cor. 12:27

8 "Let him seek peace, and _____ it." 1 Peter 3:11

9 "He went out, and wept _____." Matt. 26:75

10 "_____ that found the mules in the wilderness." Gen. 36:24

11 "That their _____ might be broken." John 19:31

16 Theater sign.

20 Son of Simeon. Gen. 46:10

22 "The LORD our God, that giveth _____." Jer. 5:24

23 Nip.

25 "Every one that passeth. . .shall. . .

	1	2	3	4		5	6	7		8	9	10	11
	12					13				14			
	15				16					17			
	18						19	20					
			21		22	23		24					
	25	26	27		28		29			30	31	32	
	33			34						35			
	36			37					38				
		39	40			41		42					
	43	44			45			46		47	48	49	
	50				51	52	53			56			
	54				55					56			
	57				58					59			

_____ his hand." Zeph. 2:15

26 Son of Caleb. I Chron. 4:15

27 "They that seek their lives, shall _____ them." Jer. 19:9

29 "When _____ was executing judgment." 2 Chron. 22:8

31 Color or tint.

32 "The _____ number of them is to be redeemed." Num. 3:48

34 "There was a continual _____ given him." Jer. 52:34

38 "But he _____, saying, I know not." Mark 14:68

40 "Every day they _____ my words." Ps. 56:5

42 "With all thy getting _____ understanding." Prov. 4:7

43 "Though your sins be as scarlet, they shall be as white as _____." Isa. 1:18

44 " _____ the son of Imnah the Levite, the porter." 2 Chron. 31:14

45 "The border. . .round about shall be a _____." Ezek. 43:13

47 Eight: comb. form.

48 "He. . .was _____ with zeal as a cloak." Isa. 59:17

49 Blood: comb. form.

52 "The whole _____ of Jacob was a hundred forty and seven years." Gen. 47:28

53 "A tree that will not _____." Isa. 40:20

ACROSS

1 "The _____ are a people not strong." Prov. 30:25
5 "The snare is laid. . .and a _____ for him." Job 18:10
9 "Upon the _____ of it thou shalt make pomegranates." Exod. 28:33
12 "They have. . .perished in the gainsaying of _____." Jude 11
13 "Wherein shall go no galley with _____." Isa. 33:21
14 "She hath also conceived a son in her _____ age." Luke 1:36
15 "I have given you. . .the fruit of a _____ yielding seed." Gen. 1:29
16 Self.
17 "Take heed that ye do not your _____ before men." Matt. 6:1
18 "They. . ._____ the sacrifices of the dead." Ps. 106:28
20 "Things wherewith one may _____ another." Rom. 14:19
22 "The habitation of dragons, where each lay, shall be grass with reeds and _____." Isa. 35:7
25 A mighty man of valor. 1 Chron. 7:7
26 Yrs. before Christ.
28 A son of Caleb. 1 Chron. 4:15
29 "Peleg lived after he begat _____ two hundred and nine years." Gen. 11:19
31 "Hezron's wife bare him _____ the father of Tekoa." 1 Chron. 2:24
33 Fairy tale monster.
35 "_____ cried unto the Lord his God." 2 Chron. 14:11
37 "Joseph, which was the son of _____." Luke 3:23
38 Youth.
40 Ht.
42 "He had one only daughter, about twelve years of _____." Luke 8:42
43 Pierre's state: abbr.
44 "I came to them of the captivity at _____-abib." Ezek. 3:15

46 "Open before him the two _____ gates." Isa. 45:1
48 "When _____ was come down out of the ship." Matt. 14:29
50 "What _____ we, that ye murmur against us?" Exod. 16:7
51 The day _____ arise in your hearts." 2 Peter 1:19
53 House cat or dog.
55 "She. . .bare a son; and she called his name _____." Gen. 38:4
58 "I am like an _____ of the desert." Ps. 102:6
59 "Woe unto _____! for it is spoiled." Jer. 48:1
60 Highly seasoned dish.
61 "One _____ is past." Rev. 9:12
62 "A _____(is laid) for him in the way." Job 18:10
63 "Hiram came out from _____ to see the cities." 1 Kings 9:12

DOWN

1 "The _____ of violence is in their hands." Isa. 59:6
2 "Fight neither with small _____ great." 1 Kings 22:31
3 "A man. . .bringeth forth out of his _____ things new and old." Matt. 13:52
4 "The next day John _____ Jesus coming." John 1:29
5 "Put it. . .upon the great _____ of their right foot." Exod. 29:20
6 "Why do the heathen _____?" Ps. 2:1
7 One of Gad's sons. Gen. 46:16
8 Afterthought of a letter.
9 "_____ and reverend is his name." Ps. 111:9
10 Deciduous tree.
11 Doctors: abbr.
17 "If he ask _____ _____, will he give him a serpent?" Matt. 7:10
19 Ever: poetic.

21 Retirement money.
22 Prison disturbances.
23 "His father-in-law _____ him."
   Judg.19:7
24 "I saw. . .a _____ of glass."
   Rev. 15:2
26 A swelling.
27 "Jesus stood and _____, saying, If
   any man thirst." John 7:37
30 Our country.
32 "Your _____ Father will also for-
   give you." Matt. 6:14
34 "_____ into his gates with thanksgiving." Ps. 100:4
36 "The LORD is good to _____."
   Ps. 145:9
39 "I will _____ a sign among them."
   Isa. 66:19
41 Hot or iced drink.

45 "In the house of Simon the
   _____." Mark 14:3
47 "There shall be _____ _____ of
   Jesse." Rom. 15:12
48 "Neither shall his face now wax
   _____." Isa. 29:22
49 One of the five kings of Midian
   slain by Moses' army. Num. 31:8
51 "They that _____ in tears shall
   reap in joy." Ps. 126:5
52 "There come _____ woes more
   hereafter." Rev. 9:12
54 "A tower, whose _____ may reach
   unto heaven." Gen. 11:4
56 "They. . .threw dust into the
   _____." Acts 22:23
57 "As it was in the days of _____."
   Luke 17:26
59 Division of the Bible: abbr.

ACROSS

1 "He was seen many _____ of them." Acts 13:31

5 "Trees. . .whose leaf shall not _____." Ezek. 47:12

9 "Fifteen shekels, shall be your _____." Ezek. 45:12

10 "Pay me that thou _____." Matt. 18:28

12 "The voice of the _____ is heard in our land." Song of Sol. 2:12

13 Amount of a lease.

15 "_____, and it shall be given you." Matt. 7:7

16 "Ye _____ men with burdens grievous to be borne." Luke 11:46

18 Sister to Hotham. 1 Chron. 7:32

19 "Blessed be the LORD God of _____." Gen. 9:26

21 Volcano ash.

23 "The work that God maketh from the beginning to the _____." Eccles. 3:11

24 City of Judah toward the coast of Edom. Josh. 15:22

26 "They wandered in _____, and in mountains." Heb. 11:38

28 One of David's mighty men. 1 Kings 1:8

30 Mythical bird.

31 "She also bare a son, and called his name _____." Gen. 19:38

35 A stage of mitosis.

39 Suffix meaning "little one."

40 "They toil not, neither do they _____." Matt. 6:28

42 "_____ my voice, and I will be your God." Jer. 7:23

43 "Their _____ caused them to err." Amos 2:4

45 "Gather of it. . .an _____ for every man." Exod. 16:16

47 "The ungodly _____ not so." Ps. 1:4

48 "Her wise _____ answered her, yea." Judg. 5:29

50 "If the salt have lost his savour, wherewith shall it be _____?" Matt. 5:13

52 "_____ the LORD with gladness." Ps. 100:2

53 "Many shall be purified. . .and _____." Dan. 12:10

54 "What _____ is this that ye have done?" Gen. 44:15

55 "I will bring forth a _____ out of Jacob." Isa. 65:9

DOWN

1 "I will _____ the earth in the clear day." Amos 8:9

2 "Go to the _____, thou sluggard." Prov. 6:6

3 "They shall _____ as lions' whelps." Jer. 51:38

4 A son of Bai. Ezra 10:29

5 "The LORD shall endure _____." Ps. 9:7

6 "My heart standeth in _____ of thy word." Ps. 119:161

7 "They wandered in deserts. . .and in _____ and caves." Heb. 11:38

8 "_____ spake yet again before the king." Esther 8:3

9 "Mahli, and _____. These are the families of the Levites." Num. 3:20

11 "It shall be a reproach and a _____." Ezek. 5:15

12 "Wherefore have ye not fulfilled your _____?" Exod. 5:14

14 "The Angel which redeemed me from all evil, bless the _____." Gen. 48:16

17 Father.

20 "Call be not Naomi, call me _____." Ruth 1:20

22 "He it is, to whom I shall give _____ _____." John 13:26

25 "They made upon the _____ of the robe pomegranates." Exod. 39:24

27 Repeat or imitate.

29 "Which stood only in. . .carnal ordinances, _____ on them." Heb. 9:10

31 "As a wild _____ in a net." Isa. 51:20

32 "This man calleth for _____." Matt. 27:47

33 "As though he _____ any thing." Acts 17:25

34 "They departed from _____, and pitched in Dibon-gad." Num. 33:45

36 "At the end of the 150 days the waters were _____." Gen. 8:3

37 Withered.

38 "Leah was tender _____." Gen. 29:17

41 "Where the birds make their _____." Ps. 104:17

44 Male parent.

46 "It is a _____ thing that the king requireth." Dan. 2:11

49 "As the serpent beguiled _____." 2 Cor. 11:3

51 "The highways _____ waste." Isa. 33:8

ACROSS

1 "The Lord _____ out. . .the Amorites." Josh. 24:18
6 "I am an _____ in their sight." Job 19:15
11 "There went out a decree from _____ Augustus." Luke 2:1
12 "She had a _____ called Mary." Luke 10:39
14 "The country. . .of _____ king of Bashan." 1 Kings 4:19
15 "The ark of God had David brought up from _____-jearim." 2 Chron. 1:4
17 Exclamation of surprise.
18 "She was of a great _____." Luke 2:36
20 "Craftiness, whereby they _____ in wait to deceive." Eph. 4:14
21 One of the priests who went up with Zerubbabel. Neh. 12:4
23 "And for this cause God shall _____ them strong delusion." 2 Thess. 2:11
25 "I went down into the garden of _____." Song of Sol. 6:11
28 "The LORD hath appeared of _____ unto me." Jer. 31:3
29 "_____ up a child in the way he should go." Prov. 22:6
31 "The _____ of the LORD of hosts shall do this." Isa. 37:32
33 Apiece: abbr.
34 "Thou art _____, O LORD." Ps. 119:151
36 Composition for two.
38 "Bear ye one another's burdens, and _____ fulfil the law of Christ." Gal. 6:2
40 "Ye shall find an ass _____." Matt. 21:2
42 David's wife was given to Phalti, son of _____. 1 Sam. 25:44
45 "Then shall _____ be in the field." Matt. 24:40

47 "Thou hast not _____ unto men." Acts 5:4
49 To erase.
50 "There was one _____, a prophetess." Luke 2:36
52 Jephunneh and Pispah's brother. 1 Chron. 7:38
54 Women's organization: abbr.
55 Third bk. of the OT.
56 "I. . .was _____ toward God." Acts 22:3
60 Three ft.
61 "Who can understand his _____?" Ps. 19:12
63 "There fell from his eyes as it had been _____." Acts 9:18
65 "As _____ obeyed Abraham." 1 Peter 3:6
66 The fourth son of Obededom. 1 Chron. 26:4

DOWN

1 "Ehud made him a _____." Judg. 3:16
2 Last bk. of the Bible.
3 "We know that he hear us, whatsoever we _____." 1 John 5:15
4 "The _____ of the temple was rent." Luke 23:45
5 "They _____ _____ vision." Isa. 28:7
6 "_____ did that which was good." 2 Chron. 14:2
7 When he has lighted or _____ a candle. Luke 8:16
8 "At that day. . .thou shalt call me _____." Hosea 2:16
9 Latin conjunction.
10 "It is easier for a camel to go through the eye of a _____." Mark 10:25
11 "Capernaum, which is upon the sea _____." Matt. 4:13
13 "A damsel came to hearken, named _____." Acts 12:13

16 One of the heads of the fathers. I Chron. 8:10

19 "This was the offering of Ahira the son of _____." Num. 7:83

22 "So likewise shall my heavenly Father _____." Matt. 18:35

24 "There was a continual _____ given him of the king." Jer. 52:34

26 Dry hay.

27 "_____, why persecuteth thou me?" Acts 9:4

30 "I will fasten him as a _____ in a sure place." Isa. 22:23

32 "_____ me to the rock that is higher than I." Ps. 61:2

35 One of David's mighty men. I Kings 1:8

37 "Ye shall find an ass _____." Matt. 21:2

38 Dry and moldy. Josh. 9:12

39 "The _____ thereof said. . .Why loose ye the colt?" Luke 19:33

41 "In the land of uprightness will he _____ unjustly." Isa. 26:10

43 "A city of refuge for the _____." Josh. 21:38

44 "With our flocks and with our _____ will we go." Exod. 10:9

46 "Poti-pherah, priest of _____." Gen. 41:45

48 "Take away the _____ from the silver." Prov. 25:4

51 Sadoc's father. Matt. 1:14

53 South American Indian tribe.

57 Geological age.

58 "He planteth an _____." Isa. 44:14

59 Seed pouch.

62 Sun god.

64 The _____ of Jeremiah: abbr.

ACROSS

1 "He struck it into the _____, or kettle." 1 Sam. 2:14
4 "They filled them up to the _____." John 2:7
8 "That _____ after the dust of the earth." Amos 2:7
12 "Adam was first formed, then _____." 1 Tim. 2:13
13 "Jacob shall return, and be in rest and at _____." Jer. 46:27
14 Hezekiahs's son. Ezra 2:16
15 "_____, captain of the host of the king of Syria." 2 Kings 5:1
17 Children of _____ returned from captivity. Ezra 2:57
19 "He saith among the trumpets, _____." Job 39:25
20 "A _____ caught in a thicket by his horns." Gen. 22:13
21 "I took the little book...and _____ it up." Rev. 10:10
22 "Cause the _____ of the tender herb to spring forth?" Job 38:27
23 "A wicked _____ giveth heed to false lips." Prov. 17:4
25 Pounds: abbr.
26 "Go _____ to thy friends." Mark 5:19
27 "Give _____, O Shepherd of Israel." Ps. 80:1
28 Distress signal.
29 "If I _____ but touch his garment." Matt. 9:21
30 Division of the Bible: abbr.
31 "The fashion of his countenance was _____." Luke 9:29
33 "Thou savourest not the things that _____ of God." Mark 8:33
35 "He turneth...watersprings into _____ ground." Ps. 107:33
36 "Leave us _____." Jer. 14:9
37 "Which shall devour the palaces of _____-hadad." Amos 1:4
38 "The _____ which dwelt in Hazerim...destroyed them." Deut. 2:23
40 "The _____ of violence is in their hands." Isa. 59:6
41 "As a vesture shalt thou _____ them up." Heb. 1:12

42 "Hiss...for the _____ that is in... Assyria." Isa. 7:18
43 "My heart standeth in _____ of thy word." Ps. 119:161
44 "The archers _____ him." 1 Sam. 31:3
45 "Gibeon...was greater than _____." Josh. 10:2
46 _____ la, la.
47 "Our God, that giveth rain, both the former and the _____." Jer. 5:24
50 Disparaging remark.
52 "Lest...ye _____ up also the wheat." Matt. 13:29
54 "They that _____ wait for my soul take counsel together." Ps. 71:10
55 "Moses...sent me...to _____ out the land." Josh. 14:7
56 "He causeth the vapours to ascend from the _____ of the earth." Ps. 135:7
57 "How long will it be _____ they attain to innocency?" Hosea 8:5

DOWN

1 "My tongue is the _____ of a ready writer." Ps. 45:1
2 "The king of Assyria brought men from Babylon...and from _____." 2 Kings 17:24
3 "There is a kinsman _____ than I." Ruth 3:12
4 "A _____ is in thine own eye?" Matt. 7:4
5 "The whole herd of swine _____ violently." Matt. 8:32
6 "Forbid them not: for of such _____ the kingdom of God." Luke 18:16
7 "Abstain from _____ offered to idols." Acts 15:29
8 The name of Hadad's city. 1 Chron. 1:50
9 "The word of God was preached of Paul _____ Berea." Acts 17:13
10 Part of the company of Zerubbabel. Neh. 7:7
11 "Their _____ hath been to feed cattle." Gen. 46:32
16 "After this manner will I _____ the

pride of Judah." Jer. 13:9

18 "Why callest thou _____ good?" Matt. 19:17

21 "Now much more in my _____." Phil. 2:12

22 "They. . .have given a _____." Joel 3:3

23 "He shall be cast into the _____ of lions." Dan 6:7

24 Cereal grain.

25 "_____ sat in the gate of Sodom." Gen. 19:1

26 "He was a thief, and _____ the bag." John 12:6

28 Crafty.

29 "Then Martha. . .went and _____ him." John 11:20

31 "He shall gather the lambs with his _____." Isa. 40:11

32 "A tree that will not _____." Isa. 40:20

33 "I will punish _____ in Babylon." Jer. 51:44

34 "Seal the book, even to the time of the _____." Dan. 12:4

35 "Neither can they _____ any more."

Luke 20:36

37 "Put thou my tears into thy _____." Ps. 56:8

38 "_____ him that is high." Ezek. 21:26

39 "The Lord will take away. . .the _____." Isa. 3:18, 23

40 "Or ever I was _____." Song of Sol. 6:12

41 "Submit yourselves. . .as it is _____ in the Lord." Col. 3:18

43 "In the night _____ of Moab is laid waste." Isa. 15:1

44 "Bound in their coats, their hosen, and their _____." Dan. 3:21

46 "And I will _____ them for thee there." Judg. 7:4

47 "_____, and Ono, the valley of craftsmen." Neh. 11:35

48 "Incline thine _____ unto me." Ps. 17:6

49 "Scatter the cummin. . .and the _____ in their place." Isa. 28:25

51 "They filled them _____ to the brim." John 2:7

53 "Power. . .to them that believe _____ his name." John 1:12

ACROSS

1 "The first came out _____, all over." Gen. 25:25
4 "My feet did not _____." Ps. 18:36
8 "A pillar, which is in the king's _____." 2 Sam. 18:18
12 One of Caleb's sons. 1 Chron. 4:15
13 "The women _____ hangings for the grove." 2 Kings 23:7
14 Affirm.
15 "Christ our _____ is sacrificed." 1 Cor. 5:7
17 "There is a _____ for the silver." Job 28:1
18 "That ye may be perfect and _____." James 1:4
19 "Can a bird fall in a snare... where no _____ is?" Amos 3:5
20 "_____ to your faith virtue." 2 Peter 1:5
21 "The borders were between the _____." 1 Kings 7:28
24 "For my _____ are many." Lam. 1:22
27 "Thou art neither cold nor _____." Rev. 3:15
28 Priest of Israel. 1 Sam. 1:9
29 _____ the son of Issachar. Gen. 46:13
30 "Thou shalt not have in thy _____ divers weights." Deut. 25:13
31 Colonnade.
32 "One of the villages in the plain of _____." Neh. 6:2
33 "_____ them out of the hand of the wicked." Ps. 82:4
34 Sadoc's son. Matt. 1:14
35 "(The river) was _____, and became into four heads." Gen. 2:10
37 "Lamech took unto him _____ wives." Gen. 4:19
38 One of the five heads of the house of Bela. 1 Chron. 7:7
39 Returning exiles: Children of _____. Neh. 7:54

43 "I am continually with _____." Ps. 73:23
45 "Their foolish heart was _____." Rom. 1:21
47 "Fret not thyself in any _____ to do evil." Ps. 37:8
48 Curved molding.
49 Crude metal.
50 "The _____ are a people not strong." Prov. 30:25
51 "Smote him on the head with a _____." Mark 15:19
52 "Thy men shall fall...and thy mighty in the _____." Isa. 3:25

DOWN

1 "My soul desired the first _____ fruit." Micah 7:1
2 Son of Shuthelah. Num. 26:36
3 "All turn to _____ again." Eccles. 3:20
4 "There is a generation, whose teeth are as _____." Prov. 30:14
5 "The Son of God, who ___ me, and gave himself for me." Gal. 2:20
6 Contraction.
7 Apiece.
8 "Hosanna to the son of _____." Matt. 21:9
9 "It is God that _____ me." Ps. 18:47
10 Hawaiian garland.
11 Sea eagle.
16 The Nethinims: the children of _____. Ezra 2:43-44
19 "_____ you to the mountain, lest the pursuers meet you." Josh. 2:16
21 "A meat offering, mingled with oil, and one _____ of oil." Lev. 14:10
22 One of the words Jesus spoke from the cross. Mark 15:34
23 Thailand.
24 "No man shall _____ me of this boasting." 2 Cor. 11:10
25 Early Celtic church center.

26 "Wherefore _____ thou in the valleys?" Jer. 49:4

27 "And they _____ no light." Jer. 4:23

30 "_____ me come unto thee on the water." Matt. 14:28

31 "Isaac was three _____ years old when she bare them." Gen. 25:26

33 "Shimei, and _____, and the mighty men. . .were not with Adonijah." 1 Kings 1:8

34 "Upon this I _____, and beheld." Jer. 31:26

36 "The rest of the _____ of his forest shall be few." Isa. 10:19

37 "There were born unto him. . . _____ daughters." Job 1:2

40 "He giveth _____ like wool." Ps. 147:16

41 Queen goddess.

42 Descendant of Benjamin. 1 Chron. 8:15

43 U.S. airline.

44 "An _____ of oil for an ephah." Ezek. 45:24

45 "The son of Abinadab in all the region of _____." 1 Kings 4:11

46 "Every man with his staff. . .for very _____." Zech. 8:4

ACROSS

1 "The time is now _____."
Matt. 14:15

5 "The king of _____, which is
Zoar." Gen. 14:2

9 "Every knee shall _____ to me."
Rom. 14:11

12 The bk. of the Bible which follows
Nehemiah.

13 The son of Nathan of Zobah.
Num. 13:7

14 Geological age.

15 "His branches shall _____."
Hosea 14:6

17 "There is a friend that sticketh
_____ than a brother." Prov. 18:24

19 "His _____ and his feet like in
colour to polished brass."
Dan. 10:6

20 One vegetable they ate in Egypt
was the _____. Num. 11:5

21 "Joab and Abishai his brother slew
_____." 2 Sam. 3:30

23 Filled to excess.

25 "Ye see the man is _____."
1 Sam. 21:14

26 "_____ the son of Omri did evil. . .
above all that were before him."
1 Kings 16:30

28 "A place where two _____ met,
they ran the ship aground."
Acts 27:41

31 "Either the sun, _____ moon."
Deut. 17:3

32 "Poor widow. . .threw in two
_____." Mark 12:42

34 "How can these things _____?"
John 3:9

35 "Adam. . .begat a son. . .and called
his name _____." Gen. 5:3

38 "Valley of Shaveh, which is the
king's _____." Gen. 14:17

39 "_____ them about thy neck."
Prov. 6:21

40 "These men were bound in their
coats, their _____." Dan. 3:21

42 Solomon was wiser than _____.
1 Kings 4:31

44 "God is gone up with a _____."
Ps. 47:5

46 Consumer.

47 "Not be afraid for the _____ by
night." Ps. 91:5

49 "Among the smooth stones of the
_____." Isa. 57:6

52 "To Riblah, on the east side of
_____." Num. 34:11

53 "The words of the LORD are
_____ words." Ps. 12:6

55 "That which cometh of the _____
of his patrimony." Deut. 18:8

56 "The king's life: and his
_____(abbr.) as many genera-
tions." Ps. 61:6

57 "He that received _____ into the
good ground." Matt. 13:23

58 "The LORD. . .put him into the garden of _____." Gen. 2:15

DOWN

1 Footlike part.

2 "The child shall play on the hole
of the _____." Isa. 11:8

3 _____ of pearls.

4 "Fear took hold upon them
_____." Ps. 48:6

5 He who _____ someone
Godspeed is a partaker of his evil
deeds. 2 John 11

6 For example.

7 Varnish: abbr.

8 Apportion.

9 "I will go out and stand _____ my
father." 1 Sam. 19:3

10 Popular cookie.

11 "As my beloved sons I _____
you." 1 Cor. 4:14

16 Son of Kahath. Num. 3:19

18 "I have commanded my sanctified
_____." Isa. 13:3

Across/Down Clues:

21 "_____ hath conspired against thee." Amos 7:10

22 "Who his own self _____ our sins." 1 Peter 2:24

23 "He was. . .tempted of _____." Mark 1:13

24 "The LORD had respect unto _____." Gen. 4:4

27 "Jesus. . .did _____ himself from them." John 12:36

29 Samuel's second son was _____ 1 Sam. 8:2

30 "The Galileans received him, having _____ all. . .he did." John 4:45

33 "Thou God _____ me." Gen. 16:13

36 "I will hedge up thy way with _____." Hosea 2:6

37 "Ye know neither the day nor the _____." Matt. 25:13

39 "He brake the withs, as a _____ of tow." Judg. 16:9

41 He who _____ his ears from hearing shall dwell on high. Isa. 33:15–16

43 Concise.

44 "Let no man _____ him." Prov. 28:17

45 "If a son, then an _____ of God." Gal. 4:7

46 Previously owned.

48 "Ye tithe mint and _____." Luke 11:42

50 Lager.

51 "The flock of my pasture, are _____." Ezek. 34:31

54 Reason: abbr.

ACROSS

1 "Aaron, and _____ went up to the top of the hill." Exod. 17:10
4 "The snare is laid...and a _____ for him." Job 18:10
8 "But be _____ with sandals." Mark 6:9
12 Compass point.
13 "These men were bound in their coats...and their _____." Dan. 3:21
14 "When I looked, behold a _____ in the wall." Ezek. 8:7
15 "Let your light so shine before _____." Matt. 5:16
16 "He casteth forth his _____ like morsels." Ps. 147:17
17 "Every kind of beasts, and of _____." James 3:7
18 "Repent...or _____ I will come." Rev. 2:5
20 "They did so at the going up to _____." 2 Kings 9:27
21 "The _____ soweth the word." Mark 4:14
23 "Hornets...shall drive out the Hivite, the Canaanite, and the _____." Exod. 23:28
27 "Believest thou not that I am _____ the Father?" John 14:10
28 "He..._____ unto the mighty God." Ps. 132:2
30 Tangle.
31 "Can a bird fall...where no _____ is for him?" Amos 3:5
33 "Some of the children of Judah dwelt...at _____." Neh. 11:25
35 "The Spirit of adoption, whereby we _____, Abba, Father." Rom. 8:15
36 "There shall not an _____ be left behind." Exod. 10:26
38 "_____ hath forsaken me." 2 Tim. 4:10
40 To: Prefix.
41 Tennis shoe.

43 Miserly.
44 "The kingdom of heaven be likened unto _____ virgins." Matt. 25:1
45 "They cast _____, that is, the lot." Esther 3:7
46 "How good...for brethren to dwell together in _____." Ps. 133:1
49 "Shut the doors, and _____ them." Neh. 7:3
50 "Delivered me out of the _____ of the lion." 1 Sam. 17:37
53 Cloy.
54 "He set it up in the plain of _____." Dan. 3:1
55 "_____ no man any thing." Rom. 13:8
56 "Saul _____ David from that day." 1 Sam. 18:9
57 "Thou...shalt remain by the stone _____." 1 Sam. 20:19
58 "Child shall put his hand on the cockatrice' _____." Isa. 11:8

DOWN

1 "Touched the _____ of his garment." Matt. 9:20
2 To employ.
3 "_____ a right spirit within me." Ps. 51:10
4 "Thou shalt take _____ _____ in thine hand." Exod. 4:17
5 "As a strong man to run a _____." Ps. 19:5
6 "I _____ no pleasant bread." Dan. 10:3
7 The bk. of the Bible that has the most chapters.
8 Jerseys.
9 "The children of Israel...came unto mount _____." Num 20:22
10 "Our _____ man is crucified with him." Rom. 6:6
11 French article.
17 "They have mouths, _____ they speak not." Ps. 115:5

Across / Down clues:

19 Third bk. of the OT.

20 "They...pursued hard after them unto _____." Judg. 20:45

21 "My _____ are many." Lam. 1:22

22 Some things they ate in Egypt were cucumber, melon, garlic, and _____. Num. 11:5

23 "Blessed above women shall Jael the wife of _____ the Kenite be." Judg. 5:24

24 Barbour Publishing _____.

25 "They departed from Tahath, and pitched at _____." Num. 33:27

26 "_____ was glad when they departed." Ps. 105:38

29 Jabez asked the Lord to enlarge, or _____, his coasts. I Chron. 4:10

32 "As it was in the days of _____, so shall it be." Luke 17:26

34 "The _____ man receiveth not the things of the Spirit." I Cor. 2:14

37 "Her hired men are in the midst of her like _____ bullocks." Jer. 46:21

39 "_____, thou hast nothing to draw with." John 4:11

42 "He that hath the _____ of David." Rev. 3:7

45 "She shall shave her head, and _____ her nails." Deut. 21:12

46 "That which is good to the _____ of edifying." Eph. 4:29

47 "I tell you _____; but rather division." Luke 12:51

48 Follower.

49 "Dedan, and Tema, and _____, and all that are in the utmost corners. Jer. 25:23

50 Like two peas in a _____.

51 "Stand in ___, and sin not." Ps. 4:4

52 "Maimed, or having a _____, or scurvy." Lev. 22:22

54 _____ facto.

ACROSS

1 "The _____, which is an homer of ten baths." Ezek. 45:14
4 "We sailed under _____, over against Salmone." Acts 27:7
9 "Moses stretched forth his hand over the _____." Exod. 14:27
12 "I am one of them that _____ peaceable." 2 Sam. 20:19
13 "One loaf of bread, and one cake of _____ bread." Exod. 29:23
14 "The earth. . .and the heavens. . . _____ no light." Jer. 4:23
15 "The sea may _____ _____ unto us." Jonah 1:11
17 "Cleanse the _____." Matt. 10:8
19 "_____ thou become like unto us?" Isa. 14:10
20 "The stork, and the _____ after her kind." Deut. 14:18
21 "One of the officers. . .struck Jesus with the _____ of his hand." John 18:22
23 Stage of sleep: abbr.
24 "He took one of his _____, and closed up the flesh." Gen. 2:21
27 "Come unto me, _____ ye that labour." Matt. 11:28
28 Indian weight.
29 "They should take nothing. . .no _____, no bread." Mark 6:8
30 Greek letter P.
31 "The _____ angel sounded." Rev. 11:15
33 "What must I do _____ be saved?" Acts 16:30
34 "One _____ happeneth to them all." Eccles. 2:14
36 "Who will show us _____ good?" Ps. 4:6
37 "See that she reverence _____ husband." Eph. 5:33
38 Californian fish.
39 Compass point.
40 "Pray, _____ ye enter into temptation." Mark 14:38
41 "Thou shalt _____ upon the lion." Ps. 91:13
43 "Unto me every knee shall _____." Isa. 45:23
44 Customer.
46 "The king's commandment was _____." Dan. 3:22
49 "_____ Father which art in heaven." Matt. 6:9
50 Taunt.
52 "Shimei, and _____, and the mighty men which belonged to David." 1 Kings 1:8
53 Psalm.
54 "I _____ not from thy precepts." Ps. 119:110
55 "The gods. . .which _____ not, nor hear." Dan. 5:23

DOWN

1 "The fourth part of a _____ of dove's dung." 2 Kings 6:25
2 Mineral.
3 "This I _____ to my mind." Lam. 3:21
4 "Thy king cometh. . .riding. . .upon a _____." Zech. 9:9
5 Border.
6 "He built there an altar, and called the place _____-bethel." Gen. 35:7
7 One of the porters. Ezra 10:24
8 "Sons of Mushi; Mahli, and _____, and Jeremoth." 1 Chron. 23:23
9 "Look. . .from the top of _____ and Hermon." Song of Sol. 4:8
10 "Incline thine _____ unto me." Ps. 17:6
11 Paid notices.
16 "Thou hast a mighty _____." Ps. 89:13
18 "Jesus walked in the temple in Solomon's _____." John 10:23
20 "Tarry ye _____ _____ watch with me." Matt. 26:38

21 "I would not write with _____ and ink." 2 John 12

22 "My son was dead, and is _____." Luke 15:24

23 Last bk. of the NT.

25 "At the last it biteth (or _____) like a serpent." Prov. 23:32

26 "It is as _____ to a fool to do mischief." Prov. 10:23

28 "They _____ forward my calamity." Job 30:13

29 Pen.

31 "The fear of man bringeth a _____." Prov. 29:25

32 Compass point.

35 "Ye may be perfect and _____." James 1:4

37 "They shall march. . .as _____ of wood." Jer. 46:22

39 "It may give. . .bread to the _____." Isa. 55:10

40 "Flour for a meat offering. . .and one _____ of oil." Lev. 14:10

42 Grafted.

43 "It _____ worms, and stank." Exod. 16:20

44 Dove cry.

45 "They of Persia and of _____ and of Phut were in thine army." Ezek. 27:10

46 "A vessel. . .meet for the master's _____." 2 Tim. 2:21

47 French for "born."

48 "_____ the kine to the cart." 1 Sam. 6:7

51 "A fire. . .hath consumed _____ of Moab." Num. 21:28

ACROSS

1 "A man shall nourish a young _____." Isa. 7:21
4 "As many as were possessors of _____ or houses sold them." Acts 4:34
9 "Him that rideth upon the heavens by his name _____." Ps. 68:4
12 "_____ no man any thing." Rom. 13:8
13 "I was _____ to write." Rev. 10:4
14 Guido's high note.
15 "Without _____ ye can do nothing." John 15:5
16 "Whose trust shall be a _____ web." Job 8:14
18 Two: Roman.
19 "He which hath the sharp sword with two _____." Rev. 2:12
21 Fall flower.
23 "Punish the men that are settled on their _____." Zeph. 1:12
25 Dock.
26 "_____ of every sort shalt thou bring into the ark." Gen. 6:19
28 "[He] saw. . .a great _____ knit at the four corners." Acts 10:11
30 Shoshonean.
33 "All that handle the _____, the mariners." Ezek. 27:29
34 Son of Jether. 1 Chron. 7:38
35 "Lest I _____ mine own inheritance." Ruth 4:6
36 Son of Bela, a mighty man of valor. 1 Chron. 7:7
37 Carve.
39 Before: prefix.
40 "Shook off. . .into the fire, and _____ no harm." Acts 28:5
42 "Give me children, or _____ I die." Gen. 30:1
44 Undecided.
46 "Of the Assyrians, upon whom she _____." Ezek. 23:9
49 Homeland of Abraham.
50 "A friend of the world _____ an enemy of God." Jas. 4:4 NIV
54 "Yea, hath God said, _____ shall not eat. . .?" Gen. 3:1
55 Eye problem.
57 Window _____.
58 Honey maker.
59 Compass point.
60 "And the water was _____ in the bottle." Gen. 21:15
61 "The Lord shall _____ to me another son." Gen. 30:24

DOWN

1 "Therefore shall his calamity _____." Prov. 6:15
2 "_____ him ten thousand talents." Matt. 18:24
3 "My herdmen and thy herdmen; for _____ be brethren." Gen. 13:8
4 Intervals.
5 "His mother's name also was _____." 2 Kings 18:2
6 "Dwelt in the land of _____." Gen. 4:16
7 "I will give you rain in _____ season." Lev. 26:4
8 "Enter ye in at the _____ gate." Matt. 7:13
9 Major prophet bk.
10 "Changed the truth of God into _____ _____." Rom. 1:25
11 "Mary. . .wiped his feet with her _____." John 11:2
16 "They shall _____ the glory of the LORD." Isa. 35:2
17 Compass point.
20 "God shall also _____ him in himself." John 13:32
22 "They have blown the _____." Ezek. 7:14
24 "Thou _____ not revile the gods." Exod. 22:28
25 "And he said, _____ be to you."

Gen. 43:23

26 "_____ king of Hamath." 2 Sam. 8:9

27 "He teacheth my hands to _____." Ps. 18:34

29 "Of _____, the family of the Erites." Num. 26:16

31 Noah put pitch (which is _____) on the ark. Gen. 6:14

32 "Sir, come down _____ my child die." John 4:49

37 "Our friend Lazarus _____." John 11:11 NKJV

38 "The three _____ sons of Jesse went." 1 Sam. 17:13

41 Wane.

43 Distress signal.

44 Contemplate.

45 "Many of them also which used curious _____ brought their books." Acts 19:19

47 "Leah was tender _____." Gen. 29:17

48 "Love...in _____ and in truth." 1 John 3:18

51 Cover.

52 "_____ event happeneth to them all." Eccles. 2:14

53 "And ye shall be holy _____ unto me." Exod. 22:31

56 "For _____ are bought with a price." 1 Cor. 6:20

58 College degree.

ACROSS

1 "Let him. . ._____ upon his God." Isa. 50:10

5 "I am the LORD your God, and none _____." Joel 2:27

9 "He it is, to whom I shall give a _____." John 13:26

12 "Take thine _____, eat, drink." Luke 12:19

13 One of Zibeon's sons. 1 Chron. 1:40

14 Son of Benjamin. Gen. 46:21

15 "I ___ the living bread." John 6:51

16 "Go rather to the _____ sheep of the house of Israel." Matt. 10:6

18 "Seek. . .unto wizards that _____, and that mutter." Isa. 8:19

19 "The wicked. . .seeketh to _____ him." Ps. 37:32

20 Parents organization.

22 Third bk. of the OT.

23 "I will ___ thee with my tears." Isa. 16:9

25 "Samson. . .put a firebrand. . . between two _____." Judg.15:4

27 "There is _____ _____ here." John 6:9

28 "The iron did _____." 2 Kings 6:6

29 "The _____ number of them is to be redeemed." Num. 3:48

32 Buffalo.

33 "All that I have is _____." Luke 15:31

34 "_____ up for yourselves treasures in heaven." Matt. 6:20

35 Compass point.

36 "All our righteousnesses are as filthy _____." Isa. 64:6

37 "Tarry _____ today also." 2 Sam. 11:12

38 "He. . .shall save the _____ of the needy." Ps. 72:13

40 "Every kind of beasts. . .hath been _____ of mankind." James 3:7

41 "_____, Judah's firstborn, was wicked." Gen. 38:7

43 "He hath spread a _____ for my feet." Lam. 1:13

44 "The lion, which hath _____ him, and slain him." 1 Kings 13:26

45 "Hate the evil, and _____ the good." Amos 5:15

47 "It _____ worms and stank." Exod. 16:20

48 "_____ are all the children of light." 1 Thess. 5:5

50 "Why make ye this _____, and weep?" Mark 5:39

51 "Let the oppressed go _____." Isa. 58:6

53 "The land is as the garden of _____." Joel 2:3

55 Cut down.

56 "The first year of Darius the _____." Dan. 11:1

57 "Whither have ye made a _____ today?" 1 Sam. 27:10

DOWN

1 "There shall be signs. . .the _____ and the waves roaring." Luke 21:25

2 Beret.

3 "The nations are _____ a drop of a bucket." Isa. 40:15

4 "The young lions roared. . .and _____." Jer. 2:15

5 "My yoke is _____." Matt. 11:30

6 Railroad sleeping car: wagon-_____.

7 Continent: abbr.

8 Exclamation.

9 "Hasten his work, that we may _____ it." Isa. 5:19

10 Son of Zerubbabel. 1 Chron. 3:20

11 "The tabret, and _____, and wine, are in their feasts." Isa. 5:12

17 "All that handle the _____, the mariners." Ezek. 27:29

18 Chum.

19 "Not one of the _____ thereof shall ever be removed." Isa. 33:20

20 "God. . .loosed the _____ of death." Acts 2:24

21 "Tomorrow about this _____ I will cause it to rain." Exod. 9:18

23 "They have not known my _____." Heb. 3:10

24 "___! for that day is great." Jer. 30:7

25 "He cropped off the top of his young _____." Ezek. 17:4

26 "Upon the harp with a _____ sound." Ps. 92:3

28 "Thou _____ love the Lord thy God." Mark 12:30

30 "We _____ not make ourselves of the number." 2 Cor. 10:12

31 "Who. . .cometh from Edom, with _____ garments." Isa. 63:1

33 "We know that thou art _____." Matt. 22:16

37 "They have made their faces _____ than a rock." Jer. 5:3

39 "Despise not _____ of these little ones." Matt. 18:10

40 "Put it. . .upon the great _____ of their right foot." Exod. 29:20

41 A duke of Edom. Gen. 36:41

42 "Absalom _____ upon a mule." 2 Sam. 18:9

44 "Rest yourselves under the _____." Gen. 18:4

46 "Paul. . .having shorn his head. . . for he had a _____." Acts 18:18

47 "If I make my _____ in hell." Ps. 139:8

48 "_____, though I walk through the valley." Ps. 23:4

49 "He that endureth to the _____ shall be saved." Matt. 10:22

51 Radio frequency.

52 Last bk. of the Bible.

54 "I will tell you what I will _____." Isa. 5:5

ACROSS

1 "Arise, take up thy _____." Matt. 9:6

4 "Tomorrow is the new _____."
1 Sam. 20:18

8 "_____ offered unto God a more
excellent sacrifice." Heb. 11:4

11 "How long will it be _____ thou be
quiet?" Jer. 47:6

12 "In _____ time and in harvest thou
shalt rest." Exod. 34:21

14 "Thou canst _____ every thing."
Job 42:2

15 Train (or ____) up a child. Prov. 22:6

17 An unclean animal: the _____ eagle.
Lev. 11:18

19 "I have sojourned with _____."
Gen. 32:4

21 "God _____ them in the firmament." Gen. 1:17

22 "Go to the _____, thou sluggard."
Prov. 6:6

24 "The rain is _____ and gone."
Song of Sol. 2:11

25 "Put thou my tears into thy bottle."
Ps. 56:8. Another word for bottle is
_____.

26 "_____, our eye hath seen it."
Ps. 35:21

27 Southeastern state: abbr.

28 "They...have given a _____ for an
harlot." Joel 3:3

29 A Christian _____ to God.

31 "She sitteth...on a _____ in the
high places." Prov. 9:14

33 In Babylon an _____ will never pitch
his tent. Isa. 13:20

34 "If thy brother be...fallen in _____
with thee." Lev. 25:35

36 "Why make ye this _____?"
Mark 5:39

37 "_____ of the Chaldees." Neh. 9:7

38 "If thou _____ this man go, thou art
not Caesar's friend." John 19:12

39 Son of Benjamin. Gen. 46:21

40 "_____, the beloved physician, and
Demas, greet you." Col. 4:14

42 "The _____ shall take him by the
heel." Job 18:9

43 "The archers _____ him; and he
was sore wounded." 1 Sam. 31:3

44 "All men _____ in their hearts of
John." Luke 3:15

45 "His _____ drew the third part of
the stars." Rev. 12:4

47 Sludge.

48 "We...be no more children, tossed
_____ and fro." Eph. 4:14

50 "Beat...your pruning hooks into
_____." Joel 3:10

52 "The star, which they _____ in the
east." Matt. 2:9

55 "Who hath established all the
_____ of the earth?" Prov. 30:4

56 "There was a continual _____ given
him." Jer. 52:34

57 "Blessed be God, even _____ Father
of our Lord Jesus Christ." 2 Cor. 1:3

DOWN

1 "Many there _____ which go in
thereat." Matt. 7:13

2 "She...bare a son; and he called his
name _____." Gen. 38:3

3 "They...fled unto Lystra and
_____." Acts 14:6

4 "What _____ ye to weep and to
break mine heart?" Acts 21:13

5 "All that handle the _____, the
mariners." Ezek. 27:29

6 "Ask it either in the depth, _____ in
the height above." Isa. 7:11

7 "Teachers; as Barnabas, and Simeon
that was called _____." Acts 13:1

8 "He is of _____; ask him." John 9:21

9 "The children of Gad called the
altar _____." Josh. 22:34

10 "I have found my sheep which was
_____." Luke 15:6

13 Insect egg.

16 "Incline thine _____ unto me."
Ps. 17:6

18 "Only _____ the harlot shall live."
Josh. 6:17

19 "For God so _____ the world."
John 3:16

20 "The king of Assyria brought men
from..._____." 2 Kings 17:24

21 "They..._____, Blessed be the
LORD." Zech. 11:5

23 "I tell you, _____; except ye repent."
Luke 13:3

A crossword puzzle grid with numbered cells: 1, 2, 3, 4, 5, 6, 7, 8, 9, 10 (top row); 11, 12, 13, 14; 15, 16, 17, 18; 19, 20, 21, 22, 23; 24, 25, 26; 27, 28, 29, 30; 31, 32, 33; 34, 35, 36, 37; 38, 39, 40, 41; 42, 43, 44; 45, 46, 47; 48, 49, 50, 51, 52, 53, 54; 55, 56, 57.

25 "One _____ or one tittle shall in no wise pass." Matt. 5:18

26 Son of Jether. I Chron. 7:38

28 "The fourth chariot grisled and _____ horses." Zech. 6:3

29 For.

30 "One. . .came and _____ them into the pot." 2 Kings 4:39

31 "Yet through the _____ of water it will bud." Job 14:9

32 "He did _____ with the Gentiles." Gal. 2:12

33 "_____ to your faith virtue." 2 Peter 1:5

35 "He ran unto _____, and said, Here am I." I Sam. 3:5

36 "Rabbi, thou _____ the Son of God." John 1:49

37 Musical instrument: abbr.

39 "What _____ thee, O thou sea?" Ps. 114:5

40 "The name of that city was called _____ at the first." Gen. 28:19

41 "Be merciful unto me, as thou _____ to do." Ps. 119:132

42 "Mordecai sat in the king's _____." Esther 2:19

43 "He smote them _____ and thigh." Judg. 15:8

44 "_____ men will proclaim. . .his own goodness." Prov. 20:6

46 "The _____ knoweth. . .his master's crib." Isa. 1:3

47 Raw mineral.

49 "Poti-pherah, priest of _____." Gen. 41:45

51 "Gibeon. . .was greater than _____." Josh. 10:2

53 "_____, Lord GOD! surely thou hast greatly deceived this people." Jer. 4:10

54 "For _____ are labourers together with God." I Cor. 3:9

ACROSS

1 "Maintain good works for neces-
sary _____." Titus 3:14
5 "He...chooseth a tree that will
not _____." Isa. 40:20
8 The book of Psalms has more
than one _____ in it.
12 "_____ only remained alive." Gen.
7:23
13 Compass point.
14 "_____ was a cunning hunter."
Gen. 25:27
15 "(The Lord will take away) the
rings, and _____ jewels." Isa. 3:21
16 "God shall let me _____my desire."
Ps. 59:10
17 Soaks flax.
18 "I ask...for what _____ ye have
sent for me?" Acts 10:29
20 "O LORD...that _____ the reins
and the heart." Jer. 11:20
22 "_____ the kine to the cart."
1 Sam 6:7
23 God asks Job if he _____an arm
like God. Job 40:9
24 "He commandeth, and _____ the
stormy wind." Ps. 107:25
28 The lioness brought up a _____
and it became a young lion.
Ezek. 19:3
32 Son of Gad. Num. 26:16
33 "A woman...touched the _____of
his garment." Matt. 9:20
35 "_____ to thee, Moab!" Num.
21:29
36 "For _____ hath forsaken me."
2 Tim. 4:10
39 "If any widow have children or
_____." 1 Tim 5:4
42 "I will come in to him, and will
_____ with him." Rev. 3:20
44 "I tell you, _____; but rather division." Luke 12:51
45 "We wrestle...against spiritual
wickedness in high _____."
Eph. 6:12

48 "_____ is laid in the walls."
Ezra 5:8
52 "_____ your beasts, and go."
Gen. 45:17
53 "_____ the son of Abdiel."
1 Chron. 5:15
55 "There is _____ righteous, no, not
one." Rom. 3:10
56 "The young men of _____ shall
fall by the sword." Ezek. 30:17
57 Constellation.
58 "He that heareth the word, and
_____ with joy receiveth it."
Matt. 13:20
59 Three feet.
60 "An open door, and no _____ can
shut it." Rev. 3:8
61 "Friend, _____ me three loaves."
Luke 11:5

DOWN

1 "Brethren of the second degree,
Zechariah...Jehiel, and _____."
1 Chron. 15:18
2 "They _____ forgat his works."
Ps. 106:13
3 "They shall come from the _____,
and from the west." Luke 13:29
4 "I will give you thirty _____ and
thirty change of garments."
Judg. 14:12
5 "Wisdom _____ in the heart of
him." Prov. 14:33
6 "Not _____ thing hath failed of all
the good things." Josh. 23:14
7 "His _____ shall be set on edge."
Jer. 31:30
8 "The law shall not _____ from the
priest." Jer. 18:18
9 The same name as Hosea.
Rom. 9:25
10 Consumes.
11 "There _____ be an inheritance."
Judg. 21:17
19 Never: German.

21 "Eat not of it _____." Exod. 12:9
24 "By faith they passed through the _____ sea." Heb. 11:29
25 "Where _____ their gods?" Deut. 32:37
26 "They departed from _____, and pitched in Dibon-gad." Num. 33:45
27 "Would I have gathered thy children. . .as a _____ doth gather her brood." Luke 13:34
29 "One _____ lamb of the first year." Lev. 14:10
30 "A man's pride shall bring him _____." Prov. 29:23
31 Foot-like part.
34 "I will _____ the loving-kindnesses of the LORD." Isa. 63:7
37 "If I _____ up into heaven, thou art there." Ps. 139:8

38 "If any man will _____ thee at the law." Matt. 5:40
40 "Hadad reigned. . .his city was _____." 1 Chron. 1:50
41 Book of worship songs.
43 "Sing unto the LORD with. . .the voice of a _____." Ps. 98:5
45 "_____ skillfully with a loud noise." Ps. 33:3
46 Molten rock.
47 Son of Beriah. 1 Chron. 8:15–16
49 "This is now _____ of my bones." Gen. 2:23
50 "John also was baptizing in _____." John 3:23
51 "Let us not _____ it, but cast lots for it." John 19:24
54 Babylonian god.

ACROSS

1 "The lot is cast into the _____."
Prov. 16:33

4 "Hold up my goings. . .that my
footsteps _____ not." Ps. 17:5

8 "Praise Him with the psaltery and
_____." Ps. 150:3

12 "_____ no man any thing."
Rom. 13:8

13 "Bind the _____ of thine head
upon thee." Ezek. 24:17

14 "_____, lama sabachthani?"
Mark 15:34

15 Apiece.

16 "The high priest. . .said unto him,
_____ thou nothing?" Matt. 26:62

18 "Every bird of every _____."
Gen. 7:14

20 Only.

21 "A sepulchre that was hewn in
_____." Luke 23:53

23 "Whosesoever sins ye _____, they
are remitted unto them." John
20:23

25 "Ye shall _____ away for your
iniquities." Ezek. 24:23

26 "Dip it in the blood that is in the
_____." Exod. 12:22

27 "He saith among the trumpets,
_____." Job 39:25

29 Paid notices.

30 "The angels shall. . ._____ the
wicked from among the just."
Matt. 13:49

31 Steep flax.

32 Ezra, _____ (abbr.), Esther.

33 "_____ the Ammonite." 1 Chron.
11:39

34 "These made war with _____ king
of Sodom." Gen. 14:2

35 "To keep thee from the evil
_____." Prov. 6:24

36 "Take one lamb for a trespass
offering to be _____." Lev. 14:21

37 Thin strip.

38 "The people shall. . .gather a certain _____ every day." Exod. 16:4

39 "At the _____ _____ his chariots." Jer. 47:3

42 "Fight neither with small _____
great." 1 King 22:31

45 Greek letter.

46 "My couch shall _____ my complaint." Job 7:13

47 "_____ ye out of the way."
Isa. 30:11

48 River flowing to the Elbe.

49 "Southward were Kabzeel, and
_____, and Jagur." Josh. 15:21

50 "Sir, come down _____ my child
die." John 4:49

DOWN

1 "Behold, the Lord. . .shall _____
the bough." Isa. 10:33

2 "My heart standeth in _____ of
thy word." Ps. 119:161

3 "He that followeth vain _____ is
void of understanding."
Prov. 12:11

4 "They look and _____ upon me."
Ps. 22:17

5 Yarn fluff.

6 Tax agency.

7 Church seat.

8 "_____ is love. . .that He loved
us." 1 John 4:10

9 He was aware of, or _____ to, the
fact. Song of Sol. 6:12

10 "I am the _____ of Sharon."
Song of Sol. 2:1

11 "One sheep, and if it fall into a
_____ on the sabbath." Matt. 12:11

17 "Of the sons of _____."
Acts 7:16

19 "_____ basket had very good figs."
Jer. 24:2

21 "A _____ shall be the length
thereof." Exod. 28:16

22 Current.

23 "The owl also and the _____ shall dwell in it." Isa. 34:11

24 "He called the name of the well _____." Gen. 26:20

26 "The king of _____, which is Zoar." Gen. 14:2

27 "What hast thou _____?" Judg.18:3

28 "They came to the threshing floor of _____." Gen. 50:10

30 "_____, which was the son of Joseph." Luke 3:26

31 "O LORD. . .visit me, and _____ me of my persecutors." Jer. 15:15

33 "Then answered _____ the Naamathite." Job 11:1

34 "The lapwing, and the _____. . . shall be an abomination unto you." Lev. 11:19–20

35 "She is empty, and void, and _____." Nahum 2:10

36 "One unleavened cake. . .and one unleavened _____." Num. 6:19

37 The third day of the week: abbr.

38 "Pharaoh _____ up in the night." Exod. 12:30

39 Baseball statistic.

40 Born.

41 "She called his name _____." Gen. 30:11

43 Above: poetic.

44 Cross-country highway: abbr.

ACROSS

1 "Joseph _____ the governor over the land." Gen. 42:6

4 "Orpah kissed her mother-in-law; but ___ clave unto her." Ruth 1:14

8 "We have seen his _____ in the east." Matt. 2:2

12 "_____ also the Jairite was a chief ruler." 2 Sam. 20:26

13 The court was the uncovered _____ enclosed within the walls of the tabernacle.

14 "The _____, because he cheweth the cud." Lev. 11:6

15 Powder.

17 Devil.

18 "___! for that day is great." Jer. 30:7

19 "He hath made my mouth like a _____ sword." Isa. 49:2

21 "Keep me as the _____ of the eye." Ps. 17:8

23 "The sons of Benjamin were... Naaman, _____, and Rosh." Gen. 46:21

25 "Love worketh no _____." Rom. 13:10

26 "That, _____ whether they both shall be alike good." Eccles. 11:6

28 "He gave unto Moses...two tables of _____." Exod. 31:18

32 "The king of Assyria brought men...from _____." 2 Kings 17:24

33 "I am, and none _____ beside me." Isa. 47:8

34 Before.

35 "All the promises of God...are yea, and in him _____." 2 Cor. 1:20

36 "Ye cannot bear them _____." John 16:12

37 "Sitting there, and _____ in their hearts." Mark 2:6

39 Palm lily.

40 "_____ God so loved the world." John 3:16

41 Droop.

42 "We do you _____ _____ of the grace of God." 2 Cor. 8:1

44 "Only _____ not ye against the LORD." Num. 14:9

48 Son of Eliphaz. Gen. 36:11

50 "They that were foolish...took no _____ with them." Matt. 25:3

52 "He that loveth his life shall _____ it." John 12:25

53 "He put them all together into _____ three days." Gen. 42:17

54 "Breastplate of judgment the _____ and the Thummim." Exod. 28:30

56 His face will not now wax pale, or look _____. Isa. 29:22

57 "The _____ of the LORD run to and fro." 2 Chron. 16:9

58 "Amaziah said unto Amos, O thou _____, go, flee." Amos 7:12

59 "Escape...to Tarshish, Pul, and _____." Isa. 66:19

DOWN

1 "They...are at their _____ end." Ps. 107:27

2 775 children of _____ came out of captivity from Babylon. Ezra 2:5

3 Cainan's son. Luke 3:35

4 Egyptian sun god.

5 "Geber the son of _____ was in the country of Gilead." 1 Kings 4:19

6 "The troops of _____ looked, the companies of Sheba waited for them." Job 6:19

7 The Lord brings us joy and _____.

8 "They that wait upon the LORD _____ renew their strength." Isa. 40:31

9 "Yet shall ye deliver the _____ of bricks." Exod. 5:18

10 Son of Jether. 1 Chron. 7:38

11 Legal action suit.

16 "They might attain to Phenice... an haven of _____." Acts 27:12

20 Greek letter.
22 Layer.
24 "Work of an _____ whorish woman." Ezek. 16:30
26 "Grass. . .tomorrow is cast into the _____." Matt. 6:30
27 "So that the earth _____ again." 1 Sam. 4:5
28 "The _____ which he placed among men." Ps. 78:60
29 "_____, lama sabachthani?" Mark 15:34
30 Compass point.
31 Danish money.
32 Returners from Babylon: children of _____. Ezra 2:57
35 "The _____ of the LORD found her." Gen. 16:7
37 "A _____ of new timber." Ezra 6:4
38 "All that handle the _____, the mariners." Ezek. 27:29

40 "The daughters of Moab shall be at the _____ of Arnon." Isa. 16:2
42 "The king arose, and _____ his garments." 2 Sam. 13:31
43 "Bind the _____ of thy head upon thee." Ezek. 24:17
45 "A candlestick all of gold, with a _____ upon the top." Zech. 4:2
46 "_____ despised his birthright." Gen. 25:34
47 "Friend, _____ me three loaves." Luke 11:5
48 "_____ no man any thing." Rom. 13:8
49 "If this cup _____ not pass away from me." Matt. 26:42
51 "They _____ in wait for my soul." Ps. 59:3
55 Man's title: abbr.

ACROSS

1 Exclamation of surprise!
4 "Abram's wife _____ him no children." Gen. 16:1
8 "So then because thou art lukewarm. . .I will _____ thee out of my mouth." Rev. 3:16
12 "_____, my Lord, hear me." Gen. 23:11
13 A certain place.
14 Cable car.
15 "Women went out after her with _____." Exod. 15:20
17 Related to aircraft.
18 "_____ turned back, and saw the angel." 1 Chron. 21:20
19 "For seasons, and for days, and _____." Gen. 1:14
21 "And _____ his son reigned in his stead." 1 Kings 15:8
23 "The _____ of the river shall dry up." Zech. 10:11
26 "Hanani the _____ came to Asa." 2 Chron. 16:7
29 "The son of _____, a man of Issachar." Judg. 10:1
32 "The one preach Christ of contention, _____ sincerely." Phil. 1:16
33 "And Adoniram the son of _____." 1 Kings 4:6
34 Compass point.
35 Measure of property size.
36 _____ the lion.
37 "David prepared _____ in abundance." 1 Chron. 22:3
38 "Daughters of Israel, _____ over Saul." 2 Sam. 1:24
39 "The children of Ephraim, being _____, and carrying bows." Ps. 78:9
41 Health resort.
43 "Friend, I do thee no _____." Matt. 20:13
46 The people heard Herod _____ from his throne. Acts 12:21

50 "An handmaid that is _____ to her mistress." Prov. 30:23
52 "And they _____ the angel of the LORD." Zech. 1:11
54 "The inhabitant of this _____." Isa. 20:6
55 "The vultures. . .every one with her _____." Isa. 34:15
56 Brew.
57 "Things which were _____ them by the shepherds." Luke 2:18
58 Pitcher.
59 "The tabernacle of God is with _____." Rev. 21:3

DOWN

1 "Then I went _____ _____ the gate of the fountain." Neh. 2:14
2 "There shall not an _____ of him fall. . ." 1 Kings 1:52
3 "When they had sung an _____." Matt. 26:30
4 "I will pull down my _____." Luke 12:18
5 "The balances of deceit _____ in his hand." Hosea 12:7
6 "Because thou didst _____ on the LORD." 2 Chron. 16:8
7 "My couch shall _____ my complaint." Job 7:13
8 "All my bones: they look and _____ upon me." Ps. 22:17
9 "In thy _____ is fulness of joy." Ps. 16:11
10 "Thou incline thine _____ unto wisdom." Prov. 2:2
11 World Meteorological Organization: abbr.
16 "Hushim and _____ were his wives." 1 Chron. 8:8
20 'Why make ye this _____?" Mark 5:39
22 One of the chief men of Aijalon. 1 Chron. 8:15
24 Meditate on, or _____ over, the

Word of God.

25 "There is but a _____ between me and death." 1 Sam. 20:3

26 One of Jesus' ancestors, Cainan's son. Luke 3:35

27 "Ships. . .shall afflict _____." Num. 24:24

28 "Over _____ _____ I cast out my shoe." Ps. 60:8

30 "The sons of Elpaal. . .who built _____." 1 Chron. 8:12

31 "When they couch in their _____, and abide." Job 38:40

35 "Men that walk over them are not _____ of them." Luke 11:44

37 "The works that _____ _____ in my Father's name." John 10:25

40 "Who concerning the truth have _____." 2 Tim. 2:18

42 "I give unto you _____ to tread on serpents." Luke 10:19

44 "O give thanks unto the LORD; call upon his _____." Ps. 105:1

45 "They _____ not the bones till the morrow." Zeph. 3:3

47 "Balak. . .brought me from _____." Num. 23:7

48 Far: comb. form.

49 "The land is as the garden of _____ before them." Joel 2:3

50 "The archers _____ him." 1 Sam. 31:3

51 Within: comb. form.

53 Holy person (female): abbr.

ACROSS

1 "Thrust through with a _____."
 Heb. 12:20
5 "And Joshua _____ peace with
 them." Josh. 9:15
9 "He _____ them forth by the
 right way." Ps. 107:7
12 Ir and Hushim were sons of
 _____. I Chron. 7:12
13 Jesus went out of the temple
 _____ the people. John 8:59
14 "The sons of Elpaal. . .who built
 _____." I Chron. 8:12
15 "Father, glorify thy _____."
 John 12:28
16 "His father. . ._____ and fell on his
 neck." Luke 15:20
17 "Ye _____ men with burdens
 grievous to be borne." Luke 11:46
18 Conger.
20 "God came to _____. . .in a
 dream." Gen. 31:24
22 "A _____ came unto him."
 Matt. 26:69
25 "I _____ rather be a doorkeeper in
 the house of my God." Ps. 84:10
26 Paid notice.
28 Decline.
29 "Submit yourselves therefore to
 _____." James 4:7
31 "Isaac dwelt in _____." Gen. 26:6
33 "If any be a hearer of the word
 and not a _____." James 1:23
35 "If it fall into a _____ on the sabbath day." Matt. 12:11
37 One of Jesus' ancestors. Luke 3:27
38 "We were driven up and down in
 _____." Acts 27:27
40 "They _____ not the land in pos-
 session by their own sword."
 Ps. 44:3
42 American author.
43 Ezra, _____ (abbr.), Esther.
44 "Who _____ no sin, neither was
 guile found in his mouth."
 I Peter 2:22
46 "I have an _____ to thee, O
 captain." 2 Kings 9:5

48 "The stork, the _____ after her
 kind. . .shall be an abomination."
 Lev. 11:19–20
50 Three: Roman numeral.
51 "Amaziah said unto Amos, O thou
 _____, go, flee." Amos 7:12
53 "Ye take _____ much upon you."
 Num. 16:3
55 "The Lord God to _____ every
 tree that is pleasant." Gen. 2:9
58 "Love the Lord thy God with
 _____ thy heart." Matt. 22:37
59 "_____ out thy light and thy
 truth." Ps. 43:3
60 "Behold, _____ I am." I Sam. 12:3
61 "Let Asher. . ._____ his foot in oil."
 Deut. 33:24
62 "A prophet of the LORD. . .whose
 name was _____." 2 Chron. 28:9
63 Horse's gait.

DOWN

1 "These are his sides east and
 west; a portion for _____." Ezek.
 48:1
2 "_____, our eye hath seen it."
 Ps. 35:21
3 "_____, O LORD, thy tender mercies." Ps. 25:6
4 "I see men as _____, walking."
 Mark 8:24
5 "They _____ my path." Job 30:13
6 Helem's son. I Chron. 7:35
7 "Afterwards she bare a daughter,
 and called her name _____."
 Gen. 30:21
8 "The children of Reuben and the
 children of Gad called the altar
 _____." Josh. 22:34
9 "For the _____ which is lent to
 the Lord." I Sam. 2:20
10 "Seal the book, even to the time
 of the _____." Dan. 12:4
11 Female deer.
17 "Jesse took an ass _____ with
 bread." I Sam. 16:20
19 "Make bare the _____, uncover
 the thigh." Isa. 47:2

21 "He was a thief, and had the
_____." John 12:6

22 "_____ was thy merchant in precious clothes for chariots."
Ezek. 27:20

23 "David _____ in the wilderness."
1 Sam. 23:14

24 "Behold, the Lord. . .shall _____
the bough." Isa. 10:33

26 "_____ thy brother shall be thy
prophet." Exod. 7:1

27 "They saw the fig tree _____ up
from the roots." Mark 11:20

30 "I cannot _____; to beg I am
ashamed." Luke 16:3

32 "Thou shalt be called, The _____
of the breach." Isa. 58:12

34 "She scorneth the horse and his
_____." Job 39:18

36 "Upon the great _____ of their
right foot." Exod. 29:20

39 "Birds of the _____ have nests."
Matt. 8:20

41 Three: prefix.

45 "The Assyrians, upon whom she
_____." Ezek 23:9

47 "Do that which is _____ in his
sight." Exod. 15:26

48 "Fear thou not. . .I will _____
thee." Isa. 41:10

49 "There is _____ to help." Ps. 22:11

51 "What manner. . .as ye walk and
are _____?" Luke 24:17

52 "They. . .brought the child to
_____." 1 Sam. 1:25

54 "The _____ number of them is to
be redeemed." Num. 3:48

56 Gold: Spanish.

57 "They are _____ with the showers of the mountains." Job 24:8

59 "If the will of God be _____."
1 Peter 3:17

ACROSS

1 "When he came unto _____, the Philistines shouted." Judg. 15:14

5 "Cedars. . .as the sycamore trees that are in the _____." 1 Kings 10:27

9 Unclean fowls: the stork, the _____. Deut. 14:18

10 "_____, Jesus Christ maketh thee whole: arise." Acts 9:34

12 "Though it were but for a _____." 2 Cor. 7:8

13 Begins.

15 "The _____ number of them is to be redeemed." Num. 3:48

16 "I. . .have the _____ of hell and of death." Rev. 1:18

18 "There was a continual _____ given him of the king." Jer. 52:34

19 "In the _____ to come he might show the exceeding riches." Eph. 2:7

21 Fishing equipment.

23 Depression agency.

24 "We gat our bread with the _____ of our lives." Lam. 5:9

26 More than one _____ smote Kirharaseth. 2 Kings 3:25

28 "I will give you rain in _____ season." Lev. 26:4

30 "I will dry up her _____, and make her springs dry." Jer. 51:36

31 "God hast punished us less than our iniquities _____." Ezra 9:13

35 "He took three _____ in his hand and thrust them." 2 Sam. 18:14

39 Christmas log.

40 Two unclean fowl are the vulture and the _____. Lev. 11:14

42 "I _____ on the work of thy hands." Ps. 143:5

43 "We abode in the valley over against _____-peor." Deut. 3:29

45 "The valley of Shaveh, which is the king's _____." Gen. 14:17

47 "The commandment is a lamp; and the _____ is light." Prov. 6:23

48 Irony.

50 "That thou shouldest. . .ordain _____ in every city." Titus 1:5

52 "They of _____ shall fall by the sword." Ezek. 25:13

53 Sulks.

54 "The _____ is made worse." Mark 2:21

55 "A glorious _____ throne from the beginning." Jer. 17:12

DOWN

1 "I have given him. . .a _____ and commander." Isa. 55:4

2 Bitter vetch.

3 "I will put my _____ in thy nose." 2 Kings 19:28

4 "Esther. . .stood in the _____ court of the king's house." Esther 5:1

5 "The _____ of the LORD's house shall. . .be brought. . .from Babylon." Jer. 27:16

6 "Go to the _____, thou sluggard." Prov. 6:6

7 "_____ me to the rock that is higher than I." Ps. 61:2

8 "In _____ time. . .thou shalt rest." Exod. 34:21

9 "The most upright is sharper than a thorn _____." Micah 7:4

11 Cubic meter.

12 Cleanser.

14 "Lo, the _____, which they saw in the east, went before them." Matt. 2:9

17 "And she answered and said unto him, _____, Lord." Mark 7:28

20 "Who is on the LORD's _____?" Exod. 32:26

22 "They _____ unto him with their tongues." Ps. 78:36

25 "Let us _____ privily for the innocent." Prov. 1:11

27 Caleb's sons were Iru, Elah, and
   _____. I Chron. 4:15
29 "It is _____ that our Lord sprang
   out of Judah." Heb. 7:14
31 Dresses leather.
32 The men of Gath slew him. I
   Chron. 7:21
33 "He seemeth to be a _____ forth
   of strange gods." Acts 17:18
34 Greek letter.
36 "One that _____ well his own
   house." I Tim. 3:4
37 Russian emperors.

38 No man _____ a piece of new
   cloth on an old garment.
   Mark 2:21
41 One of fourteen cities inherited by
   the children of Benjamin. Josh.
   18:28
44 "_____ me under the shadow of
   thy wings." Ps. 17:8
46 "_____, lama sabachthani." Mark
   15:34
49 "They _____ the ship aground."
   Acts 27:41
51 They digged (or _____) down the
   altars. Rom. 11:3

ACROSS

1 "Satan hath desired to. . ._____ you as wheat." Luke 22:31
5 "It was planted in a good _____." Ezek. 17:8
9 "Thou shalt not call her name Sarai, but _____." Gen. 17:15
10 "An altar unto the LORD in the threshingfloor of _____." I Chron. 21:18
12 "I will _____ her, and bring her into the wilderness." Hosea 2:14
13 Learned by a pupil.
15 An unclean bird. Deut. 14:18
16 "The earth shall reel to and _____." Isa. 24:20
18 ". . .and _____ the kine to the cart." I Sam. 6:7
19 "When he speaketh a _____, he speaketh of his own." John 8:44
20 Articles.
22 Compass point.
23 "He shall surely _____ her to be his wife." Exod. 22:16
25 "The voice of the trumpet _____ long." Exod. 19:19
27 _____ Miserables.
29 Never: German.
30 "Give him as many as he _____." Luke 11:8
34 "He cropped off the top of his young _____." Ezek. 17:4
38 "Brought him to an _____, and took care of him." Luke 10:34
39 Snoops or spies.
41 Pinch.
42 Third bk. of the Bible.
43 Greek letter.
44 Truth: Chinese.
45 Girl's name.
48 "Be _____, O all flesh, before the LORD." Zech. 2:13
51 Leavening agent.
52 "One _____ happeneth to them all." Eccles. 2:14
53 Health resorts.
54 "Rams' skins _____ red." Exod. 25:5

DOWN

1 "Wherewith shall it be _____?" Matt. 5:13
2 Son of Caleb. I Chron. 4:15
3 "The LORD saith, Be it _____ from me." I Sam. 2:30
4 "Neither repented they of their. . . _____." Rev. 9:21
5 "At that time_____ held a feast." I Kings 8:65
6 Iron _____.
7 Opposite of outs.
8 Endured.
9 "I have _____ them by the words of my mouth." Hosea 6:5
11 "Making a _____ with psalteries and harps." I Chron. 15:28
12 "Our God whom we serve is _____ to deliver us." Dan. 3:17
14 "What further _____ have we of witnesses?" Matt. 26:65
17 Legal case.
20 "Did not _____ _____ for him?" Job 30:25
21 "The changeable _____ of apparel." Isa. 3:22
24 "They shall still bring forth fruit in _____ age." Ps. 92:14
26 "I saw a _____ heaven." Rev. 21:1
28 "She uttereth her voice in the _____." Prov. 1:20
30 Egyptian river.
31 "Thou makest us to turn back from the _____." Ps. 44:10
32 "Laying aside all malice. . .and _____." I Peter 2:1
33 "The archers _____ him." I Chron. 10:3
35 "Take heed to yourself what ye _____ to do." Acts 5:35
36 "He runneth upon me like a _____." Job 16:14
37 "A glorious church, not having _____, or wrinkle." Eph. 5:27

40 "I mean not that other men be
_____." 2 Cor. 8:13

46 "Gathered...wild gourds his
_____ full." 2 Kings 4:39

47 "There _____ _____ spirit in man."
Job 32:8

49 Climbing vine.

50 In Ps. 107:30 a desired haven
could also be called a _____.

ACROSS

1 "Meted out heaven with the
   _____?" Isa. 40:12
5 "_____ not thyself because of evildoers." Ps. 37:1
9 "The fourth part of a _____."
   2 Kings 6:25
12 "Take thine _____, eat, drink, and
   be merry." Luke 12:19
13 "Simeon and _____ are brethren."
   Gen. 49:5
14 "He is of _____; ask him." John
   9:21
15 Handle: French.
16 City of Judah in the valley. Josh.
   15:34
17 "They of Persia and of _____ . . .
   were in thine army." Ezek. 27:10
18 "Giants, that dwelt at Ashtaroth
   and at _____." Josh. 12:4
20 "Whose _____ are in the book of
   life." Phil. 4:3
22 Rigid.
24 "The _____ of deceitful weights."
   Micah 6:11
25 Rodent.
26 One of the five sons of Zerah.
   1 Chron. 2:6
29 "Cut off the Anakim from the
   mountains. . .from _____."
   Josh. 11:21
33 "Yet have _____ _____ my king
   upon my holy hill." Ps. 2:6
35 "When the chief priests. . .saw the
   wonderful things that he _____."
   Matt. 21:15
36 "King Asa built with them _____
   of Benjamin." 1 Kings 15:22
37 "The first year of Darius the
   _____." Dan. 11:1
38 "And Cain talked with _____ his
   brother." Gen. 4:8
40 "Love worketh no _____ to his
   neighbor." Rom. 13:10
41 "Hast with thine _____ redeemed
   thy people." Ps. 77:15
43 "The Lord hath sent his _____."
   Acts 12:11

45 "They look and _____ upon me."
   Ps. 22:17
48 Kore was the son of _____ the
   Levite, the porter toward the
   east. 2 Chron. 31:14
50 One of Shamer's four sons.
   1 Chron. 7:34
51 Zerubbabel's grandfather.
   Luke 3:27
53 "They called his name _____."
   Ruth 4:17
56 "Jacob _____ the rest of Laban's
   flocks." Gen. 30:36
57 "Sons of Shuthelah: of _____, the
   family of Eranites." Num. 26:36
58 "Let me pull out the _____ out of
   thine eye." Matt. 7:4
59 "I will guide thee with mine
   _____." Ps. 32:8
60 "He took them, and _____ aside
   privately." Luke 9:10
61 "I have made thee this day. . .an
   _____ pillar." Jer. 1:18

DOWN

1 "Even the winds and the _____
   obey him." Matt. 8:27
2 "Take thou unto thee an iron
   _____." Ezek. 4:3
3 "The Jews also _____, saying that
   these things were so." Acts 24:9
4 "If I must _____ glory, I will."
   2 Cor. 11:30
5 "Jonah rose up to _____ unto
   Tarshish." Jonah 1:3
6 Italian painter.
7 Harriet Beecher Stowe character.
8 "And _____ was concubine to
   Eliphaz Esau's son." Gen. 36:12
9 "He maketh the storm a _____."
   Ps. 107:29
10 "I will even appoint over you terror. . .the burning _____."
   Lev. 26:16
11 "Let them sing aloud upon their
   _____." Ps. 149:5
19 "Look not thou upon the wine

1	2	3	4		5	6	7	8		9	10	11
12					13					14		
15					16					17		
		18		19				20	21			
22	23						24					
25				26	27	28			29	30	31	32
33			34	35					36			
37				38			39		40			
			41	42			43	44				
45	46	47				48	49					
50				51	52		53			54	55	
56				57			58					
59				60			61					

when it is _____." Prov. 23:31

21 "His king shall be higher than _____." Num. 24:7

22 The virgins arose to _____ their lamps. Matt. 25:7

23 "My couch shall _____ my complaint." Job 7:13

24 "The Spirit _____ me go with them." Acts 11:12

27 "_____ gave names to all cattle." Gen. 2:20

28 "The _____, which the Lord God had taken from man, made he a woman." Gen. 2:22

30 "Who is my _____?" Luke 10:29

31 "I shall be _____ to drive them out." Josh. 14:12

32 "He will. . .turn and toss thee like a _____." Isa. 22:18

34 "The lion did _____ in pieces enough for his whelps." Nahum 2:12

39 Swedish county.

42 "_____ a right spirit within me." Ps. 51:10

44 Elimelech's wife was _____. Ruth 1:2

45 "The righteous runneth into it, and is _____." Prov. 18:10

46 "And _____ brought it to him." 2 Kings 2:20

47 Adjutant.

48 Formerly Persia.

49 "Ye pay tithe of _____ and anise." Matt. 23:23

52 "Sir, come down _____ my child die." John 4:49

54 World War II area.

55 "He lieth in wait secretly as a lion in his _____." Ps. 10:9

ACROSS

1 "There is at Jerusalem. . ._____
_____." John 5:2
6 The father of Bethlehem.
I Chron. 2:51
11 "The disciples. . .let him down. . .
in a _____." Acts 9:25
13 "I might _____unto the resurrection of the dead." Phil. 3:11
14 "Sir, come down _____ my child
die." John 4:49
15 Greek letter.
16 "See if there _____ any wicked
way in me." Ps. 139:24
17 Genetic substance.
18 Third bk. of the OT.
19 "The men of Israel _____ in the
battle." Judg. 20:39
22 Printer's measure.
23 "Jesus tarried behind in _____."
Luke 2:43
25 "_____! for that day is great."
Jer. 30:7
27 Eli's protege's nickname.
28 Fly.
31 "The sword. . .cannot hold: the
spear, the _____, nor the haber-
geon." Job 41:26
32 "I will bring it health and _____."
Jer. 33:6
33 Popular cookie.
34 Medina Arab.
37 "_____ was a cunning hunter."
Gen. 25:27
38 "Upon the wicked he shall rain
snares, fire and _____." Ps. 11:6
41 Paid notice.
43 "According to my _____ expecta-
tion and my hope." Phil.1:20
44 Exclamation of surprise.
46 Three: Roman.
48 First two letters of the last book
of the Old Testament.
49 "_____ sinful nation, a people
laden with iniquity." Isa. 1:4

50 "The king of Assyria brought men
from Babylon. . .and from _____."
2 Kings 17:24
51 "_____ _____ _____ the last."
Isa. 44:6
53 "God made. . .the _____ light to
rule the night." Gen. 1:16
55 "He shall strengthen thine _____."
Ps. 27:14
56 "Men that walk over them are not
_____ of them." Luke 11:44

DOWN

1 "_____ offered unto God a more
excellent sacrifice." Heb. 11:4
2 "She shall shave her head and
_____ her nails." Deut. 21:12
3 Simple sugar.
4 All right.
5 "Naaman. . .was a _____."
2 Kings 5:1
6 "A bow of _____is broken by
mine arms." Ps. 18:34
7 "Judgment must begin _____ the
house of God." I Peter 4:17
8 "There is a _____ here, which
hath five barley loaves." John 6:9
9 "For all the earth is _____."
Exod. 19:5
10 One of the men who sealed the
covenant. Neh. 10:26
12 "I. . .took _____ with me also."
Gal. 2:1
13 "The Lord had said unto _____,
Get thee out." Gen. 12:1
19 "I will lead him also, and _____
comforts." Isa. 57:18
20 Isaiah: abbr.
21 "At the _____ of the Mount of
Olives." Luke 19:37
23 "They. . .sent to king _____: yet
could he not heal." Hosea 5:13
24 "Eating swine's flesh. . .and the
_____, shall be consumed to-
gether." Isa. 66:17

25 "Why make ye this _____, and weep?" Mark 5:39
26 Monkey.
29 A son of Jether. I Chron. 7:38
30 "_____ lived two and thirty years and begat Serug." Gen. 11:20
34 Son of Dishon. I Chron. 1:41
35 Our country's fleet: abbr.
36 "Where thieves break through and _____." Matt. 6:19
39 "Behold, _____ _____ _____ the point to die." Gen. 25:32
40 Joshua is called Jehoshua and _____. Num. 13:16

41 Son of Zibeon. I Chron. 1:40
42 "These men shall _____ with me." Gen. 43:16
44 "My cup runneth _____." Ps. 23:5
45 "The _____. . .is unclean unto you." Lev. 11:6
47 Girl's name.
50 "Behold, the acts of _____, first and last." 2 Chron. 16:11
52 Prefix meaning non- or un-.
54 Compass point.

ACROSS

1 "And the LORD _____ respect unto Abel." Gen. 4:4

4 "I will send a very heavy hail, such _____ _____ not been seen in Egypt." Exod. 9:18 (NASB)

9 "The tenth part of a bath out of the _____." Ezek. 45:14

12 "And Hur begat _____." 1 Chron. 2:20

13 "But God shall wound. . .the hairy _____ of such an one." Ps. 68:21

14 "The children of Lod, Hadid, and _____." Ezra 2:33

15 "He rebuked the _____ _____ also." Ps. 106:9

17 "Thou shalt no more be _____ Forsaken." Isa. 62:4

19 When one thrusts with a knife, he _____.

21 "They. . ._____ the sacrifices of the dead." Ps. 106:28

22 "Father of Abner was the son of _____." 1 Sam. 14:51

24 "Even as the garden of the LORD, _____ _____ land of Egypt." Gen. 13:10

28 "Jews of _____ sought to stone thee." John 11:8

29 "And they tied unto it a _____ of blue." Exod. 39:31

30 A curse associated with witches.

31 "And every one stood _____ the door." Ezek. 10:19

32 "Thy _____ and thine alms are come up." Acts 10:4

35 Rhode Island: abbr.

36 Nickname for Rhoda.

38 "_____ the son of Jonathan." Ezra 8:6

39 "Asa destroyed her _____, and burnt it." 1 Kings 15:13

41 "What _____ thou by all this drove?" Gen. 33:8

43 "And the fat closed upon the _____." Judg. 3:22

44 Boy's name.

45 "The sons of _____ were, Zereth. . ." 1 Chron. 4:7

47 "Arab, and Dumah, and _____." Josh. 15:52

50 Famous Methodist preacher.

53 Also.

54 "_____ they have, but they smell not." Ps. 115:6

56 Intense anger.

57 Nickname for Alfred.

58 "Take away the _____ from the silver." Prov. 25:4

59 ". . .Jephunneh, and Pispah, and _____." 1 Chron. 7:38

DOWN

1 "Aaron and _____ stayed up his hands." Exod. 17:12

2 "Your fathers, where _____ they?" Zech. 1:5

3 "And the Ancient of days _____ _____, whose garment was white as snow." Dan. 7:9

4 "Shut him up, and set _____ _____ upon him." Rev. 20:3

5 "Behold, the _____ spreadeth in the skin." Lev. 13:8

6 "He saith among the trumpets, _____." Job 39:25

7 Alternate: abbr.

8 "They called. . .Paul, Mercurius, because he was the chief _____." Acts 14:12

9 "Behold, this dreamer _____." Gen. 37:19

10 "And every _____ had four faces." Ezek. 1:6

11 "Whatsoever passeth under the _____." Lev. 27:32

16 "The waters that are poured down a _____ place." Micah 1:4

18 Highway: abbr.

20 "Say before him that _____ thee, I am God?" Ezek. 28:9

22 "With sounding trumpets to cry _____." 2 Chron. 13:12

23 "He shall _____ his flesh in water." Num. 19:7

25 In winter, the car windshield can become _____.

26 "And _____ said, John have I beheaded." Luke 9:9

27 "For thou art a stranger, and also an _____." 2 Sam. 15:19

29 Where scientists do research.

33 "There was a man. . .and a measuring _____; _____ he stood." Ezek. 40:3

34 "And Paul chose _____, and departed." Acts 15:40

37 "And Joseph took an _____ _____ the children of Israel." Gen. 50:25

40 Type of flower.

42 Used to identify a woman by her maiden name.

43 "The Almighty, who shall _____ thee." Gen. 49:25

46 "Two hundred _____ and twenty rams." Gen. 32:14

47 Estimated time of arrival: abbr.

48 Solomon: abbr.

49 "Thy fathers, _____ thy fathers' fathers." Exod. 10:6

51 "Do they not _____ that devise evil?" Prov. 14:22

52 "_____, I hated all my labour which I had." Eccles. 2:18

55 "God commanded him, _____ did he." Gen. 6:22

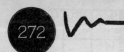

ACROSS

1 "_____ you to the mountain." Josh. 2:16
4 Fleur-de-_____.
7 "Write it. . .and _____ it in a book." Isa. 30:8
11 "All that handleth the _____, the mariners." Ezek. 27:29
12 Trigonometry function.
13 Gem.
14 "When it is grown, it is the _____ among herbs." Matt. 13:32
16 "_____ me, art thou a Roman?" Acts 22:27
17 "They came to the threshingfloor of _____." Gen. 50:10
18 "While I prayed in the temple, I was in a _____." Acts 22:17
20 "They shall walk _____ the LORD." Hosea 11:10
22 Underground: Greek.
23 Den.
24 "It is a _____ spot that groweth in the skin." Lev. 13:39
28 "Ye shall find an _____ tied." Matt. 21:2
29 "Samuel _____ and went to Eli." 1 Sam. 3:6
30 "He spake concerning the house of _____ in Shiloh." 1 Kings 2:27
31 "Whose spirit was not _____." Ps. 78:8
33 "Four cubits was the length of one _____." 1 Kings 7:27
34 "Whether he _____ or laugh, there is no rest." Prov. 29:9
35 "The Amorites would dwell in mount _____." Judg. 1:35
36 "Do according to all that they _____ thee." Deut. 17:10
39 "He shall not stand before _____ men." Prov. 22:29
40 Leak.
41 "The high and lofty One that inhabiteth _____." Isa. 57:15
45 "He hath settled on his _____." Jer. 48:11
46 "There is _____ other God but one." 1 Cor. 8:4
47 "As it was in the days of _____." Luke 17:26
48 Whirlpool.
49 "_____ the kine to the cart." 1 Sam. 6:7
50 "I _____ me servants and maidens." Eccles. 2:7

DOWN

1 "_____ and Magog, to gather them together to battle." Rev. 20:8
2 "First the blade, then the _____." Mark 4:28
3 "The former _____ have I made, O Theophilus." Acts 1:1
4 "They _____ unto him with their tongues." Ps. 78:36
5 Those in office.
6 "Thou _____ the furrows thereof." Ps. 65:10
7 "I will _____ _____, neither will I tempt the LORD." Isa. 7:12
8 "His ears are _____ unto their cry." Ps. 34:15
9 Powder.
10 Her: French.
12 "I will give him the morning _____." Rev. 2:28
15 Some of the porters were the children of Shallum and the children of _____. Neh. 7:45
19 "Let us run with patience the _____ that is set before us." Heb. 12:1
20 "_____! for that day is great." Jer. 30:7
21 "Why do. . .thy disciples _____ not?" Mark 2:18
22 Uneven as if worn away.

24 Jesus told his disciples to gather up each _____ that remained. John 6:12

25 "A wise man will hear, and will increase _____." Prov. 1:5

26 "Strangers...spent their time in nothing _____." Acts 17:21

27 Ruth tells Naomi she will die where Naomi _____. Ruth 1:17

29 "Her eyes behold _____ off." Job 39:29

32 "A certain man before him which had the _____." Luke 14:2

33 One of the vegetables Ezekiel was to put in a vessel. Ezek. 4:9

35 "I stand _____ by the well of water." Gen. 24:13

36 "A ship...which had wintered in the _____." Acts 28:11

37 "The Lord hath _____ of him." Mark 11:3

38 "I will not _____ you." Zech. 11:9

39 "The interpretation..._____; God hath numbered thy kingdom." Dan. 5:26

42 "Then _____ sent Joram his son unto king David." 2 Sam. 8:10

43 "There is nothing _____ hard for thee." Jer. 32:17

44 "I shall _____ praise him for the help." Ps. 42:5

ACROSS

1 "The ravens. . .neither sow nor _____." Luke 12:24

4 "Stand. . .having your loins girt _____ with truth." Eph. 6:14

8 "The children of Gad called the altar _____." Josh. 22:34

10 "The thoughts of the diligent _____ only to plenteousness." Prov. 21:5

12 "Shimei, and _____, and the mighty men which belonged to David." 1 Kings 1:8

13 "Bear ye one another's burdens, and _____ fulfill the law of Christ." Gal. 6:2

14 "Thy faith hath saved thee; _____ in peace." Luke 7:50

16 "Call ye upon him while he is _____." Isa. 55:6

18 "Sin no more, _____ a worse thing come unto thee." John 5:14

20 "As the serpent beguiled _____." 2 Cor. 11:3

22 "The covering narrower than that he can _____ himself in it." Isa. 28:20

24 "Faith, if it hath not works, is _____." James 2:17

26 Compass point.

28 "Eat not of it _____, nor sodden." Exod. 12:9

30 "They. . ._____ the sacrifices of the dead." Ps. 106:28

31 "He shall flee from the _____ weapon." Job 20:24

32 The son of Menan. Luke 3:31

34 Apiece: abbr.

35 "Jesus Christ the _____ yesterday, and today, and forever." Heb. 13:8

37 "_____ up the gift of God, which is in thee." 2 Tim. 1:6

39 "The glory _____ of the only begotten of the Father." John 1:14

41 Furiously.

43 "They. . .heard the word. . .both _____ and Greeks." Acts 19:10

45 "_____, a troop shall overcome him." Gen. 49:19

47 "_____, and all that live godly in Christ." 2 Tim. 3:12

48 "His mother's name also was _____, the daughter of Zachariah." 2 Kings 18:2

49 "Thy _____ and thy she goats have not cast their young." Gen. 31:38

51 "Establish the decree, and _____ the writing." Dan. 6:8

54 "_____ of me, and I shall give thee." Ps. 2:8

56 "John also was baptizing in _____." John 3:23

58 "She. . ._____ for all his camels." Gen. 24:20

60 "_____ sought where to weep." Gen. 43:30

61 "So soon _____ I shall see how it will go with me." Phil. 2:23

62 "They _____ my path." Job 30:13

64 "He. . .dwelt in the top of the rock _____." Judg. 15:8

66 "_____ is Elijah the Tishbite." 2 Kings 1:8

67 "He shall surely _____ her to be his wife." Exod. 22:16

68 "Rahab. . .had _____ them out another way." James 2:25

DOWN

1 "The chariots shall _____ in the streets." Nahum 2:4

2 "_____ the end it shall speak." Hab. 2:3

3 "Write in it with a man's _____." Isa. 8:1

4 "This house was finished on the third day of the month _____." Ezra 6:15

5 "Whether shall prosper, either this _____ that." Eccles. 11:6

6 Son of Bani. Ezra 10:34

7 "Neither voice of man, but horses _____." 2 Kings 7:10

8 "Lo, I am come to great _____." Eccles. 1:16

9 "Learn to _____ well." Isa. 1:17

11 "They are _____ every morning." Lam. 3:23

15 "Joy shall be in heaven _____ one sinner." Luke 15:7

17 "It is a _____ thing that the king requireth." Dan. 2:11

19 "He rebuketh the _____." Nahum 1:4

21 "Seth...called his name _____." Gen. 4:26

23 "My servant lieth at home sick of the _____." Matt. 8:6

25 "Take...three tenth _____ of fine flour for a meat offering." Lev. 14:10

27 One of the cities of Judah in the valley. Josh. 15:34

29 "They are _____ with the showers of the mountains." Job 24:8

31 "His molten _____ is falsehood." Jer. 10:14

32 "I will stir up the _____ against them." Isa. 13:17

33 "The children also of Benjamin from Geba dwelt at. . ._____." Neh. 11:31

36 "If I _____ but touch his garment." Matt. 9:21

38 One of the five kings of Midian slain by the Israelites. Num. 31:8

40 "When thou _____ a thief, then thou consentedst with him." Ps. 50:18

42 "The men _____ hold upon his hand." Gen. 19:16

44 "I _____ above all things that thou mayest prosper." 3 John 2

46 "He lieth in wait secretly as a lion in his _____." Ps. 10:9

50 "That I might by all means save _____." 1 Cor. 9:22

52 "Israel. . ._____and multiplied exceedingly." Gen. 47:27

53 "The kingdom of heaven is like unto a _____, that was cast into the sea." Matt. 13:47

55 "All the multitude _____ silence." Acts 15:12

57 Girl's name.

59 "He. . .forgetteth what manner of man he _____." James 1:24

61 "Howl, O Heshbon, for _____ is spoiled." Jer. 49:3

63 "Whither have ye made a _____ (abbr.) today?" 1 Sam. 27:10

65 "Let not mine enemies triumph over _____." Ps. 25:2

ACROSS

1 "He brought me up also out of an horrible _____." Ps. 40:2
4 "One _____ shall run to meet another." Jer. 51:31
8 "Because he was the son-in-law of Shechaniah the son of _____." Neh. 6:18
12 "Your fathers, where _____ they?" Zech. 1:5
13 "God. . .confirmed it by an _____." Heb. 6:17
14 "In the name of Jesus Christ of Nazareth _____ up and walk." Acts 3:6
15 "There appeared a great _____ in heaven." Rev. 12:1
17 "It shall not be lawful to _____ toll." Ezra 7:24
19 "As a jewel of gold in a swine's _____." Prov. 11:22
20 Orderly.
21 "The birds of the air have _____." Matt. 8:20
24 Girl's name.
27 "The world passeth away, and the _____ thereof." 1 John 2:17
29 Actual.
31 "Let it be wet with the _____ of heaven." Dan. 4:15
32 "Speak not to Jacob either good _____ bad." Gen. 31:24
33 "Lest by any _____, as the serpent beguiled Eve." 2 Cor. 11:3
34 Abbreviation of the book of the Bible which comes after Ezra.
35 "Many. . .shall _____ down with Abraham." Matt. 8:11
37 "I John. . .was in the _____ that is called Patmos." Rev. 1:9
38 "His idols. . .to the moles and to the _____." Isa. 2:20
40 "He that is surety for a stranger shall _____ for it." Prov. 11:15
42 "An odour of a sweet _____, a sacrifice." Phil. 4:18
44 "God, which knoweth the hearts, _____ them witness." Acts 15:8
46 "A _____ came out of the cloud." Mark 9:7
49 "They _____ upon the LORD God." 2 Chron. 13:18
51 "When I make up my _____." Mal. 3:17
52 "I will. . .cut off the inhabitants from the plain of _____." Amos 1:5
53 "John also was baptizing in _____." John 3:23
55 "Yet a little sleep." A little sleep could be called a _____. Prov. 24:33
56 Disorder.
57 Whoever _____ his father or mother and says it's not sin is a companion of a destroyer. Prov. 28:24
58 "He said, Go and _____ where he is." 2 Kings 6:13

DOWN

1 "Whatsoever goeth upon his _____ . . .shall be unclean." Lev. 11:27
2 "He shall rule them with a rod of _____." Rev. 2:27
3 "Two _____ shall there be in one board." Exod. 26:17
4 "Certain also of your own _____ have said." Acts 17:28
5 "All that handle the _____, the mariners." Ezek. 27:29
6 "Go into the _____ (abbr.) which is called Straight." Acts 9:11
7 Opposite of fat.
8 "Where is the king of Hamath, and the king of _____?" Isa. 37:13
9 Whoever is a companion to those who have _____ shames his father. Prov. 28:7
10 "Abraham rose up early. . .and saddled his _____." Gen. 22:3

11 _____ haw.
16 Composition for two.
18 Normally eaten three times a day.
22 Very: French.
23 "A book. . .sealed with seven _____." Rev. 5:1
25 "Nor men have _____ to me on usury." Jer. 15:10
26 "Thy _____ and thy she goats have not cast their young." Gen. 31:38
27 "I count all things but _____ for. . . Christ." Phil. 3:8
28 "Thou shalt put in the breastplate of judgment the _____ and the Thummin." Exod. 28:30
30 City of the tribe of Issachar. 1 Chron. 6:73
33 "With the linen _____ shall he be attired." Lev. 16:4
36 "He wrote on the _____, according to the first writing." Deut. 10:4

38 "When ye see the south wind _____." Luke 12:55
39 "Our inheritance is turned to strangers, our houses to _____." Lam. 5:2
41 The _____ fill the pools.
43 Odds and _____.
45 The uttermost city of Judah toward the coast. Josh. 15:21
47 "O _____ your hands, all ye people." Ps. 47:1
48 "Stand by the way, and _____." Jer. 48:19
49 "I saw the _____ pushing westward." Dan. 8:4
50 "For Adam was first formed, then _____." 1 Tim. 2:13
51 "Ye have heard of the patience of _____." James 5:11
54 "There hath _____ temptation taken you but such as is common to man." 1 Cor. 10:13

CryptoScripture Puzzles

by Sharon Y. Brown

Each of the CryptoScriptures is a Bible verse in substitution code. For example, JEHOVAH might become M P X S T Q V if M is substituted for J, P for E, X for H, etc. One way to break the code is to look for repeated letters: E, T, A, O, N, R, and I are the most often used. A single letter is usually A or I. OF, IT, and IS are common two-letter words. Try THE or AND for a three-letter group. The code is different for each CryptoScripture.

1. QVY OUGJ GJ OUK RKJJNAK
   OUNO ZK UKNYS QYVR OUK
   IKAGBBGBA, OUNO HK JUVPWS
   WVLK VBK NBVOUKY.

2. WV ZBZCN FMWVY YWBZ
   FMEVHO: RDC FMWO WO FMZ
   LWXX DR YDP WV KMCWOF
   QZOSO KDVKZCVWVY NDU.

3. ILER RWNIL ILJ SZYQ ILJ VNMU
   ZC NRYWJS, WMQ LNR YJQJJGJY
   ILJ SZYQ ZC LZRIR; N WG
   ILJ CNYRI, WMQ N WG ILJ SWRI;
   WMQ HJRNQJ GJ ILJYJ NR MZ
   UZQ.

4. QTDN NCKQT QTY VZSI, VYQ
GZQ QTY UKNY ACG EVZSW KG
TKN UKNIZA, GYKQTYS VYQ QTY
AKETQW ACG EVZSW KG TKN
AKETQ, VYQ GZQ QTY SKMT ACG
EVZSW KG TKN SKMTYN.

5. PLO WFGI WFPW ELDV WFI LPSG
VZMM RJW WFGZC WCJYW ZL
WFGG: TDC WFDJ, MDCO, FPYW
LDW TDCYPEGL WFGS WFPW
YGGE WFGG.

6. XAT BVJ YTJKEVDZQ AX BVJ
ETAHH DH BA BVJO BVKB
YJTDHV XAAGDHVZJHH; UPB PZBA
PH RVDEV KTJ HKIJS DB DH
BVJ YARJT AX QAS.

7. OYXR WXOXH VRJ OYX IOYXH
VWIBOUXB VRBCXHXJ VRJ BVSJ,
CX IGFYO OI IAXM FIJ HVOYXH
OYVR LXR.

8. KRUO WOOY KWRK QO YS ZSK
QSPX RIDG MOJSXO DOZ, KS MO
GOOZ SJ KWOD: SKWOXLTGO
QO WRFO ZS XOLRXY SJ QSPX
JRKWOX LWTAW TG TZ WORFOZ.

9. FYT CBD ZEGT, BD WC WN
CBFC TECB KE ODVEGD CBDD:
BD QWZZ OD QWCB CBDD, BD
QWZZ YEC VFWZ CBDD,
YDWCBDG VEGNFID CBDD: VDFG
YEC, YDWCBDG OD TWNSFADT.

10. V PVW VZFU UT OUPVW LEVL
    EVLE V KVPSZSVT FMSTSL, UT
    LEVL SF V OSIVTX, FEVZZ
    FBTDZQ GD MBL LU XDVLE:
    LEDQ FEVZZ FLUWD LEDP OSLE
    FLUWDF: LEDST GZUUX FEVZZ
    GD BMUW LEDP.

11. YZR FA MDYOO TXPQ AX VYMM,
    ADYA LSXP XZQ ZQG PXXZ AX
    YZXADQS, YZR LSXP XZQ
    MYWWYAD AX YZXADQS, MDYOO
    YOO LOQMD TXPQ AX GXSMDFV
    WQLXSQ PQ, MYFAD ADQ OXSR.

12. ULQT OE EZQT RXZK EZR, LKS
    FTLYK ZN OT; NZY V LO OTTQ
    LKS FZHFE VK ITLYU: LKS ET
    MILFF NVKS YTMU RKUZ EZRY
    MZRFM.

13. XNB DWM IWFFUPMUBZ ZKJ
    VWHU BWQOTM NJ, KP BZOB,
    QZKVU QU QUTU LUB JKPPUTJ,
    IZTKJB MKUM YWT NJ.

14. UEE CQZGDKSZH GC AGLHY JN
    GYCDGZUKGRY RP ARV, UYV GC
    DZRPGKUJEH PRZ VRQKZGYH,
    PRZ ZHDZRRP, PRZ QRZZHQKGRY,
    PRZ GYCKZSQKGRY GY
    ZGATKHRSCYHCC.

15. R ZSIQ MJXM, UJXMVITATC BIW
    WITMJ, RM VJXFF PT NIC TATC:
    SIMJRSB DXS PT OEM MI RM,
    SIC XSK MJRSB MXZTS NCIL
    RM: XSW BIW WITMJ RM, MJXM
    LTS VJIEFW NTXC PTNICT JRL.

16. JXZQP UX JR IR JPD LGWW;
KRH JPRV ZHJ UD BRI: JPD
OSGHGJ GO BRRI; WXZI UX
GYJR JPX WZYI RK
VSHGBPJYXOO.

17. VUS BWS AYVZZ LQGK VLVC
VZZ RKVMA XMWD RYKQM
KCKA; VUS RYKMK AYVZZ NK
UW DWMK SKVRY, UKQRYKM
AWMMWL, UWM FMCQUB,
UKQRYKM AYVZZ RYKMK NK VUC
DWMK GVQU; XWM RYK XWMDKM
RYQUBA VMK GVAAKS VLVC.

18. MV EXDPMF ZUM VGES VLLSDSN
FV QSUD FXS MPGM VL TUGH;
UGN KGFV FXST FXUF AVVW
LVD XPT MXUAA XS URRSUD
FXS MSEVGN FPTS ZPFXVKF MPG
KGFV MUABUFPVG.

19. ZXQ   QWNQ   SWHRW   YXPQW
    HZQX   QWP   UXBQW   JPAHDPQW
    N   UNZ;   FBQ   QWNQ   SWHRW
    RXUPQW   XBQ   XA   QWP   UXBQW,
    QWHK   JPAHDPQW   N   UNZ.

20. NQIWI   FH   ZAZI   QAXM   TH   NQI
    XAWG: SAW   NQIWI   FH   ZAZI
    OIHFGI   NQII: ZIFNQIW   FH
    NQIWI   TZM   WAYD   XFDI   ACW
    BAG.

21. AX   CZI   A   HAEE   NDWATG   KAT
    HZDI,   AX   CZI   A   KWBG   NOJ   RL
    JDOTJ;   A   HAEE   XZJ   UGWD
    HKWJ   UEGTK   MWX   IZ   OXJZ   RG.

22. VTRZBW QP GOSOQUVBD, TEG
    IOTBUM QP RTQE: IBU T FZNTE
    UATU VOTWOUA UAO DZWG,
    PAO PATDD IO CWTQPOG.

23. ECU SG VWEXX RCTL HWEH O
    ED OC HWG DOUVH TY OVNEGX,
    ECU HWEH O ED HWG XTNU
    STPN KTU, ECU CTCG GXVG: ECU
    DS AGTAXG VWEXX CGJGN QG
    EVWEDGU.

24. GBI CSORO OGMI RBZQ ZUSK, M
    GK ZUS WTSGI QX AMXS: US
    ZUGZ EQKSZU ZQ KS OUGAA
    BSJST URBYST; GBI US ZUGZ
    WSAMSJSZU QB KS OUGAA BSJST
    ZUMTOZ.

25. GWU SDPX EN MYYX, O
NGPYFMWYSX EF GWU XOI YH
GPYVKSU; OFX WU JFYLUGW GWUC
GWOG GPVNG EF WEC.

26. AZC EY FYQQHDC FYUUHEPFXCPYE
DQYFZZK YHC YG OYHQ UYHCY,
RHC CVXC JVPFV PL TYYK CY
CVZ HLZ YG ZKPGOPET, CVXC
PC UXO UPEPLCZQ TQXFZ HECY
CVZ VZXQZQL.

27. GVD DUS OHIMHTDST, BUKOU KN
DUS UHYX CUHND, BUHI DUS
MQDUST BKYY NSPE KP IX PQIS,
US NUQYY DSQOU XHV QYY
DUKPCN, QPE GTKPC QYY DUKPCN
DH XHVT TSISIGTQPOS,
BUQDNHSLST K UQLS NQKE
VPDH XHV.

28. DYZ UB ILP LPUNPKB UZP LCVLPZ
ILUK ILP PUZIL, BY UZP EX
RUXB LCVLPZ ILUK XYWZ RUXB,
UKT EX ILYWVLIB ILUK XYWZ
ILYWVLIB.

29. MNSWS HNQVV GYM QGK PQG
FS QFVS MY HMQGL FSAYWS
MNSS QVV MNS LQKH YA MNK
VJAS: QH J IQH IJMN PYHSH,
HY J IJVV FS IJMN MNSS: J
IJVV GYM AQJV MNSS, GYW
AYWHQDS MNSS.

30. FRU TDJI RKFR KSSUKJUI DB
DTI OYFD PU, VKAXYW, AUK, X
RKCU TDCUI FRUU LXFR KY
UCUJTKVFXYW TDCU: FRUJUBDJU
LXFR TDCXYWGXYIYUVV RKCU X
IJKLY FRUU.

31. QXKIXGIK HBXQ BI TET UKITILCEZYCI, CBIQ BI YNLX SYNNIT: YZT HBXQ BI SYNNIT, CBIQ BI YNLX FDLCEJEIT: YZT HBXQ BI FDLCEJEIT, CBIQ BI YNLX ANXKEJEIT.

32. UHN SJKSEESDZ QX ZUF EHRQDYIQDODSXX, H YHO! ZUSTSWHTS ZUS KUQEOTSD HW ASD LVZ ZUSQT ZTVXZ VDOST ZUS XUCOHN HW ZUF NQDYX.

33. BAM PYFVFQTQS VYBGG VJQBL B PFSM BWBRAVX XYQ VFA FU CBA, RX VYBGG EQ UFSWRTQA YRC: EZX ZAXF YRC XYBX EGBVJYQCQXY BWBRAVX XYQ YFGH WYFVX RX VYBGG AFX EQ UFSWRTQA.

34. EGBAB JD EGZE RZNBEG
    GJRDBOC AJVG, PBE GZEG
    YXEGJYF: EGBAB JD EGZE
    RZNBEG GJRDBOC UXXA, PBE
    GZEG FABZE AJVGBD.

35. USC CN BUSC HIVH JSP
    INVMNHI USH KFUUNMK: TGH FL
    VUW ZVU TN V CSMKIFQQNM
    SL JSP, VUP PSNHI IFK CFXX,
    IFZ IN INVMNHI.

36. UOADDAY UA EVY, AIAT FGA
    CSFGAB VC VHB OVBY KADHD
    WGBJDF, FGA CSFGAB VC
    QABWJAD, STY FGA EVY VC SOO
    WVQCVBF;

37. L SLV, GRLF ZIG NB SLV; UZIAB
DQAA Q HUUO GRUU: NB HLFA
GRQIHGUGR TLI GRUU, NB
TAUHR ALMSUGR TLI GRUU QM
Z VIB ZMV GRQIHGB AZMV,
DRUIU ML DZGUI QH.

38. DSP GYKLX CSLWW XYD GPLB
DSLD GSTNS ZPBDLTXPDS EXDY
L KLX, XPTDSPB CSLWW L KLX
ZED YX L GYKLX'C RLBKPXD:
QYB LWW DSLD OY CY LBP
LMYKTXLDTYX EXDY DSP WYBO
DSI RYO.

39. WXL NPC HAZL MWQL OXNA
TAMCM, Q FQHH LA NPQM
NPQXU WHMA NPWN NPAO PWMN
MBAGCX: DAZ NPAO PWMN
DAOXL UZWKC QX TI MQUPN,
WXL Q GXAF NPCC VI XWTC.

40. GVRXSV ELV CXHQEPYQO BVSV
    GSXHDLE RXSEL, XS VWVS ELXH
    LPFOE RXSCVF ELV VPSEL PQF
    ELV BXSTF, VWVQ RSXC
    VWVSTPOEYQD EX VWVSTPOEYQD,
    ELXH PSE DXF.

41. CIALZI H JTYYBQ RA BETU HY
    ILYRQBR CTOBJ, HYR ITJ RHNJ
    WB VQAUAYZBR, NBC JLQBUN T
    MYAG CIHC TC JIHUU WB GBUU
    GTCI CIBO CIHC XBHQ ZAR,
    GITKI XBHQ WBXAQB ITO.

42. IJF OBIRWKXPXE MX FK AJ
    OKEF KE FXXF, FK ITT AJ RBX
    JISX KD RBX TKEF VXWQW,
    CAPAJC RBIJUW RK CKF IJF
    RBX DIRBXE HM BAS.

43. BGF RYWP HDYAFBG GYA BY
PFRTUFW BGF OYPRI YSB YV
BFLKBMBTYDJ, MDP BY WFJFWZF
BGF SDNSJB SDBY BGF PMI YV
NSPOLFDB BY EF KSDTJGFP.

44. QAAS CYFIDAGBAD ZU MJA GYBA
YX TYL, GYYQZUT XYI MJA
RAIEC YX YFI GYIL VADFD
EJIZDM FUMY AMAIUOG GZXA.

45. JKT LHOFO CWWPZKR FBWK
SEHX OJZSE, MZSE XHK ZS ZO
ZXBWOOZVCH, VFS KWS MZSE
RWT: NWI MZSE RWT JCC
SEZKRO JIH BWOOZVCH.

46. DM DJ NZZS MUKM K PKQ
JUZEHS YZMU UZRF KQS
LEDFMHV CKDM XZA MUF
JKHTKMDZQ ZX MUF HZAS.

47. RNY BEC IOV NR BEC WNYI
UM QCOY JZNQ OWW BEC
ECOBECQ: OM BENJ EOMB INQC,
UB MEOWW LC INQC JQBN
BECC: BEV YCHOYI MEOWW
YCBJYQ JZNQ BEUQC N HQ
ECOI.

48. RSM FOAX AX HAKW WFWNSRH,
FORF FOWU TACOF VSQB FOWW
FOW QSHU FNLW CQM, RSM
IWXLX YONAXF, BOQT FOQL
ORXF XWSF.

49. W UPRTYN NRUYUATYU, NRDN, AWYJN TA DII, JLBBIWMDNWTCJ, BYDHUYJ, WCNUYMUJJWTCJ, DCK ZWFWCZ TA NRDCOJ, QU GDKU ATY DII GUC.

50. CRTFQRY, JFTTFG WFK KPLK GPNSP NX RQNT, CDK KPLK GPNSP NX EFFY. PR KPLK YFRKP EFFY NX FJ EFY: CDK PR KPLK YFRKP RQNT PLKP WFK XRRW EFY.

51. TNO JQI ONP NT JQI HUDXIP EQKFF SNJ OIEJ MWNS JQI FNJ NT JQI OUBQJINME; FIEJ JQI OUBQJINME WMJ TNOJQ JQIUO QKSPE MSJN USUYMUJR.

52. JLU WV GLX D FDG, XQDX QR

VQLBKU KWR; GRWXQRS XQR

VLG LE FDG, XQDX QR VQLBKU

SRARGX: QDXQ QR VDWU, DGU

VQDKK QR GLX UL WX? LS

QDXQ QR VALPRG, DGU VQDKK

QR GLX FDPR WX JLLU?

53. SWK RENY LWUYK KLWYWZEYW

DW TWYZWJK BQKL KLW SEYO

ENY FEO, KE BUSX QV LQC

CKUKNKWC, UVO KE XWWT LQC

JEAAUVOAWVKC, UC UK KLQC

OUR.

54. PU KZPQJ JQJLE HJ ZBQFGE,

FPOJ ZPL HGJNC KD JNK; NQC

PU ZJ HJ KZPGVKE, FPOJ ZPL

INKJG KD CGPQA.

55. EGVYNGXY, G XUR QDJT RTQ,
JWYCY GX MTR GD JWY
ZCYXYDSY TA JWY UDPYEX TA
PTI TBYC TDY XGDDYC JWUJ
CYZYDJYJW.

56. RCN JQV FHNF PFQXBK NFB
OQQYTXF NFTKJX QO NFB
GQIYV NQ PQKOQCKV NFB GTXB;
HKV JQV FHNF PFQXBK NFB
GBHD NFTKJX QO NFB GQIYV
NQ PQKOQCKV NFB NFTKJX
GFTPF HIB UTJFNZ.

57. RSI BWJ XSLJ SR OSYJN FQ BWJ
ISSB SR KXX JLFX: EWFDW
EWFXJ QSOJ DSLJBJU KRBJI, BWJN
WKLJ JIIJU RISO BWJ RKFBW,
KYU CFJIDJU BWJOQJXLJQ
BWISGHW EFBW OKYN QSIISEQ.

58. JFMUMXZUM JM UMQMKEKVD S
YKVDWZI JFKQF QSVVZL OM
IZEMW, TML RN FSEM DUSQM,
JFMUMOC JM ISC NMUEM DZW
SQQMALSOTC JKLF UMEMUMVQM
SVW DZWTC XMSU.

59. QT JD MQT VPOW, QJD KPVW JD
ZTVLTOM: LPV YHH QJD KYXD
YVT FBCARTUM: Y APC PL
MVBMQ YUC KJMQPBM JUJNBJMX,
FBDM YUC VJAQM JD QT.

60. GC GRBG IRNC BGC CRYBG EH
GKM DQVCY, GC GRBG
CMBREUKMGCN BGC VQYUN EH
GKM VKMNQI, RTN GRBG
MBYCBZGCN QOB BGC GCRFCTM
EH GKM NKMZYCBKQT.

61. XQB DC LNF LDTF QX LBQGEWF
NF ONPWW NDVF TF DC NDO
MPADWDQC: DC LNF OFZBFL QX
NDO LPEFBCPZWF ONPWW NF
NDVF TF; NF ONPWW OFL TF
GM GMQC P BQZH.

62. OWK OHH BER BGBER TX BER
HOWK, FERBERY TX BER LRRK
TX BER HOWK, TY TX BER
XYPGB TX BER BYRR, GL BER
HTYK'L: GB GL ETHV PWBT BER
HTYK.

63. JSZ PBI FNYZ TNZ HJLZ, LP LH
SNP TNNZ PBJP PBI RJS HBNCFZ
OI JFNSI; L ULFF RJQI BLR JS
BIFA RIIP WNY BLR.

64. WTC OF BTEM CBT XPDXWOFQPD
PJ CBT KBPWT RECCTM: JTEM
ZPN, EDN GTTY BQF
XPRREDNRTDCF: JPM CBQF QF
CBT KBPWT NOCH PJ RED.

65. EWT HRWZWUAUT HKYY ZQAU
RKZ YKEU ZRQYY YWZU KD; JND
HRWZWUAUT ZRQYY YWZU RKZ
YKEU EWT OG ZQFU QLM DRU
CWZIUY'Z, DRU ZQOU ZRQYY
ZQAU KD.

66. TX BO VWOZ, QOTZC OKTA,
UZRD WRD VR CTKO CRRE
CTXVN GZVR BRGP SWTAEPOZ:
WRD JGSW JRPO NWIAA BRGP
WOIKOZAB XIVWOP CTKO VWO
WRAB NHTPTV VR VWOJ VWIV
INU WTJ?

67. KSR VJDKLB UHCLB K LJLDB,
KSR VAL JL CS LGB MHCQQ.
KSR LGB UHJLJST UKQ, OBQAQ
CW SKIKHBLG LGB XJST CW
LGB OBUQ.

68. XYST DYP, WDA CTB NR GTWRYD
BYJTBVTG, RWEBV BVT CYGA:
BVYNJV MYNG REDR QT WR
RXWGCTB, BVTM RVWCC QT WR
PVEBT WR RDYP; BVYNJV BVTM QT
GTA CELT XGESRYD, BVTM
RVWCC QT WR PYYC.

69. ATBL KLYIH JDZU KL, Z PZV,
TIIZYVXUP OZ OAH
CZBXUPRXUVULMM: TIIZYVXUP
JUOZ OAL KJCOXOJVL ZE OAH
OLUVLY KLYIXLM NCZO ZJO KH
OYTUMPYLMMXZUM.

70. DGT NQ FIWE BVV BLLQBT
MQDGTQ EJQ OIHXFQYE WQBE GD
RJTUWE; EJBE QCQTK GYQ FBK
TQRQUCQ EJQ EJUYXW HGYQ UY
JUW MGHK, BRRGTHUYX EG EJBE
JQ JBEJ HGYQ, NJQEJQT UE MQ
XGGH GT MBH.

71. NVZOPB IVBF IVZI ZOB OHNV
HM IVHW GAOTX, IVZI IVBE LB
MAI VHPVFHMXBX, MAO IOCWI
HM CMNBOIZHM OHNVBW, LCI HM
IVB THQHMP PAX, GVA PHQBIV CW
OHNVTE ZTT IVHMPW IA BMDAE.

72. LE ANQI FNI! KHENAI, SENT
ELRS ZLIH SEH EHLUHM LMI
SEH HLQSE KW SEW FQHLS
ONVHQ LMI RSQHSJEHI NTS LQZ,
LMI SEHQH DR MNSEDMF SNN
ELQI GNQ SEHH.

73. UVN YHMF QG JZ GUMNOTUV
BOF JZ GVQNYF; JZ VNBMU
UMEGUNF QO VQJ, BOF Q BJ
VNYANF: UVNMNCHMN JZ VNBMU
TMNBUYZ MNWHQPNUV; BOF
XQUV JZ GHOT XQYY Q
AMBQGN VQJ.

74. NEZ OR IOMS PUDZ DESS, Z
IZBA, YKZUQ DES QZAR? NEZ
OR IOMS DESS, QIZBOZPR OU
EZIOUSRR, CSYBCPI OU XBYORSR,
AZOUQ NZUASBR?

75. CYDU ZAD ZOO FKJD KTC KE
CYD HZU, CYDU ZAD CKFDCYDA
PDQKWD TJLAKEXCZPOD; CYDAD
XB JKJD CYZC RKDCY FKKR, JK,
JKC KJD.

76. DJVIPJ WJGZ IKX SIK GHRFW
XRA ZTPRABT HTFWRGRHTX IKU
EIFK UJQJFZ, IOZJP ZTJ
ZPIUFZFRK RO SJK, IOZJP ZTJ
PAUFSJKZG RO ZTJ VRPWU, IKU
KRZ IOZJP QTKFGZ.

77. FCQ, JT AFYVTBW, NBHSHMT CHY
JHZB OVRIQBTC YH PBFYV: KZY
KBRCX YVTG ZN RC YVT
CZBYZBT FCQ FQGHCRYRHC HA
YVT IHBQ.

78. EC YEJY QDTCYE KNQTCW KEJQQ
IDY XC KJYNKLNCS MNYE
KNQTCW; IDW EC YEJY QDTCYE
JXBISJIUC MNYE NIUWCJKC:
YENK NK JQKD TJINYV.

79. MUL IOW ZUUL VOFXX CWAWL
KWFVW UNI UM IOW XFCE:
IOWLWMULW D KUHHFCE IOWW,
VFSDCJ, IOUN VOFXI UZWC
IODCW OFCE QDEW NCIU IOS
TLUIOWL, IU IOS ZUUL, FCE IU
IOS CWWES, DC IOS XFCE.

80. DCCH FWWX, KLX LWR CIMA,
RZKR GC OKG AMIC: KLX DW
RZC AWPX, RZC FWX WS ZWDRD,
DZKAA EC TMRZ GWB, KD GC
ZKIC DYWHCL.

81. WUC A HR IUV HMYHRNT UW
VYN JUMGNK UW DYCAMV: WUC
AV AM VYN GUBNC UW JUT
EIVU MHKPHVAUI VU NPNCL UIN
VYHV ONKANPNVY; VU VYN QNB
WACMV, HIT HKMU VU VYN
JCNNX.

82. KBO NB HN MIV THEE BK JBW,
MIZM THMI TVEE WBHCJ RV
DZR ALM MB NHEVCXV MIV
HJCBOZCXV BK KBBEHNI DVC.

83. TLIFWR, IUEEM ZB AIL VUY
OIFV JFR SFCCLSALAI: AILCLKFCL
RLBEZBL YFA AIFQ AIL
SIUBALYZYJ FK AIL UWVZJIAM.

84. FNIW WLEFN FNV ZXMH;
RIMWVH CV FNV OLG FNLF
FMIWFVFN EG OLG, LGH OLJVFN
AZVWN NEW LMO, LGH UNXWV
NVLMF HVQLMFVFN AMXO FNV
ZXMH.

85. FGZ ZWNF BNQSQ ZPQ JAQNF
NPJDX RVN OAJQR MPX GO RVN
ZNNC, VN PHHNPJNM OAJQR RG
EPJX EPUMPDNFN, GSR GO ZVGE
VN VPM LPQR QNTNF MNTADQ.

86. RGMFLI GVIG MNONNZNO HL
KMTZ IGN RHMLN TK IGN XVD,
SNFUJ ZVON V RHMLN KTM HL:
KTM FI FL DMFIINU, RHMLNO FL
NENMW TUN IGVI GVUJNIG TU
V IMNN.

87. QTA MK SK UCTA GTK NG
QTGNXKB, NKTAKBXKQBNKA,
OGBHCZCTH GTK QTGNXKB, KZKT
QE HGA OGB FXBCEN'E EQUK
XQNX OGBHCZKT SGL.

88. MEK XLK VMUK BEJL ELMO, JOR REK LA MHH AHRVO UV FLZR SRALGR ZR; ALG JOR RMGJO UV AUHHRK TUJO NULHREFR JOGLBXO JORZ; MEK, SROLHK, U TUHH KRVJGLD JORZ TUJO JOR RMGJO.

89. PHSHSJHP QCN NWH ALQA CY ST SCGNW, QCP ST NPRQAOPHAALCQA: RBBCPZLQO NC NWT SHPBT PHSHSJHP NWCG SH YCP NWT OCCZQHAA' ARXH, C ECPZ.

90. OEN QUN POG BVIFT GUTXP, BVOB BVIM BHTEIN CTUR BVIFT IYFA GOM; OEN QUN TIDIEBIN UC BVI IYFA, BVOB VI VON POFN BVOB VI GUHAN NU HEBU BVIR; OEN VI NFN FB EUB.

SPOTTY HEADLINE PUZZLES

by Sara Stoker

———————————————————⎯ᐯ\/

Fill in the missing letters of each "headline," which relates
a Bible story. Then unscramble the letters you've added
to the headline to form a name which is the object of the
headline.

OLD TESTAMENT HEADLINES

1.

BLI●D C●PTIVE
DE●TROY● TE●PLE

__ __ __ __ __ __

2.

LUNATIC ●AS
TH●USANDS OF A●IM●LS

__ __ __ __

3.

K●NG ●OUBLY
●IOLATES SACRE● L●WS

__ __ __ __ __

4.

ⒷELIEVING WⒶNDERER PⓄOⒷISED LⒶND FOR ⒽIS MⒶNY HEIRS

_ _ _ _ _ _ _ _

5.

FIRⓈT KING OF ISRⒶEⓁ COMMITS SⓊICIDE

_ _ _ _

6.

CⒶPTIVE BOY'S THRⒺE FRIENⒹS DEⓁIVERED FROM FⒾRE UⓃHURT

_ _ _ _ _ _

7.

**FIRST ●AN CON●EMNS
●LL FUTURE GENER●TIONS**

— — — —

8.

**●LAVE BABY RAIS●D AS
PHARA●H'S ●IGHTY ●ON**

— — — — —

9.

**●UST PROP●ET
L●MENTS D●STRUCT●ON OF
TH● L●OD'S TE●PLE**

— — — — — —

10.

FORST MURDER
●OMMITTED O● E●RTH
BY A MAN

— — — —

11.

Y●UNG BROT●ER ●ULLED
FROM PIT AND UN●USTLY
●OLD AS SLAV●

— — — — — —

12.

KING THREATE●ING T● CUT
CHI●D IN TW● ●AY SETTLE
●WNERSHIP DI●PUTE

— — — — — —

13.

PROP●ET   HAS   BE●UN
ENCOUR●G●N●   EX-C●PTIVES   TO
REBUILD   TEMPLE

— — — — — —

14.

P●●EST   RENEWS
●EAL   TOW●RD   T●MPLE
RE●AB   AMONGST   T●E
EX-●●PTIVES

— — — — — —

15.

OLD   CHILDLESS   M●N
●ELIEVES   PRO●ISE   TO
●●VE   M●NY   CHILD●EN

— — — — — —

16.

**COU●AGEOU● QU●EN OU●WITS
●ATEFUL PLOTTING ●NEMY**

_ _ _ _ _ _

17.

**M●THER RETURNS HO●E
AFTER YE●RS OF A●GU●SH**

_ _ _ _

18.

**W●RRIOR CROSSES ●ORDAN,
CONQ●ERS LAND, AND
●LAYS PREVIOUS IN●ABITANTS**

_ _ _ _ _ _

19.

SHEPHERD TRICKED ●Y ●N UN●UST UN●LE'S PROMISE

— — — — —

20.

BROTHER ●ELLS BIRTHRIGHT IN RET●RN FOR A M●●L

— — — —

21.

MAN'S WIFE BEC●MES SA●T S●ATUE

— — —

22.

CONNIVING MOTH●R ●NOWINGLY H●LPED SON LIE TO F●T●ER FO● ●LESSING

— — — — — — —

23.

GOV●RNMENT OFF●CI●L SPEN●S ●IGHT WITH ●IONS

— — — — — —

24.

●EALOUS ●ING BUILDS ●UGE W●TER TUNNELS UNDERN●AT● B●S●EGED CITY

— — — — — — —

25.

WEALTHIEST ●AN IS A●S●
W●RLD'● M●ST WISE KI●G

— — — — — — — —

26.

●GYPTIAN FUGITIVE BECO●E●
GOD'S CH●●EN LEADER

— — — — —

27.

AUTHOR OF
TEN COMMAN●MENTS
EN●RAVES THEM IN ST●NE

— — —

28.

PROPHET'S ●OURNEY
●INKED TO FI●RY CHOR●OT RIDE
UP TO ●EAVEN

— — — — — —

29.

●UST KING RE●T●RES
●EBREW P●SSOVER TO
OR●GINAL SPECIFICATIONS

— — — — — —

30.

●RAFTY ●●URNEYMAN
WRESTLES WITH ●NGEL AND
LIVES TO TELL A●OUT IT

— — — — — —

31.

WOMAN H●S FI●ST CHILD W●EN
●HE'S ONE HUNDRED YE●RS OLD

— — — — —

32.

BOY ORDERED TO BE
●●CRIF●●ED TO TE●T FATHER

— — — — —

33.

UNGODLY KI●G T●ROW●
●●NY CHILDREN INTO FIR●;
L●TER REPENT●

— — — — — — — —

34.

OVEROEAOOUS QUEEN MURDORS
INNOCONT POOPLE AND
OUMOLES RELIGION

— — — — — — — —

35.

SYRION MON CURED OF
LEPROSY AFTER BOTHIOG
SEVEO TIOES IN RIVER

— — — — — — —

36.

KING DIES FROM
POINFUL INCUOABLE DISOASE
AS GOD'S OUST PUNISOOENT

— — — — — — — —

37.

**BRAVE ●AN L●ADS TH●U●ANDS
ON DRY PATH THROUGH ●EA**

— — — — —

38.

**RIGHTEOUS MAN COPES WITH
SUDDEN L●SS OF
●UST A●OUT EVERYTHING**

— — —

39.

**●AN ●IV●S TO ●EE HIS
NINE H●NDR●D AND
SIX●Y-NINT● BIRT●D●Y**

— — — — — — — —

40.

DIS●BEDIENT PROPHET E●DURES THREE DAYS IN ●UMBO FISH'S STOM●C●

— — — — — —

41.

WOMAN'S ●NGUIS●ED PRAYERS ●●SWERED T●ROUGH BIRTH OF SO●

— — — — — —

42.

RIG●TEOUS PRI●ST KILLED BY ●NTENTION●LLY FO●GETFUL KING AND OVER●E●LOUS ●O●●ORTS

— — — — — — — — —

43.

WOAK MAN SUBOUES
MIOHTY ARMY WOTH ONLY
THREE HUODRED MEN

— — — — — — —

44.

DAOOLING KIOG OOMOLOD
AND FOROEO TO
EOT GOOSS LIKO OXEO

— — — — — — — — — — — — — — —

45.

GOO CHOOSES
SONGING SHEPHERO TO BECOME
FOOORED KING

— — — — — —

46.

INNOCEN● LA●D●WNER MURDERED FOR ●IS ●E●UTIFUL PLOT OF LAND

— — — — — —

47.

M●N'S DONKEY ST●RTS SCO●DING HI● IN HE●REW LANGU●GE

— — — — —

48.

●EALOUS EX-CAPTIVE T●ACES LIN●AGE BACK TO HIGH PRIEST ●ARON

— — — —

49.

EX-SPY RE●EIV●S PORTION OF ●EAUTIFUL PROMISED ●●ND

— — — — —

50.

IMMORA● WOMAN
TRICKS JU●GE ●NTO
REVE●●ING S●CRET STRENGT●

— — — — — —

51.

MAN TW●CE CHALLE●●ES GOD
TO ●EWDR●P T●STS

— — — — —

52.

WOMAN DRIVES WOODEN P●G ●UST THROUGH S●EEPING ENEMY'S HE●D

— — — — —

53.

RUL●R PU●●LED ●Y MY●TE●IOUS ●●ND WRITING ON THE W●L●

— — — — — — — — —

54.

●ABITUALLY STUBBORN EGY●TI●N ●ULER ●ASN'T LET GOD'S PE●PLE LE●VE

— — — — — — — —

55.

PROPHET FORETELLS JESUS' BIRTH, DEATH, AND RESURRECTION

__ __ __ __ __ __

56.

MAN'S NEWBY GIVEN NAME TO REPRESENT AN ENTIRE NATION

__ __ __ __ __ __

57.

WICKED MAN PLOTS TO HANG QUEEN'S ADOPTED FATHER

__ __ __ __ __ __

58.

TALKING SNAKE
DECEIVES WOMAN

— — —

59.

SLUMBERING MAN IS BARRED
WHEN HE CAN SEE
STAIRWAY TO HEAVEN IN DREAM

— — — — —

60.

YOUNG BOY HEARS
GOD CALL HIS NAME
THREE TIMES IN ONE NIGHT

— — — — —

BIBLE QUOTATION PUZZLES

by G. Rebecca Shodin

Place the letters in each column into the puzzle grid preceding to form words. The letters may or may not fit into the grid in the same order in which they're given; black spaces indicate the ends of words. When a letter has been used, cross it off and do not use it again. When the grid has been properly filled in, you'll be able to read a Bible verse by scanning the lines of the grid from left to right.

JOHN 1:4

A	L	I	T	F	I	A	E	N	S
H	S	E	O	E	M	F	W	A	W
I	T	N	H	L	E	M	N	D	G
T	N		F	H		E	E	I	
	H			I		L			

ISAIAH 12:5

T	H	E	O	E	U	S	X	C	A
G	S	L	T	E	O	H	T	O	H
R	I	O	N	L	H	E	D	T	E
A	R	E	N	W	N	E	A	N	N
L	D	H	H	H	I	N	I	I	S
S	K	N	G	T		R	H	I	F
O	L	N		T		T		E	
	T								

3 JOHN 4

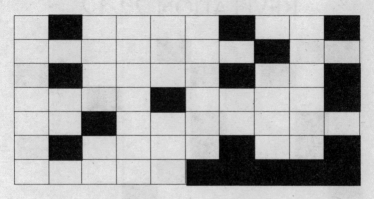

I	R	H	C	V	N	R	N	J	O
G	R	E	A	T	T	H	D	O	E
Y	E	T	A	A	I	L	A	T	
H	Y	A	H	H	K		I	R	
M		U	A	L	E		T	N	
N		W	A	E	E			O	
T			R	H					

REVELATION 22:12

Q D A Y O L L L A O
D U I S H R S M A E
M A M T H W D E H N
R A I C O R E I A G
E K V C R W B M V N
L E C N D Y O A N R
D E S I K C Y N W O
        C A I W H B
        S   I T E
            E E

ECCLESIASTES 3:1

T O O E P A D P A R

E I I N A N E R E A

E R I E G T T H E H

H H N S E U O S Y S

S T H N D E R N T V

E   U   A V R   O

T   Y   V E   E

     M

ISAIAH 59:1

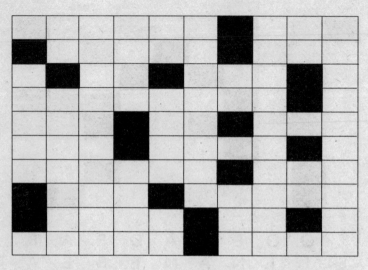

```
B   E   H   O   L   D   E   H   A   E
H   I   T   R   E   N   I   A   V   N
N   E   A   S   I   T   H   T   I   R
E   T   H   T   A   A   V   E   H   S
D   N   N   R   S   R   E   T   A   N
H   O   R   A   E   S   O   D   A   S
A   A   T   O   D   N       C   A   Y
    L   O   H   T   H       E   B   C
        I               H       N
```

EXODUS 20:3

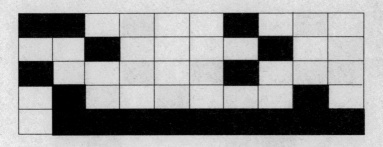

L	T	B	E	F	U	E	S	N	D
S	O	T	H	A	V	R	G	H	O
E		T	H	O	R		E	O	M
			H	E	O				A

PSALM 145:1

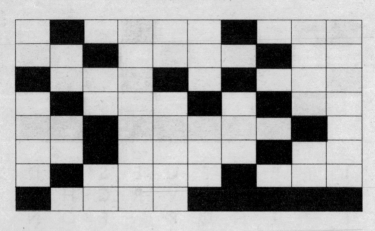

H   Y   O   V   L   O   E   K   X   N
R   G   V   T   L   M   S   A   F   Y
G   L   A   D   H   E   I   S   W   T
L   L   V   N   D   E   E   E   N   O
O   E   W   I   E   L   I   T
I   N   A   R   M   D
                        B   R   D

JOHN 6:47

E	E	R	I	A	Y	S	V	E	V
I	L	Y	H	T	T	O	A	Y	R
M	N	T	A	A	H	H	U	E	H
E	E	L	E	S	T	I	B	N	L
I	E	F	O	L	T		O	E	
V	R	T	H	I	Y		N	G	
L	L	V	E						
U									

HABAKKUK 3:18

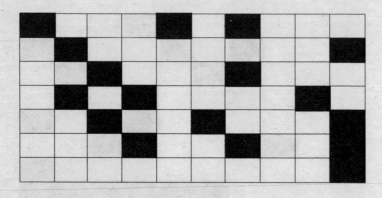

L	Y	I	I	J	E	L	W	E	R
I	O	L	E	H	I	T	C	O	J
D	Y	E	T	W	T	I	L	Y	L
S	N	D	T	N	I	I	L	N	
G	A	R	V	A	O	L	H	I	
O				O	F		H	E	
							M	O	
							O		

Proverbs 15:1

```
A   E   E   S   W   A   Y   W   A   E
D   S   V   R   O   F   R   R   U   R
S   W   N   S   E   T   T       W   R
I   A   H   G   U   R   T       O   P
T   T       A   T   S   U       N   N
    A       O   B   I           G   R
    H           U
```

MATTHEW 11:29

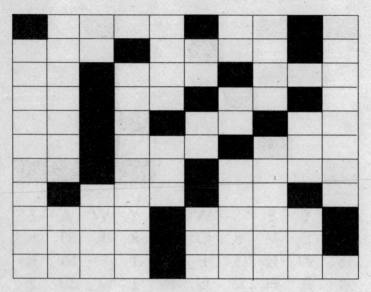

O	K	L	K	U	P	M	N	M	E
R	R	A	R	N	D	H	E	A	E
E	T	S	T	N	S	N	Y	E	F
T	K	E	N	D	A	O	N	O	S
O	U	A	I	I	F	M	E	L	Y
H	A	U	A	N	D	O	E	D	Y
L	O		O	E	U	Y	L	O	A
O	N		L	F		M	T		R
R	Y		A			I	U		W
Y	E		I				L		S

PROVERBS 2:20

M Y Y N F A H W H L
K M I G O H G E U W
A E P T H T N O U D
T H S E S T E O A K
T R A N T F H O P A
E H I O   T E D O E
   A E   T T D   S
```
```

JUDE 2

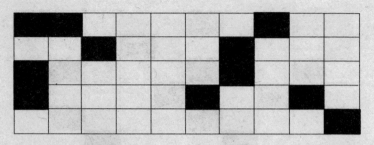

```
U   O   E   A   R   U   B   A   N   N
T   P   O   V   O   E   Y   E   N   D
    L   M   E   C   L   I   E   D   M
    L   T   I   E   C       A   U   D
            Y   P
```

PSALM 76:4

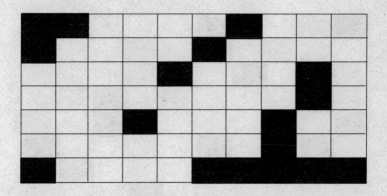

```
X    O    T    A    L    A    G    D    M    T
H    C    O    E    T    E    N    T    O    O
I    A    U    H    O    U    S    A    O    T
U    M    E    R    E    N    E    L    R    R
     P    N    L    I    H         L         F
     N    T    S    Y                        E
          R
```

LUKE 14:11

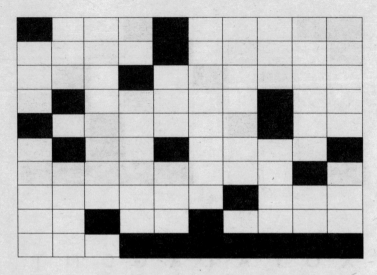

D	F	O	A	H	W	X	H	S	O
H	V	E	E	A	E	M	S	L	T
I	T	H	B	L	I	L	A	E	L
E	U	S	R	E	L	E	O	H	A
E	M	D	H	S	L	H	X	A	L
F	L	B	R	L	E	D	A	A	E
L	A	H	E	B	T	H	X	T	N
T	E	S	B		E	T	S	B	H
	M	M			F				

Hebrews 13:8

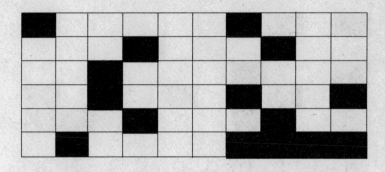

M	E	Y	Y	U	S	E	T	O	O
A	Y	E	A	T	D	T	C	F	A
D	A	T	S	E	N	D	E	S	D
I	J	E	V	N	S			R	R
R	S	E		A	H			H	
				E	R				

JAMES 1:8

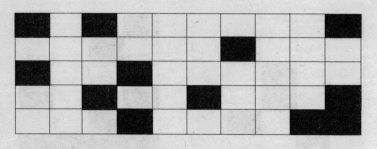

M	I	S	D	O	D	S	T	E	B
H	E	N	I	E	N	A	L	A	N
L	A	S	D	U	U	B	L	L	
	I			N	A	Y	S	A	
	I			W		M			

JOB 23:10

N
N
I
E
T

G
R
S
W
O

T
H
I
B
W
F
O
A
H

U
E
Y
A
E
A
O
L
L

T
T
R
D
K
L

E
H
H
T
T
H
L

H
M
M
H
A
H

T
A
W
C
E
T
E

H
T
H
A
H
O

E
S
K
E
I
M

ROMANS 12:17

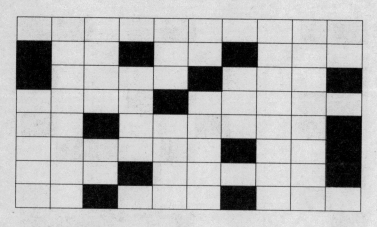

H	E	O	L	N	P	F	M	A	N
T	T	V	T	L	I	R	O	R	E
E	E	I	E	S	T	G	O	V	I
O	V	E	O	S	P	E	G	T	I
R	E	C	A	M	O	N	M	E	
D	O	N	I	L	L		N	S	
	H			H	I		I	S	
	F						H	N	

HEBREWS 3:15

```
I    S    H    I    L    V    F    E    T    O
A    D    E    S    L    E    H    I    T    E
T    W    I    Y    A    R    O    V    Y    R
R    H    A    O    A    R    D    I    A    C
T    T    I    L    P    E    N    H    C    O
     H    I    R    N    I    O    I    N    A
     T    Y    S    D    S         N    E    E
     W    S    O    U    I              N
          A         U                   O
```

PSALM 133:1

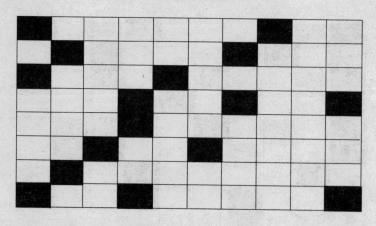

W	N	O	O	I	P	T	I	H	O
L	I	T	W	B	T	I	T	N	D
F	B	E	O	O	R	I	W	A	L
A	O	N	H	U	L	D	A	S	R
E	H	G	T	O	E	E	E	H	S
	N	R		O	D	L	T	E	R
		T		G	N	D	H	E	
								Y	

LUKE 2:14

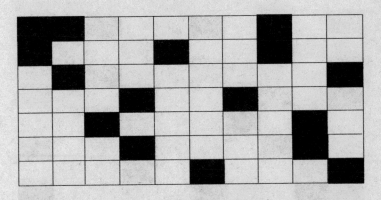

E	G	D	L	E	R	C	S	A	R
A	N	R	D	I	I	L	E	T	G
T	H	O	I	G	H	N	N	T	H
W	A	H	D	O	N	E	E	T	O
O	O	G	W	O	A	Y	E	T	O
		D	P		L	E			
					M				

JONAH 2:7

```
R   E   E   F   N   M   N   T   L   Y
R   D   I   T   E   I   H   M   Y   O
P   R   E   N   A   I   Y   M   A   D
W   W   D   M   H   M   N   C   O   E
U   H   I   N   P   H   N   T   S   M
E   H   E   Y   E   D   N   T   E   O
T   L   A   N   T   R   E   O   O   E
T   L   I   R   U   U   E       M
    I       E   I   E   B       B
            A   L           L
```

JOHN 1:5

L N A H T A R H A N
E H G E I M P D D R
K S H S S M T N N H
T T D N O N A K I E
S I E C D   I T E N
E N E   D   S H R E
O T   D   N

PROVERBS 15:33

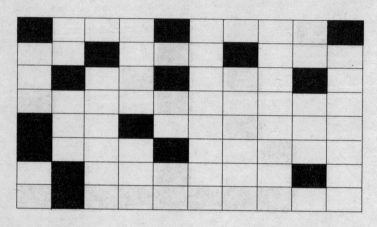

```
O   T   T   E   M   F   S   A   O   I
D   F   F   T   H   E   E   L   O   N
S   A   N   D   W   T   E   E   O   M
N   O   H   O   U   C   H   R   T   Y
E   S   I   R   N   I   L   I   R   R
        H   U       B   T   D       I
        H   S       O   U   F       R
                    I
```

James 5:8

S	U	P	R	Y	E	E	N	L	Y
O	F	A	N	T	I	S	H	D	S
A	M	R	A	L	R	A	R	G	C
H	E	E	B	O	E	O	I	T	T
O	B	O	L	H	I	D	A	T	R
O	W	E	T	H	T	H	E		H
	T	I		G			F		S

ISAIAH 60:1

```
L   T   F   S   R   R   S   H   O   H
O   S   G   O   T   L   T   S   D   N
P   R   E   E   A   H   I   R   I   U
A   I   N   R   T   N   D   N   Y   C
E   M   I   H   E   S   Y   H   T   F
I   O   G   L   O       O   E
E       H   I   I       E
                        E
```

PSALM 70:1

E E O L E O D E A T
T M E A G V E O L O
E M E K I E L R S P
   D A T K   H A T M
      M   O   H H R D
            O   S

PSALM 119:10

U   H   A   T   T   H   M   E   R   T
O   O   G   H   E   A   D   E   E   S   O
O   G   R   M   V   H   N   I   E   N   T
S   R   W   I   N   N   T   H   Y   R   W
F   O   O   L   M   E   T   M   E   N   N
O   M   T   O   A   H   D   Y   C
H   M   L   T   H   A
                E

Psalm 121:1

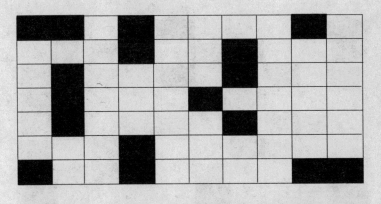

E	T	I	H	W	P	H	U	N	T
O	F	T	Y	U	S	L	I	L	L
N	M	E	R	E	O	L	W	H	L
I	C	Y		O	I	M	P	I	H
S		F		C	M		L	T	N
		T		H	E		E		E
							M		

366

PROVERBS 9:10

R O F I E N F H A R
B D L I T S E N L O
O E H W S H T E E T
I F T H N G I R G F
A S G E T D D O Y N
A N D U D H E L S K
O N D I N H E O M
W E N O E
T I E M

LUKE 2:11

```
F   U   H   I   S   V   B   O   R   R
O   T   R   T   H   H   D   A   Y   D
C   H   R   F   A   N   I   C   I   T
I   L   H   S   C   E   T   V   U   Y
Y   O   O   I   S   D   A   O   S   N
    N   O   R   D   T       I   I   E
    A       I   U           T   H
    W       I   S
```

1 SAMUEL 12:24

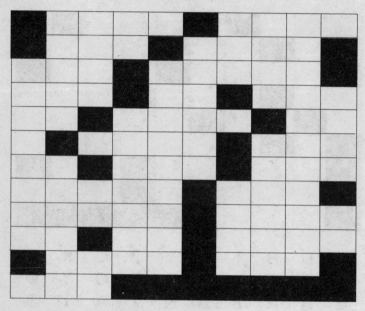

Y O Y L I L H R A R

G T U E I E O V D N

G R M E I R R T E H

A S D A U R T O R U

H D N W O N H H A L

T O H O Y T H A E N

L I E N T   F E O A

R H O F E   F C W

S T D H S   H I

   I   R   C T

   N   O R

JOEL 2:21

```
R   G   J   E   A   C   L   O   N   E
S   E   T   L   D   R   D   O   O   D
R   R   F   A   I   T   D   N   B   T
R   O   A   O   L   N   D   N   R   G
    W   L   H   A       A   I   F   O
        I   L   E       H   D   D   G
            T
```

PSALM 145:9

L	M	H	L	L	I	L	D	D	R
S	E	T	O	T	O	O	N	E	A
H	I	S	H	V	E	A	D	R	T
R	I	S	R	E	E	N	O	R	K
O		E	I	S		E	S	A	D
		A		G		R	O		L
				C		W			

PROVERBS 16:7

O	W	S	C	N	T	S	M	A	H
E	S	D	M	A	E	H	A	M	K
P	A	A	E	B	V	W	E	T	A
N	R	H	W	E	Y	E	I	P	L
I	T	O	E	E	E	A	N	T	S
E	S	H	E	H	E	M	E	E	L
	T	I		N					H
	E								
	H								

PROVERBS 22:6

R	R	A	D	W	A	Y	I	H	O
T	C	H	I	U	L	D	T	G	O
T	H	N	W	I	T	U	E	D	E
T	S	M	I	P	D	L	P	N	F
H	A	E	I	I	L	H	L	N	A
H	E	H	E	N	W	O		N	
	E	E	O	L	A	R			
	O	D		S					

1 SAMUEL 2:2

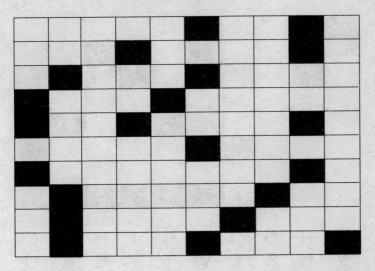

O	F	E	D	C	H	E	S	E	N
S	I	E	I	R	R	E	Y	D	A
Y	S	T	H	E	O	I	O	R	D
E	H	O	R	H	K	L	H	R	K
E	N	S	U	N	T	G	R	A	B
T	N	I	H	E	O	N	E	I	E
S		E	R	E		T	L		I
		T	O	T		H	O		E
		R		E					N
		O							

GENESIS 27:8

N   H   O   O   G   H   T   M   R   O
V   N   R   E   W   T   I   C   S   O
R   O   O   E   M   Y   H   O   D   E
F   D   I   B   E   M   A   E   C   T
T   A   I   C   M   M   Y   N   Y
H   O   T   W   A   C   H
I   C   N
          E

EPHESIANS 6:11

A W H A E T Y V L D
E T T B S S A G D M
P U W I N N A E T E
O T H E L E S B O F
A Y H O T E S N I L
  T O I O D E T R M
  G A   O F   A H H
  U   L   E

PSALM 91:1

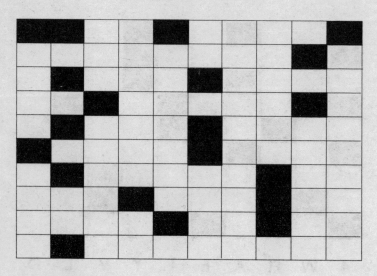

D	W	T	E	L	A	H	E	C	I
N	E	I	L	E	T	S	H	S	R
E	D	A	H	L	E	C	A	T	O
D	T	O	G	E	O	M	H	S	H
A	H	A	B	M	I	E	E	A	Y
E		H	W	H	D	O	O	T	T
F		E	P	I	H	H	U	U	L
L		R	H	T		E			H
			L			E			N
						F			
						G			

John 10:11

R	G	O	O	S	H	S	T	E	E
O	E	R	D	I	V	H	E	H	P
H	O	S	T	A	I	F	S	H	F
E	D	I	G	D	M	E	T	H	E
O	I	D		H	E	E	H	H	G
O	R			L	T		P		E
	P						E		

EPHESIANS 2:8

F	G	L	A	B	A	A	G	R	F
C	N	R	E	R	H	Y	Y	E	N
S	T	O	T	D	E	O	H	R	A
U	O	H	O	E	G	T	I	T	R
A	E	V	F	H	Y	I	G	I	O
O	E	D	V	T	E		T	H	
S	S			F	S		T	U	
I	A			F			O		
T							D		

TELEPHONE SCRAMBLE PUZZLES

by Nancy Bernhard

Each set of telephone push-buttons contains a hidden Bible word—and you'll need to determine which letter of each three-letter combination is part of the word.

ALLEGORIES

| GHI 4 | ABC 2 | GHI 4 | ABC 2 | PRS 7 |

| JKL 5 | GHI 4 | MNO 6 | MNO 6 | DEF 3 | PRS 7 | PRS 7 |

| PRS 7 | ABC 2 | PRS 7 | ABC 2 | GHI 4 |

| TUV 8 | GHI 4 | MNO 6 | DEF 3 |

| TUV 8 | GHI 4 | MNO 6 | DEF 3 | WXY 9 | ABC 2 | PRS 7 | DEF 3 |

PRISONERS

GHI 4	MNO 6	PRS 7	GHI 4	DEF 3	ABC 2

JKL 5	MNO 6	PRS 7	DEF 3	PRS 7	GHI 4

PRS 7	ABC 2	TUV 8	JKL 5

PRS 7	DEF 3	TUV 8	DEF 3	PRS 7

PRS 7	ABC 2	MNO 6	PRS 7	MNO 6	MNO 6

PRS 7	GHI 4	JKL 5	ABC 2	PRS 7

PRS 7	GHI 4	MNO 6	DEF 3	MNO 6	MNO 6

GENEALOGIES

ABC 2	ABC 2	PRS 7	ABC 2	GHI 4	ABC 2	MNO 6

DEF 3	PRS 7	ABC 2	TUV 8

GHI 4	PRS 7	ABC 2	ABC 2	ABC 2

JKL 5	DEF 3	PRS 7	TUV 8	PRS 7

JKL 5	MNO 6	PRS 7	DEF 3	PRS 7	GHI 4

MNO 6	ABC 2	PRS 7	WXY 9

PRS 7	GHI 4	MNO 6	DEF 3	MNO 6	MNO 6

MEASUREMENTS

| ABC 2 | TUV 8 | PRS 7 | GHI 4 | DEF 3 | JKL 5 |

| ABC 2 | TUV 8 | ABC 2 | GHI 4 | TUV 8 |

| DEF 3 | DEF 3 | MNO 6 | ABC 2 | PRS 7 | GHI 4 | TUV 8 | PRS 7 |

| DEF 3 | PRS 7 | ABC 2 | ABC 2 | GHI 4 | MNO 6 | ABC 2 |

| MNO 6 | MNO 6 | DEF 3 | PRS 7 |

| PRS 7 | GHI 4 | DEF 3 | JKL 5 | DEF 3 | JKL 5 |

| TUV 8 | ABC 2 | JKL 5 | DEF 3 | MNO 6 | TUV 8 |

ANIMALS IN THE OLD TESTAMENT

| ABC 2 | PRS 7 | PRS 7 |

| ABC 2 | ABC 2 | MNO 6 | DEF 3 | JKL 5 |

| DEF 3 | MNO 6 | TUV 8 | DEF 3 |

| DEF 3 | ABC 2 | GHI 4 | JKL 5 | DEF 3 |

| DEF 3 | GHI 4 | PRS 7 | GHI 4 |

| GHI 4 | MNO 6 | ABC 2 | TUV 8 |

| JKL 5 | ABC 2 | MNO 6 | ABC 2 |

Offerings

| GHI 4 | MNO 6 | ABC 2 | TUV 8 |

| GHI 4 | PRS 7 | ABC 2 | GHI 4 | MNO 6 |

| JKL 5 | ABC 2 | MNO 6 | ABC 2 |

| MNO 6 | DEF 3 | ABC 2 | JKL 5 |

| MNO 6 | DEF 3 | ABC 2 | TUV 8 |

| MNO 6 | GHI 4 | JKL 5 |

| PRS 7 | MNO 6 | MNO 6 |

CONVERSIONS IN THE OLD TESTAMENT

| ABC 2 | ABC 2 | PRS 7 | ABC 2 | GHI 4 | ABC 2 | MNO 6 |

| ABC 2 | WXY 9 | PRS 7 | TUV 8 | PRS 7 |

| DEF 3 | ABC 2 | PRS 7 | GHI 4 | TUV 8 | PRS 7 |

| DEF 3 | ABC 2 | TUV 8 | GHI 4 | DEF 3 |

| JKL 5 | ABC 2 | ABC 2 | MNO 6 | ABC 2 |

| PRS 7 | TUV 8 | TUV 8 | GHI 4 |

| PRS 7 | ABC 2 | MNO 6 | TUV 8 | DEF 3 | JKL 5 |

City Walls

ABC 2	DEF 3	TUV 8	GHI 4	PRS 7	GHI 4	ABC 2	MNO 6
DEF 3	ABC 2	MNO 6	ABC 2	PRS 7	ABC 2	TUV 8	PRS 7
JKL 5	DEF 3	PRS 7	GHI 4	ABC 2	GHI 4	MNO 6	
JKL 5	DEF 3	PRS 7	TUV 8	PRS 7	ABC 2	JKL 5	DEF 3	MNO 6
MNO 6	MNO 6	ABC 2	ABC 2				
PRS 7	ABC 2	ABC 2	ABC 2	ABC 2	GHI 4		
PRS 7	ABC 2	MNO 6	ABC 2	PRS 7	GHI 4	ABC 2	

GOD KNOWS OUR. . .

DEF 3	DEF 3	DEF 3	DEF 3	PRS 7

DEF 3	PRS 7	ABC 2	GHI 4	JKL 5	TUV 8	GHI 4	DEF 3	PRS 7

MNO 6	DEF 3	DEF 3	DEF 3	PRS 7

PRS 7	MNO 6	PRS 7	PRS 7	MNO 6	WXY 9	PRS 7

TUV 8	GHI 4	MNO 6	TUV 8	GHI 4	GHI 4	TUV 8	PRS 7

WXY 9	MNO 6	PRS 7	DEF 3	PRS 7

PRIESTS

ABC 2	ABC 2	PRS 7	MNO 6	MNO 6

ABC 2	MNO 6	ABC 2	MNO 6	GHI 4	ABC 2	PRS 7

ABC 2	MNO 6	MNO 6	ABC 2	PRS 7

DEF 3	JKL 5	GHI 4

DEF 3	QZ 0	PRS 7	ABC 2

JKL 5	MNO 6	PRS 7	GHI 4	TUV 8	ABC 2

QZ 0	ABC 2	ABC 2	GHI 4	ABC 2	PRS 7	GHI 4	ABC 2	PRS 7

JUDGES

| ABC 2 | ABC 2 | DEF 3 | MNO 6 | MNO 6 |

| DEF 3 | DEF 3 | ABC 2 | MNO 6 | PRS 7 | ABC 2 | GHI 4 |

| DEF 3 | GHI 4 | TUV 8 | DEF 3 |

| GHI 4 | GHI 4 | DEF 3 | DEF 3 | MNO 6 | MNO 6 |

| JKL 5 | ABC 2 | GHI 4 | PRS 7 |

| MNO 6 | TUV 8 | GHI 4 | MNO 6 | GHI 4 | DEF 3 | JKL 5 |

| TUV 8 | MNO 6 | JKL 5 | ABC 2 |

DEACONS

| MNO 6 | GHI 4 | ABC 2 | ABC 2 | MNO 6 | MNO 6 | PRS 7 |

| MNO 6 | GHI 4 | ABC 2 | MNO 6 | JKL 5 | ABC 2 | PRS 7 |

| PRS 7 | ABC 2 | PRS 7 | MNO 6 | DEF 3 | MNO 6 | ABC 2 | PRS 7 |

| PRS 7 | GHI 4 | GHI 4 | JKL 5 | GHI 4 | PRS 7 |

| PRS 7 | PRS 7 | MNO 6 | ABC 2 | GHI 4 | MNO 6 | PRS 7 | TUV 8 | PRS 7 |

| PRS 7 | TUV 8 | DEF 3 | PRS 7 | GHI 4 | DEF 3 | MNO 6 |

| TUV 8 | GHI 4 | MNO 6 | MNO 6 | MNO 6 |

AUTHORS

| DEF 3 | ABC 2 | TUV 8 | GHI 4 | DEF 3 |

| JKL 5 | MNO 6 | GHI 4 | MNO 6 |

| JKL 5 | MNO 6 | PRS 7 | GHI 4 | TUV 8 | ABC 2 |

| JKL 5 | TUV 8 | JKL 5 | DEF 3 |

| MNO 6 | ABC 2 | TUV 8 | TUV 8 | GHI 4 | DEF 3 | WXY 9 |

| PRS 7 | ABC 2 | MNO 6 | TUV 8 | DEF 3 | JKL 5 |

| PRS 7 | MNO 6 | JKL 5 | MNO 6 | MNO 6 | MNO 6 | MNO 6 |

BOOKS OF THE OLD TESTAMENT

DEF 3	ABC 2	MNO 6	GHI 4	DEF 3	JKL 5

DEF 3	PRS 7	TUV 8	GHI 4	DEF 3	PRS 7

GHI 4	DEF 3	MNO 6	DEF 3	PRS 7	GHI 4	PRS 7

JKL 5	DEF 3	PRS 7	DEF 3	MNO 6	GHI 4	ABC 2	GHI 4

MNO 6	TUV 8	MNO 6	ABC 2	DEF 3	PRS 7	PRS 7

PRS 7	PRS 7	MNO 6	TUV 8	DEF 3	PRS 7	ABC 2	PRS 7

PRS 7	PRS 7	ABC 2	JKL 5	MNO 6	PRS 7

FOODS IN THE NEW TESTAMENT

ABC 2	MNO 6	GHI 4	PRS 7	DEF 3

TUV 8	DEF 3	ABC 2	JKL 5

DEF 3	GHI 4	PRS 7	GHI 4

MNO 6	GHI 4	MNO 6	TUV 8

MNO 6	TUV 8	PRS 7	TUV 8	ABC 2	PRS 7	DEF 3

MOUNTAINS

| ABC 2 | PRS 7 | ABC 2 | PRS 7 | ABC 2 | TUV 8 |

| ABC 2 | ABC 2 | PRS 7 | MNO 6 | DEF 3 | JKL 5 |

| GHI 4 | MNO 6 | PRS 7 |

| GHI 4 | MNO 6 | PRS 7 | DEF 3 | ABC 2 |

| MNO 6 | MNO 6 | PRS 7 | GHI 4 | ABC 2 | GHI 4 |

| MNO 6 | JKL 5 | GHI 4 | TUV 8 | DEF 3 |

| PRS 7 | GHI 4 | MNO 6 | ABC 2 | GHI 4 |

PEOPLE IN THE OLD TESTAMENT

ABC 2	ABC 2	PRS 7	MNO 6	MNO 6	

DEF 3	ABC 2	TUV 8	GHI 4	DEF 3	

DEF 3	JKL 5	GHI 4	JKL 5	ABC 2	GHI 4

DEF 3	JKL 5	GHI 4	PRS 7	GHI 4	ABC 2

JKL 5	ABC 2	ABC 2	MNO 6	ABC 2	

MNO 6	MNO 6	PRS 7	DEF 3	PRS 7	

PRS 7	MNO 6	JKL 5	MNO 6	MNO 6	MNO 6	MNO 6

Heaven Is a Place of. . .

| ABC 2 | MNO 6 | GHI 4 | DEF 3 | JKL 5 | PRS 7 |

| ABC 2 | DEF 3 | ABC 2 | TUV 8 | TUV 8 | WXY 9 |

| DEF 3 | TUV 8 | DEF 3 | PRS 7 | MNO 6 | GHI 4 | TUV 8 | WXY 9 |

| GHI 4 | MNO 6 | JKL 5 | GHI 4 | MNO 6 | DEF 3 | PRS 7 | PRS 7 |

| JKL 5 | MNO 6 | WXY 9 |

| PRS 7 | DEF 3 | PRS 7 | DEF 3 | DEF 3 | ABC 2 | TUV 8 | GHI 4 | MNO 6 | MNO 6 |

| TUV 8 | MNO 6 | GHI 4 | TUV 8 | WXY 9 |

CURSED

ABC 2	ABC 2	GHI 4	MNO 6

ABC 2	ABC 2	MNO 6	ABC 2	ABC 2	MNO 6

GHI 4	PRS 7	MNO 6	TUV 8	MNO 6	DEF 3

JKL 5	DEF 3	GHI 4	MNO 6	GHI 4	ABC 2	ABC 2	GHI 4	GHI 4	MNO 6

MNO 6	ABC 2	TUV 8	TUV 8	PRS 7	DEF 3

PRS 7	DEF 3	PRS 7	PRS 7	DEF 3	MNO 6	TUV 8

ANAGRAM
PUZZLES

by Paul Kent

Unscramble the letters of the nonsensical message to spell the name of a Bible person, place, or thing. Each letter will be used once.

BOOKS OF THE BIBLE. . .

E v i c t   L u i s

_ _ _ _ _ _ _ _

BIBLE CITIES. . .

T h e y   b a n

_ _ _ _ _ _ _

PAUL'S MISSIONARY JOURNEYS. . .

t o   a   c h i n

_ _ _ _ _ _ _

WOMEN OF THE BIBLE. . .

Ham art

— — — — — —

PLACES. . .

Hog gloat

— — — — — — — —

RIVERS/BODIES OF WATER. . .

Pure haste

— — — — — — — — —

BOOKS OF THE BIBLE. . .

Sox due

_ _ _ _ _ _

NEW TESTAMENT PEOPLE. . .

Huey cuts

_ _ _ _ _ _ _

BAD GUYS. . .

This tin car

_ _ _ _ _ _ _ _ _

BIBLE CITIES. . .

Dooms

_ _ _ _ _

KINGS. . .

Race hen and buzz

_ _ _ _ _ _ _ _ _ _ _ _

EVENTS. . .

Star of grain unit

_ _ _ _ _ _ _ _ _ _ _ _

BOOKS OF THE BIBLE. . .

A voter line

— — — — — — — — —

WOMEN OF THE BIBLE. . .

Her beak

— — — — — — —

PLACES. . .

Doe can aim

— — — — — — — — —

BOOKS OF THE BIBLE. . .

Cats see slice

_ _ _ _ _ _ _ _ _ _

BIBLE CITIES. . .

Rule James

_ _ _ _ _ _ _ _ _

NEW TESTAMENT PEOPLE. . .

Rhine sand

_ _ _ _ _ _ _ _ _

BOOKS OF THE BIBLE. . .

She is a pen

_ _ _ _ _ _ _ _

EVENTS. . .

Sap roves

_ _ _ _ _ _ _

BOOKS OF THE BIBLE. . .

Burns me

_ _ _ _ _ _ _

BIBLE CITIES. . .

R i c h   J o e

_ _ _ _ _ _ _

BAD GUYS. . .

I n t o   a p p l e   s u i t

_ _ _ _ _ _ _   _ _ _ _ _ _

NEW TESTAMENT PEOPLE. . .

M o u s e   s i n

_ _ _ _ _ _ _

BOOKS OF THE BIBLE. . .

So scan oils

_ _ _ _ _ _ _ _ _ _

WOMEN OF THE BIBLE. . .

Hail led

_ _ _ _ _ _ _

EVENTS. . .

Puts pearls

_ _ _ _ _ _ _ _ _ _

BOOKS OF THE BIBLE. . .

A calm hi

_ _ _ _ _ _

WOMEN OF THE BIBLE. . .

Lithe base

_ _ _ _ _ _ _ _ _

KINGS. . .

Rip a gap

_ _ _ _ _ _ _

ANSWERS

DROP TWO PUZZLES

ACTS:
Smile, Cased, Match, Trace, Range, Bible, Beard, Plume, Cried, Winds, Singe, Pound, Yukon: "Behold, I see the heavens opened." Acts 7:56

ISAIAH:
Lines, Plush, Elect, Miter, Frame, Salve, Parse, Train, Elate, Cream, Clear, Fries, Surge: "Surely he hath borne our griefs." Isaiah 53:4

ZECHARIAH:
Meals, Savor, Flora, Bingo, Piece, Names, Chief, Parch, Sheer, Shoal, Cleat, Great, Speed: "I will dwell in the midst of thee." Zechariah 2:10

COLOSSIANS:
Taped, Stair, Stiff, Goner, Month, Place, Acted, Dread, Blade, Glade, Tents: "And he is before all things." Colossians 1:17

I PETER:
Heats, Plaid, Toned, Paper, Taper, Tampa, After, Spied, Sheet, Pairs, Lying, Ports: "The word of the Lord endureth." I Peter 1:25

MICAH:
Basil, Daily, Store, Peril, Dense, Spied, Ennui, Serum, Space, Stead, Bland: "What doth the LORD require?" Micah 6:8

DANIEL:
Learn, Stole, Winds, Trees, Amble, Rated, Glued, Caned, Noble, Blasé, China, Vines, Verge: "The king made Daniel a great man." Daniel 2:48

I SAMUEL:
Bahia, Oprah, Tills, Grand, Guest, Lemon, Their, Riles, Curds, Piece, Dealt, Drawn, Strap: "The LORD hath set a king over you." I Samuel 12:13

2 CHRONICLES:
Moose, Scope, Prate, Shire, Flute, Court, Inure, Start, Ceded, Chair, Plies, Claim: "Who can judge this thy people?" 2 Chronicles 1:10

NEHEMIAH:
Weird, Grits, Ravel, Rival, Shame, Riled, Miser, Daily, Eight, Dense, Dries, Clank, Sleds: "Why is the house of God forsaken?" Nehemiah 13:11

PHILEMON:
Trine, Dirts, Stray, Loath, Chain, Mired, Leash, Bikes, Malts, Eager, Legit: "Have joy of thee in the Lord." Philemon 20

DEUTERONOMY:
Files, Tunic, Prate, Fable, Earth, Cowed, Tiles, Slain, Evens, Baste, Black, Paper, Leaps: "Thou shalt love the LORD thy God." Deuteronomy 6:5

2 CORINTHIANS:
Decal, Frail, Clear, Prime, Greed, Hated, Stead, Corps, Flute, Homer, Count, Grain, Grail: "My grace is sufficient for thee." 2 Corinthians 12:9

PHILIPPIANS:
>Lanai, Tripe, Green, Teach, Trips, Share, Train, Snood, Flair, Aging, Alarm, Float, Cribs: "A name which is above every name." Philippians 2:9

2 THESSALONIANS:
>Lured, Eaten, Drags, Posed, Lends, Eased, Begin, Flake, Poise, Rites, Bring, Drive, Flare: "Therefore, brethren, stand fast." 2 Thessalonians 2:15

PROVERBS:
>Fairs, Train, Roper, Curse, Means, Realm, Drain, Doing, Coral, Agree, Fared: "Go to the ant, thou sluggard." Proverbs 6:6

ECCLESIASTES:
>Close, Plain, Laced, Lover, Cling, Steed, Slant, Least, Rosin, Regal, Glide, Shunt, Stain: "To everything there is a season." Ecclesiastes 3:1

PSALMS:
>Feint, Stone, Stile, Shred, Sting, Final, Creed, Latin, Chase, Grief, Blurt, Scone, Scare: "Thou anointest my head with oil." Psalm 23:5

EPHESIANS:
>Chair, Named, Trams, Blade, Learn, Agent, Trick, Waver, Paris, Verso, Barge, Plane, Reeds: "There is one body, and one Spirit." Ephesians 4:4

JAMES:
>Hotly, Crate, Canes, Aural, Doing, Stark, Spice, Ratio, Boles, Stain, Pride, Capes: "But the tongue can no man tame." James 3:8

DECODER PUZZLES

PSALM 27:14

Wait on the LORD: be of good courage, and he shall strengthen thine heart: wait, I say, on the LORD.

1 CORINTHIANS 3:16

Know ye not that ye are the temple of God, and that the Spirit of God dwelleth in you?

1 CORINTHIANS 13:11

But when I became a man, I put away childish things.

ECCLESIASTES 12:13

Let us hear the conclusion of the whole matter: Fear God, and keep his commandments: for this is the whole duty of man.

1 THESSALONIANS 5:9

For God hath not appointed us to wrath, but to obtain salvation by our Lord Jesus Christ.

1 TIMOTHY 4:12

Let no man despise thy youth; but be thou an example of the believers, in word, in conversation, in charity, in spirit, in faith, in purity.

COLOSSIANS 3:23

And whatsoever ye do, do it heartily, as to the Lord, and not unto men.

ROMANS 12:19

Dearly beloved, avenge not yourselves, but rather give place unto wrath: for it is written, Vengeance is mine; I will repay, saith the Lord.

PSALM 27:1

The LORD is my light and my salvation; whom shall I fear? the LORD is the strength of my life; of whom shall I be afraid?

ROMANS 14:8

For whether we live, we live unto the Lord; and whether we die, we die unto the Lord: whether we live therefore, or die, we are the Lord's.

EPHESIANS 4:31

Let all bitterness, and wrath, and anger, and clamour, and evil speaking, be put away from you, with all malice.

MATTHEW 7:8

For every one that asketh receiveth; and he that seeketh findeth; and to him that knocketh it shall be opened.

JAMES 1:2

My brethren, count it all joy when ye fall into divers temptations.

EPHESIANS 6:11

Put on the whole armour of God, that ye may be able to stand against the wiles of the devil.

PSALM 4:2

O ye sons of men, how long will ye turn my glory into shame? how long will ye love vanity, and seek after leasing?

1 CORINTHIANS 10:14

Wherefore, my dearly beloved, flee from idolatry.

PSALM 24:9

Lift up your heads, O ye gates; even lift them up, ye everlasting doors; and the King of glory shall come in.

1 CORINTHIANS 9:22

To the weak became I as weak, that I might gain the weak: I am made all things to all men, that I might by all means save some.

PSALM 18:3

I will call upon the LORD, who is worthy to be praised: so shall I be saved from mine enemies.

PROVERBS 27:1

Boast not thyself of to morrow; for thou knowest not what a day may bring forth.

ACROSTIC PUZZLES

ROMANS 14:19

MARK	HEAVY	TRANSCRIBE
FLAG	WOULD	PERSISTENCE

Let us therefore follow after the things which make for peace, and things wherewith one may edify another.

I CORINTHIANS 15:58

THIMBLE	ITCHY	TRANSFERRED
WORKING	OVERTIME	USELESS

Therefore, my beloved brethren, be ye stedfast, unmoveable, always abounding in the work of the Lord.

MATTHEW 6:24

COVER	SILENT	WEALTHY
HOME	PLANKTON	FONDUE

No man can serve two masters: for either he will hate the one, and love the other; or else he will hold to the one, and despise the other.

ISAIAH 1:18

CLOTHES	NICHE	SPICY
WHEREABOUTS	SMORGASBORD	STORY

Come now, and let us reason together, saith the LORD: though your sins be as scarlet, they shall be as white as snow.

PSALM 1:3

CAPTIVATED	FOGGY	OPTIMISTIC
HOMEWORK	CRYSTAL	BUNNY

And he shall be like a tree planted by the rivers of water, that bringeth forth his fruit in his season.

I CORINTHIANS 14:10

SLEEVES	FAMILY	THICK
MAYBE	WRONGED	UNIFIED

There are, it may be, so many kinds of voices in the world, and none of them is without signification.

I CORINTHIANS 6:20

FLAME	WISCONSIN	CARICATURE
YOUNG	BIOGRAPHY	DIET

For ye are bought with a price: therefore glorify God in your body, and in your spirit, which are God's.

I CORINTHIANS 3:17

FLIGHT	PREVIEW	SCRUTINY
DAYTIME	PSEUDONYM	ROOSTER

If any man defile the temple of God, him shall God destroy; for the temple of God is holy, which temple ye are.

PHILIPPIANS 2:14

DURATION	LAWLESS	CONFIRM
GARBAGE	EXAMPLE	HARMONY

Do all things without murmurings and disputings.

PSALM 23:6

CLAUSTROPHOBIA	MAY	REVIEW
DEFECTIVE	GLUTTON	UPSTAIRS

Surely goodness and mercy shall follow me all the days of my life: and I will dwell in the house of the LORD for ever.

PROVERBS 22:1

MUDDY	FATHER	NAUGHTY
CLOVER	GHOST	BENEFICIARY

A good name is rather to be chosen than great riches, and loving favour rather than silver and gold.

PROVERBS 17:28

| CAMOUFLAGE | FIVE | ADORATION |
| WINTER | HAPPY | LISTLESS |

Even a fool, when he holdeth his peace, is counted wise, and he that shutteth his lips is esteemed a man of understanding.

PSALM 1:2

| BEAUTIFY | WATERLOGGED | CENTENNIAL |
| MEND | UNDERTAKER | HESITANT |

But his delight is in the law of the LORD, and in his law doth he meditate day and night.

MATTHEW 6:6

| BEWILDERED | TOOTHPASTE | FLASH |
| HINDRANCE | PUTTY | SPIRIT |

But thou, when thou prayest, enter into thy closet, and when thou hast shut thy door, pray to thy Father which is in secret.

PROVERBS 25:11

| FRIEND | UT | SWAMP |
| IMAGINARY | BUCKLE | GLOVER |

A word fitly spoken is like apples of gold in pictures of silver.

PSALM 12:6

| PARTICIPATE | FLAWLESS | AUTHENTIC |
| ADVENTURE | MUTTER | ONWARD |

The words of the LORD are pure words: as silver tried in a furnace of earth, purified seven times.

COLOSSIANS 3:16

| POLITICIAN | RHYME | TURN |
| SWIRL | DOGGIE BAG | FORGET |

Let the word of Christ dwell in you richly in all wisdom; teaching and admonishing one another in psalms and hymns and spiritual songs.

PSALM 13:6

| HYDE | BUFFALO | ANCIENT |
| WRESTLE | MUGGY | HERBAL |

I will sing unto the LORD, because he hath dealt bountifully with me.

PSALM 8:1

| EXPENSIVE | BYSTANDER | AUTOGRAPH |
| LOGICAL | WHINE | EMBRACE |

O LORD our Lord, how excellent is thy name in all the earth! who hast set thy glory above the heavens.

PROVERBS 16:32

| PICKY | BUMP | CHAUFFEUR |
| SWALLOWED | GARGLE | NUTRITIOUS |

He that is slow to anger is better than the mighty; and he that ruleth his spirit than he that taketh a city.

Word Search Puzzles

Monument to a River Crossing:
BARE (9,11) CHILDREN (1,9) CLEAN (7,4) COVENANT (2,3) FIRM (4,8) FOREVER (2,8) GROUND (7,2) ISRAEL (11,3) JORDAN (13,8) LORD (4,7) MEMORIAL (8,10) MIDST (1,1) NUMBER (11,4) OVER (7,5) PASSED (14,5) PEOPLE (1,7) PRIESTS (14,5) STONES (8,11) STOOD (6,1) TOOK (9,9) TRIBES (9,9) TWELVE (5,1)

Hidden Phrase:
Waters of Jordan were cut off before the ark of the covenant (Joshua 4:7).

Defeat and Victory at Ai
ACCURSED (1,8) ACHAN (17,10) AGAINST (17,4) AMBUSH (17,10) ANGER (3,5) ANSWERED (4,1) BEATEN (4,8) CHASED (4,4) CITY (13,14) COMMITTED (16,9) ENTERED (8,5) FIRE (12,9) FIVE (5,12) FLED (1,2) GARMENT (1,9) GOLD (1,9) HEARTS (6,7) INDEED (4,12) ISRAEL (7,6) JOSHUA (9,14) KINDLED (11,11) KING (17,5) LORD (10,10) MELTED (4,14) PEOPLE (8,2) SHEKELS (10,5) SILVER (6,5) SINNED (12,4) SMOTE (5,14) SPOILS (16,13) STONED (14,12) THOUSAND (17,6) TOOK (14,5) TRESPASS (10,3) VALLEY (1,13) WATER (5,1) WEDGE (13,7) WILDERNESS (5,1)

Hidden Phrase:
The Lord said unto Joshua, Fear not, neither be thou dismayed (Joshua 8:1).

Land for Joshua and Caleb
ALIVE (8,3) BLESSED (11,3) BUILT (5,11) CALEB (13,12) CANAAN (6,12) CITIES (6,6) CITY (5,4) DIVIDING (1,5) DWELT (13,6) EPHRAIM (1,10) FEET (14,2) GAVE (2,13) HALF (14,5) HEADS (3,8) HEBRON (9,6) INHERITED (1,13) ISRAEL (10,8) JORDAN (8,2) JOSHUA (6,9) KEPT (4,2) LAND (11,13) LEVITES (11,13) LORD (4,6) MOSES (12,8) MOUNT (3,6) NINE (11,11) NOTHING (2,5) OTHER (7,6) SAVE (4,13) SIDE (14,8) STRONG (13,4) SWARE (4,13) THEREIN (13,10) TRIBES (1,1) TRODDEN (11,5)

Hidden Phrase:
For they have wholly followed the LORD (Numbers 32:12).

Gideon's Special Army
BLEW (6,10) BOWED (11,6) BRAKE (13,3) CAMP (11,4) COMPANIES (5,13) CRIED (5,9) DELIVER (2,13) DEPART (1,9) DIVIDED (17,12) FEARFUL (4,13) FELLOW (4,13) GIDEON (11,13) HAND (10,12) HOST (8,7) HUNDRED (17,6) LAPPED (2,2) MANY (17,10) MIDIANITES (14,10) MOUTH (13,2) OUTSIDE (10,2) PEOPLE (3,4) PITCHED (17,2) PITCHERS (12,7) PUTTING (12,9) REMAINED (6,6) REST (5,5) SAVE (15,11) SWORD (12,2) THEIR (10,13) THEMSELVES (1,1) THOUSAND (9,6) THREE (16,5) TRUMPETS (1,1) VAULT (6,13) WHOSOEVER (17,11)

Hidden Phrase:
By the three hundred men that lapped will I save you (Judges 7:7).

A Strong Man
ALTAR (11,8) ANGEL (14,12) APPEARED (9,14) BARREN (12,6) BEGAN (11,1) BEWARE (4,6) BLESSED (13,9) CALLED (6,10) CAMP (7,13) CHILD (10,10) CONCEIVE (7,13) DRINK (7,2) ENTREATED (10,11) FLAME (2,3) GREW (5,2) HEAD (2,14) HEARKENED (3,4) HEAVEN (7,14) LORD (1,7) MEAT (2,1) NAME (12,1) NAZARITE (15,2) OFFERING (1,5) PLEASED (14,4) RAZOR (15,12) SAMSON (1,1) SECRET (13,1) SHALL (9,13) SPIRIT (9,6) STRONG (9,12) TEACH (1,11) TIMES (7,1) TOWARD (8,8)

Hidden Phrase:
No razor shall come on his head: for the child shall be a Nazarite (Judges 13:5).

Samson and the Lion
BEES (1,3) CAME (1,10) CARCASE (6,9) COMPANION (4,9) EATER (5,11) FEAST (7,7) HAND (13,7) HONEY (13,7) LINE (1,13) LION (7,11) MEAT (2,9) MIGHTILY (12,8) NOTHING (12,1) PLEASED (9,2) RENT (10,7) RIDDLE (3,10) ROARED (5,7) SAMSON (12,10) SPIRIT (12,7) STRONG (9,8) SWARM (8,10) SWEETNESS (4,4) TALKED (1,11) VINEYARDS (3,1) WOMAN (13,12) YOUNG (2,5)

Hidden Phrase:
Samson said unto them, I will now put forth a riddle unto you (Judges 14:12).

RUTH AND BOAZ

AFTER (1,11) ANSWERED (8,1) BLESS (7,5) BOAZ (6,11) DAMSEL (1,8) FAMILY (12,4) FAVOUR (12,4)
FIELD (11,7) FIND (9,2) FRIENDLY (1,2) GLEANED (1,9) HANDMAID (3,10) HUSBANDS (10,8)
KINSMAN (11,6) LORD (10,12) MIGHTY (7,6) MOABITESS (10,1) NAME (12,2) NAOMI (11,11)
REAPERS (2,8) RUTH (9,10) SHEAVES (4,6) SPOKEN (4,12) WEALTH (8,8)

HIDDEN PHRASE:
Boaz took Ruth, and she was his wife (Ruth 4:13).

WHERE WERE YOU?

ANSWERED (4,12) BIND (5,14) CAUSE (1,13) CLOUDS (6,10) DECLARE (12,7) DEMAND (5,4)
EARTH (9,6) FOOD (2,2) FOUNDATIONS (1,4) LAID (4,11) LIGHTNINGS (14,10) LIONS (5,8)
LOOSE (8,5) LORD (7,10) MORNING (4,7) ORION (1,6) PLEIADES (14,13) PROVIDETH (7,2) RAIN (6,3)
RAVEN (15,9) SANG (7,14) SHOUTED (3,8) SNOW (2,8) SONS (11,4) STARS (14,11) THOU (1,8)
THUNDER (12,11) TOGETHER (15,2) TREASURES (15,6) WAST (6,1) WHERE (14,1) WHIRLWIND (2,10)
WISDOM (7,5)

HIDDEN PHRASE:
Hath the rain a father? or who hath begotten the drops of dew? (Job 38:28).

HOW EXCELLENT IS THE LORD

ABOVE (13,11) AVENGER (14,6) BABES (13,13) BEASTS (3,4) BECAUSE (1,10) CONSIDER (13,9)
CROWNED (3,7) DOMINION (6,8) EARTH (8,11) ENEMIES (9,9) EXCELLENT (1,9) FINGERS (8,1)
FOWL (8,8) GLORY (6,9) HEAVENS (7,12) HONOUR (9,2) LORD (7,9) MINDFUL (8,5) MOON (6,5)
MOUTH (13,7) NAME (11,14) ORDAINED (1,3) OVER (3,2) OXEN (14,14) SHEEP (13,10) STARS (5,10)
STRENGTH (11,11) SUCKLINGS (1,5) THINE (2,9) VISITEST (14,7) WORK (14,4)

HIDDEN PHRASE:
For thou hast made him a little lower than the angels (Psalm 8:5).

RASH WORDS

ABOMINABLE (10,12) ASIDE (6,5) CORRUPT (11,7) COUNSEL (2,11) DONE (4,2) FEAR (12,9)
FILTHY (14,1) FOOL (14,1) GENERATION (3,14) GLAD (9,5) GONE (8,8) GOOD (3,7) GREAT (11,11)
HEART (7,5) INIQUITY (8,13) KNOWLEDGE (10,14) LOOKED (15,4) NONE (3,11) PEOPLE (6,9)
POOR (15,2) REFUGE (4,6) REJOICE (13,3) RIGHTEOUS (14,6) SAID (15,8) SALVATION (10,3) SEEK (5,13)
SHAMED (4,1) THEY (15,10) TOGETHER (1,6) UNDERSTAND (1,2) WORKERS (7,14) WORKS (8,1)

HIDDEN PHRASE:
The LORD looked down from heaven upon the children of men (Psalm 14:2).

THE GLORY OF GOD

BRIDEGROOM (10,10) CHAMBER (4,8) DECLARE (13,2) EARTH (10,14) FIRMAMENT (3,1)
GLORY (10,7) GONE (10,5) HANDIWORK (5,12) HEARD (2,12) HEAVENS (12,1) KNOWLEDGE (13,12)
LANGUAGE (11,8) LINE (3,9) MAKING (12,8) NIGHT (8,3) PURE (10,2) RACE (12,3) SHEWETH (14,8)
SIMPLE (6,1) STATUTES (10,13) STRONG (8,9) SURE (12,5) TABERNACLE (5,13) TESTIMONY (9,6)
THROUGH (2,14) VOICE (1,8) WISE (1,3) WORDS (2,7) WORLD (2,4)

HIDDEN PHRASE:
The law of the LORD is perfect, converting the soul (Psalm 19:7).

A CRY OF ANGUISH

BRETHREN (1,7) CONGREGATION (2,12) DAYTIME (8,7) DECLARE (9,2) DELIVER (12,11) DESPISED (8,13)
DRIED (11,4) FATHERS (7,8) FORSAKEN (3,14) GLORY (6,10) HASTE (11,14) HELPING (7,1) HOLY (15,14)
LAUGH (13,14) LORD (11,2) MIDST (4,2) NAME (10,7) NIGHT (10,1) PRAISE (5,8) REMEMBER (13,5)
ROARING (13,2) SCORN (6,13) SEASON (13,9) SILENT (15,9) STRENGTH (4,14) SWORD (1,2) THEM (5,6)
TRUSTED (2,4) WORDS (3,6) WORLD (15,7) WORM (5,3) WORSHIP (15,7)

HIDDEN PHRASE:
They part my garments among them, and cast lots upon my vesture (Psalm 22:18).

THE GOOD SHEPHERD

BESIDE (15,13) COMFORT (11,2) DEATH (2,10) DOWN (2,10) DWELL (6,5) ENEMIES (14,7) EVIL (2,4)
FEAR (14,5) FOREVER (3,6) GREEN (8,14) HOUSE (2,6) LEADETH (4,7) LORD (5,10) MAKETH (15,5)
NAME (1,6) PASTURES (10,12) PATHS (10,5) PRESENCE (8,8) RESTORETH (6,2) RIGHTEOUSNESS (13,1)

SAKE (8,13) SHADOW (14,9) SHALL (9,4) SHEPHERD (3,14) SOUL (15,14) STAFF (14,1) STILL (11,8)
SURELY (10,3) TABLE (15,6) VALLEY (3,10) WALK (10,14) WANT (1,4) WATERS (9,1)

Hidden Phrase:
Surely goodness and mercy shall follow me all the days of my life (Psalm 23:6).

A Prayer for Protection
ACCORDING (1,1) ASHAMED (14,7) CAUSE (2,2) ENEMIES (9,12) GOODNESS (5,13) KINDNESSES (3,1)
LEAD (11,3) LIFT (4,5) LORD (14,10) LOVING (3,9) MERCIES (4,13) MINE (9,4) NONE (5,3) PATHS (9,5)
REMEMBER (12,1) SAKE (12,10) SALVATION (11,13) SHEW (13,13) SINS (10,5) SOUL (14,2) TEACH (9,8)
TENDER (9,6) THEE (14,12) TRANSGRESS (5,11) TRIUMPH (13,1) TRUST (5,6) TRUTH (6,11) WAIT (2,11)
WAYS (13,4) WITHOUT (3,2) YOUTH (1,5)

Hidden Phrase:
Let me not be ashamed; for I put my trust in thee (Psalm 25:20).

Wicked and Upright
AGAINST (1,11) BECAUSE (11,1) BRING (8,14) COMMIT (13,14) DELIGHT (3,2) DESIRES (1,9)
DWELL (7,8) EARTH (10,12) ENVIOUS (2,9) EVILDOERS (14,9) FRET (13,12) GIVE (2,11) GOOD (12,14)
HEART (10,6) INHERIT (14,6) INIQUITY (7,12) JUDGMENT (14,4) LAND (6,5) LORD (13,13) MEEK (7,6)
NEITHER (8,10) NOONDAY (7,4) PEACE (7,5) RIGHTEOUSNESS (13,3) SHALL (5,9) THEE (3,14)
THEMSELVES (1,1) THINE (9,5) THYSELF (13,7) TRUST (8,9) WAIT (12,5) WORKERS (5,2)

Hidden Phrase:
The steps of a good man are ordered by the LORD (Psalm 37:23).

Rejoice!
CARRIED (10,1) CITY (10,1) EARTH (8,1) FEAR (5,11) GLAD (10,11) HELP (4,4) HIGH (2,11) HOLY (13,4)
HOSTS (9,1) LORD (10,9) MELTED (7,12) MIDST (9,4) MOUNTAINS (3,11) PRESENT (9,10) REFUGE (11,7)
REMOVED (3,13) RIVER (1,11) ROAR (11,7) SHAKE (4,1) STRENGTH (6,6) SWELLING (11,13)
TABERNACLES (1,3) THEREFORE (1,3) THEREOF (1,3) THOUGH (13,8) TROUBLE (12,12) UTTERED (12,3)
VERY (2,1) VOICE (8,2) WATERS (6,12)

Hidden Phrase:
Come, behold the works of the LORD (Psalm 46:8).

Dwell in God's House
AMIABLE (7,2) ANOINTED (5,13) BLESSED (16,9) COURTS (15,3) CRIETH (6,6) DOORKEEPER (16,3)
DWELL (15,2) FACE (2,9) FLESH (1,9) FOUND (8,6) HEART (11,1) HERSELF (13,8) HOSTS (7,10)
HOUSE (15,11) LIVING (13,3) LONGETH (13,3) LORD (2,8) NEST (13,11) PRAISING (3,13) RATHER (6,5)
SHIELD (1,4) SOUL (12,11) SPARROW (7,9) STRENGTH (4,4) SWALLOW (3,1) TABERNACLES (11,12)
TENTS (1,8) THEY (3,11) UPRIGHTLY (10,11) WALK (9,4) WICKEDNESS (4,1) YOUNG (14,11)

Hidden Phrase:
I had rather be a doorkeeper in the house of my God (Psalm 84:10).

God Will Protect His People
ABIDE (1,3) AFRAID (14,6) AGAINST (13,1) ALMIGHTY (6,3) ARROW (4,14) BEAR (12,4) BEHOLD
(12,14) COVER (4,4) DASH (7,4) DELIVER (2,14) DESTRUCTION (9,11) DWELLETH (9,11) EYES (5,8)
FOOT (14,13) FORTRESS (14,5) HANDS (7,6) HIGH (7,14) LORD (11,11) MOST (8,7) NIGHT (13,4)
NOONDAY (13,4) PESTILENCE (3,4) PLACE (1,5) REFUSE (3,8) REWARD (13,13) SECRET (6,11)
SHADOW (6,14) SHIELD (6,14) SNARE (5,1) STONE (11,2) TERROR (4,2) TRUST (1,10) WICKED (2,9)

Hidden Phrase:
For he shall give his angels charge over thee (Psalm 91:11).

God the Creator
ABOVE (14,5) BEFORE (5,10) COME (13,2) DEEP (13,9) EARTH (3,4) GENERATION (2,2) GREAT (8,7)
GRIEVED (2,12) HANDS (10,8) HEAR (13,11) HILLS (1,9) JOYFUL (9,10) KING (5,11) KNEEL (12,5)
LORD (4,8) MAKE (10,13) NOISE (14,1) PASTURE (10,3) PEOPLE (10,6) PLACES (9,1) PRESENCE (3,14)
PROVED (6,5) PSALMS (14,7) ROCK (12,2) SALVATION (12,14) SHEEP (2,1) SING (2,1) STRENGTH (8,2)
TEMPTED (2,4) THANKSGIVING (1,11) VOICE (9,11) WORSHIP (9,14)

Hidden Phrase:
The sea is his, and he made it: and his hands formed the dry land (Psalm 95:5).

The Goodness of God

ANGELS (9,10) BEAST (2,8) BLESS (12,9) CHARIOT (3,8) CLOTHED (14,1) CLOUDS (3,6) CURTAIN (9,8) DOWN (2,12) DRINK (11,5) EARTH (6,9) FIELD (12,13) FIRE (12,2) FLAMING (15,7) FOUNDATIONS (8,11) FOUNDED (2,1) FRUIT (15,4) GARMENT (7,5) GIVE (7,13) GREAT (5,1) HEAVENS (16,6) HONOUR (11,13) LIGHT (9,13) LORD (9,12) MAJESTY (1,1) MOUNTAINS (1,1) SATISFIED (14,10) SOUL (15,2) SPIRITS (3,10) THUNDER (16,7) VALLEYS (10,11) VOICE (2,13) WATERS (1,13) WIND (4,6) WINGS (13,5) WORK (14,2)

HIDDEN PHRASE:
He causeth the grass to grow for the cattle (Psalm 104:14).

Joy in Zion's Return

AGAIN (11,7) AMONG (13,1) BEARING (15,4) BRINGING (16,4) CAPTIVITY (1,9) COME (3,7) DOUBTLESS (3,6) DREAM (5,3) FILLED (3,2) FORTH (16,7) GLAD (16,12) GREAT (9,11) HEATHEN (2,11) LAUGHTER (15,12) LIKE (5,1) LORD (13,5) MOUTH (15,8) PRECIOUS (7,8) REAP (12,4) REJOICING (1,3) SAID (4,4) SEED (1,1) SHEAVES (7,10) SINGING (9,12) SOUTH (9,12) STREAMS (1,1) THEM (12,7) THEY (2,8) THINGS (13,6) TONGUE (1,2) TURNED (16,10) WEEPETH (7,1) WHEN (1,11) ZION (10,8)

HIDDEN PHRASE:
They that sow in tears shall reap in joy (Psalm 126:5).

The Road to Wisdom

ABOUT (12,4) ACKNOWLEDGE (1,11) BIND (11,5) COMMANDMENTS (1,10) DAYS (3,8) DEPART (9,1) EVIL (11,7) FAVOUR (14,7) FIND (13,10) FORGET (6,6) HEART (11,11) KEEP (5,7) LENGTH (11,6) LIFE (6,7) LONG (2,11) MERCY (10,4) NECK (2,9) PATHS (7,1) PEACE (4,7) TABLE (14,9) THEM (2,3) TRUST (9,5) TRUTH (2,3) UNDERSTANDING (13,2) UPON (8,1) WRITE (6,9)

HIDDEN PHRASE:
The LORD by wisdom hath founded the earth (Proverbs 3:19).

Wisdom and Folly

BLESSINGS (9,2) COMMANDMENTS (12,1) DEATH (14,2) DELIVERETH (6,1) DILIGENT (14,2) FALL (12,6) FAMISH (11,14) FATHER (13,7) FOOLISH (4,11) FROM (9,14) GLAD (10,11) HAND (3,10) HEAD (14,14) HEAVINESS (13,12) JUST (15,11) LORD (5,9) MAKETH (8,5) MOTHER (3,2) NOTHING (2,3) POOR (4,14) PROFIT (4,14) PROVERBS (1,8) RECEIVE (5,8) RICH (9,10) RIGHTEOUSNESS (13,13) SLACK (5,7) SOLOMON (10,3) SOUL (1,10) SUFFER (10,3) TREASURES (7,13) WICKEDNESS (4,12) WILL (1,13) WISE (15,6)

HIDDEN PHRASE:
The years of the wicked shall be shortened (Proverbs 10:27).

Rich and Poor

BELIEVETH (9,13) BUILDETH (3,5) CROWNED (11,6) DEATH (14,1) DESPISETH (2,14) DOWN (13,7) EVERY (11,2) FALSE (7,14) FLOURISH (1,12) FOOLISH (7,14) GOING (10,9) HOUSE (6,1) KNOWLEDGE (7,1) LORD (11,14) OVERTHROWN (5,1) PERVERSE (8,3) PLUCKETH (15,4) PRIDE (14,12) PRUDENT (9,4) SEEMETH (4,6) SIMPLE (2,13) TABERNACLE (15,3) THEREOF (2,7) UPRIGHT (10,13) WAYS (10,4) WELL (1,4) WICKED (13,4) WISE (11,9) WITNESS (1,13) WOMAN (11,13) WORD (11,1)

HIDDEN PHRASE:
Give to the poor, and thou shalt have treasure in heaven (Mark 10:21).

Proper Training

BORROWER (1,1) CHOSEN (7,5) EVIL (6,10) FAVOUR (5,2) FORESEETH (13,1) GOLD (13,12) GOOD (2,4) GREAT (5,12) HONOUR (8,2) HUMILITY (5,9) INIQUITY (10,13) LENDER (11,8) LIFE (7,4) LION (11,11) LORD (14,2) LOVING (11,12) MAKER (3,9) NAME (6,4) PRUDENT (4,13) PUNISHED (5,10) RATHER (7,6) REAP (12,7) RICHES (9,13) SERVANT (14,6) SILVER (7,1) SIMPLE (5,13) SLAIN (13,6) SLOTHFUL (14,6) SNARES (7,1) STREETS (14,4) THEM (9,4) THORNS (2,11) VANITY (9,8)

HIDDEN PHRASE:
Train up a child in the way he should go (Proverbs 22:6).

Proper Conduct

APPETITE (1,3) CAUSE (13,10) CHILD (14,6) CONSIDER (2,9) CORRECTION (13,1) DAINTIES (8,1)
DECEITFUL (6,4) DELIVER (13,8) DESIROUS (10,9) DESPISE (1,6) DILIGENTLY (14,10) EARS (1,12)
FOOL (12,5) FROM (9,10) GIVEN (10,6) GUIDE (4,1) HEART (7,6) KNIFE (14,1) LANDMARK (14,12)
MEAT (10,10) MIGHTY (2,11) PLEAD (12,1) REDEEMER (13,2) RULER (14,11) SOUL (3,2) SPEAK (2,2)
THROAT (5,12) WHEN (2,4) WISDOM (1,5)

Hidden Phrase:
Buy the truth, and sell it not (Proverbs 23:23).

In Defense of Wisdom

BETTER (6,11) BIRTH (1,9) CONSIDER (6,10) COUNTENANCE (11,11) CROOKED (5,6) DEATH (1,8)
EARTH (9,12) FEASTING (5,1) FOOLS (7,4) GOOD (9,4) HEAR (2,12) HOUSE (6,5) JUST (14,13)
LAUGHTER (6,3) MAKE (6,9) MOURNING (8,10) NAME (2,4) OINTMENT (11,2) PATIENT (3,8)
PRECIOUS (14,1) PROFIT (3,13) PROUD (14,1) REBUKE (6,12) SADNESS (4,3) SINNETH (13,8)
SONG (9,14) SORROW (9,14) SPIRIT (9,7) STRAIGHT (12,13) WISDOM (6,14) WORK (4,14)

Hidden Phrase:
The patient in spirit is better than the proud in spirit (Ecclesiastes 7:8).

Advice to Youth

AWAY (8,9) BEHOLD (9,6) BREAD (11,5) BRING (10,2) CAST (6,6) CHILDHOOD (2,9) DAYS (1,5)
EVENING (1,12) EVIL (9,7) EYES (10,13) FIND (4,2) FLESH (4,2) HEART (9,13) JUDGMENT (4,3)
LIGHT (8,4) MORNING (2,12) PLEASANT (11,6) PROSPER (10,10) REMOVE (1,7) SEED (10,11) SHALL (9,1)
SIGHT (4,8) SORROW (13,6) SWEET (3,5) TRULY (12,9) UPON (2,1) VANITY (8,13) WATERS (13,11)
YOUTH (12,6)

Hidden Phrase:
Remember now thy Creator in the days of thy youth (Ecclesiastes 12:1).

Isaiah Tells about Jesus

ACQUAINTED (15,16) AFFLICTED (8,1) BEAUTY (16,8) BORNE (5,13) BROUGHT (9,13) BRUISED (15,3)
CARRIED (10,12) COMELINESS (5,16) DESIRE (1,6) DESPISED (8,2) DUMB (6,10) ESTEEMED (5,11)
GRIEF (7,5) HEALED (16,14) INIQUITIES (14,3) LAMB (5,14) MOUTH (12,11) OPENED (14,9)
OPPRESSED (16,2) PEACE (1,1) REJECTED (2,8) REVEALED (2,8) ROOT (12,16) SHEARERS (3,4)
SHEEP (15,4) SLAUGHTER (7,1) SMITTEN (15,4) SORROWS (2,15) STRICKEN (9,16) STRIPES (1,8)
SURELY (1,14) TENDER (9,7) TRANSGRESSIONS (14,1) TURNED (8,9) WOUNDED (10,15)

Hidden Phrase:
Philip. . .began at the same scripture, and preached unto him Jesus (Acts 8:35).

Sower, Seed, and Soils

ABUNDANCE (12,9) CARE (3,3) CHOKE (15,14) CLOSED (15,10) DEVOURED (16,4) DISCIPLES (8,5)
DULL (14,8) EARS (10,10) EARTH (6,5) EYES (9,14) FOWLS (16,9) FRUIT (4,6) GIVEN (7,1) GOOD (5,12)
GROUND (3,11) HEARING (12,1) HEART (2,5) HEAVEN (11,2) HUNDREDFOLD (11,6) KINGDOM (8,12)
KNOW (14,15) MYSTERIES (2,10) PARABLES (13,9) PLACES (10,3) RECEIVED (7,8) RICHES (8,13)
ROOT (1,8) SCORCHED (15,11) SEEDS (9,7) SIXTY (1,1) SOWER (2,13) SPAKE (12,13) SPRUNG (9,7)
STONY (3,8) TAKEN (16,10) THIRTY (9,10) THORNS (1,4) UNDERSTAND (3,2) WICKED (11,15)
WITHERED (1,13) WORLD (14,4)

Hidden Phrase:
Hear the word, and receive it, and bring forth fruit (Mark 4:20).

Scrambled Circle Puzzles

He really lost his head over Jesus. Who was he? — JOHN the BAPTIST
1. JESUS 2. PROPHETS 3. SHADOWS 4. SANDAL 5. BAPTIZE 6. NAPHTALI 7. PARABLE
8. SPIRIT 9. PHARISEES 10. BEATITUDES 11. SALT

This church had a golden lampstand named after it. — EPHESUS
1. PERSEVERE 2. PAGANS 3. BROTHER 4. REVELATION 5. SINS 6. FULLNESS
7. FELLOWSHIP

She may have had the same name, but she was *not* the wife of the famous singer. Who was she? — PRISCILLA
1. PEOPLE 2. GROANING 3. CONSIDER 4. SOVEREIGN 5. MERCY 6. SINFUL 6. STRUGGLE
7. CONTROL 8. PASSIONS

This prophet was the son of Berekiah. — ZECHARIAH
1. BAPTIZE 2. WONDER 3. SORCERY 4. YOUTH 5. DECLARE 6. STRICKEN 7. MULTIPLY
8. EARTH 9. HANDS

Such a wind was worth the wait. — PENTECOST
1. PEOPLE 2. GREAT 3. INCREASE 4. RESTORE 5. DEVOUR 6. OUTCAST 7. BEHOLD
8. PASS 9. SMITE

What is it that all believers will experience? — RESURRECTION
1. NEAR 2. GREEN 3. SIEGE 4. RULERS 5. GIRDLES 6. SISTER 7. DERISION 8. CONTAIN
9. SCATTER 10. PITY 11. HOUSE 12. HEATHEN

He threw a party for Jesus but was not prepared for the woman with the perfume. — SIMON
1. BLESSED 2. SPIRIT 3. MOURN 4. FORBADE 5. PINNACLE

Who is like the greatest in heaven? — LITTLE CHILD
1. REVILE 2. GALILEE 3. TEMPLE 4. COUNTRY 5. ANGEL 6. HEARD 7. REJOICE 8. HEROD
9. PRISON 10. PEARL 11. BLADE

Many feet meant a dramatic change for this place. — JERICHO
1. JESUS 2. DAMSEL 3. DEPART 4. TIME 5. RECEIVE 6. HONOR 7. KINGDOM

With a little oil, he made David king. Who was he? — SAMUEL
1. SHEEP 2. DANCING 3. WOMEN 4. CONTINUED 5. CAPTURE 6. PHILISTINE

This town was home to a widow and her son who were very glad to have Elijah stay with them. — ZAREPHATH
1. ZIDON 2. BATTLE 3. RISING 4. TRIBES 5. PLAINS 6. STRENGTH 7. CHARIOTS 8. TOWARD
9. DEATH

Wheels and scrolls—a vision for this prophet. Who was he? — EZEKIEL
1. ABOVE 2. ZACCUR 3. JUDGMENT 4. WORKMAN 5. WILLING 6. SERVICE 7. BOWLS

In the old days, a little water would clean one right up! — BAPTIZE
1. JOB 2. APPOINTED 3. TROOPS 4. TERRORS 5. PILLARS 6. ZEBEDEE 7. EXALTED

In the beginning, there was nothing to separate the water, until God created it. What was it? — EXPANSE
1. CONSUME 2. EXALT 3. PLEASURE 4. SERVANT 5. ANSWER 6. WORSHIP 7. PASTURE

This righteous man had a difficult time with fear. — ABRAHAM
1. EATEN 2. BONES 3. TERRIBLE 4. HEARTH 5. RIGHTEOUS 6. ORDINANCE 7. ENEMY

This son of Nun took control of a nation. — JOSHUA
1. JEREMIAH 2. TROUBLE 3. SPEAK 4. NEITHER 5. BUILD 6. TARSHISH

This couple fell in love on a threshing floor.   RUTH and BOAZ
1. WILDERNESS 2. COUNTRY 3. WHEAT 4. WEIGHT 5. REMEMBER 6. LORD 7. BRACELET 8. ZION

He should have ducked. Who was he?   GOLIATH
1. GREAT 2. HORSES 3. JEALOUS 4. MIDST 5. JERUSALEM 6. PLUMMET 7. HOSTS

Whom shall we fear when the Lord is our light and our...?   SALVATION
1. SINFUL 2. FATHER 3. ASSEMBLE 4. VISION 5. GLADNESS 6. BRETHREN 7. FAITH
8. OPENED 9. FOUND

He made the right choice and was blessed more than any other man.   SOLOMON
1. SAMARIA 2. REMOVE 3. SEPULCHRE 4. ANOINTED 5. BETHLEHEM 6. COVENANT
7. CAPTAIN

She became queen and saved Israel. Who was she?   ESTHER
1. DELIVER 2. PRESENCE 3. CERTAIN 4. HEAVEN 5. FIELDS 6. PRAISE

This book of the Bible is good for learning.   ECCLESIASTES
1. LAMENT 2. SERVICE 3. COME 4. BEHOLD 5. TWENTY 6. FORSAKE 7. BUILD 8. DEPART 9. SOUL
10. HASTE 11. VALLEY 12. SERVANTS

He asked Jesus if He was the King of the Jews.   PILATE
1. PORTER 2. WITNESS 3. DISCIPLE 4. SAVED 5. FATHER 6. STRANGER

This will lead to an abundance of grief. What is it?   SINFUL DESIRES
1. GENTILES 2. MAGNIFY 3. REPENT 4. FAITH 5. FRUIT 6. UNBELIEF 7. SOUND 8. MOSES 9. GOSPEL
10. RICHES 11. SLUMBER 12. JEALOUSY 13. BOAST

This puffs up, but charity edifies. What is it?   KNOWLEDGE
1. THINK 2. NATIONS 3. GROW 4. SPARROWS 5. LILIES 6. RAVENS 7. DELAY 8. GRAVES
9. SCRIBES

Who were these people who were bewitched?   GALATIANS
1. GLORY 2. MANNER 3. WALK 4. ANGEL 5. PRIVATE 6. PROMISE 7. PRAYING
8. ACCOUNT 9. PLEASE

Who was Paul's own son in the faith?   TIMOTHY
1. ENTER 2. TITHES 3. INFIRMITIES 4. DOCTRINE 5. MOTHER 6. HOLY 7. FORTY

Satan comes with all power, signs, and what else?   LYING WONDERS
1. FLESH 2. LIBERTY 3. WRITTEN 4. UNDER 5. GRACE 6. BESTOWED 7. ALLEGORY
8. SINAI 9. BONDAGE 10. LEAVEN 11. CHRIST 12. SEASON

What is a laborer worthy of?   HIS REWARD
1. STRENGTH 2. DOMINION 3. SAINTS 4. BREADTH 5. POWER 6. WISHFUL 7. GATHER
8. WRATH 9. PRUDENCE

The Spirit speaks in what way regarding the latter times?   EXPRESSLY
1. CERTAIN 2. EXPRESS 3. PEOPLE 4. AROSE 5. TEACHING 6. DISEASES 7. FRIENDS
8. MULTITUDE 9. RASHLY

Jesus is considered the Apostle and what of our profession?   HIGH PRIEST
1. BRETHREN 2. LIKEWISE 3. STAGGER 4. ASHAMED 5. PATIENCE 6. ETERNAL
7. LIKENESS 8. FREED 9. JUSTIFY 10. INIQUITY

Only the Lamb is worthy to open these. What are they?   SEVEN SEALS
1. TONGUES 2. BURIED 3. LOVELY 4. EARTHLY 5. MANIFEST 6. CEPHAS 7. BORNE
8. IMAGE 9. TWINKLING 10. SUBJECT

This book is the only one of its kind in the Bible.   The <u>SONG</u> of <u>SOLOMON</u>
1. PRESERVE 2. SORROWS 3. COUNSEL 4. FORGOTTEN 5. SUFFER 6. COVETOUS
7. EXALTED 8. PROUD 9. HUMBLE 10. NATIONS 11. INHERIT

Jesus made reference to this slimy story.   <u>JONAH</u> and the <u>WHALE</u>
1. JESUS 2. SWORD 3. NETHER 4. LAMENT 5. PHARAOH 6. DWELT 7. TWELFTH
8. SLAIN 9. FALLEN 10. MULTITUDE

She was a female judge who ruled Israel.   <u>DEBORAH</u>
1. HUNDRED 2. TREES 3. CHERUBIM 4. HOUSE 5. GROUND 6. MEASURES 7. ARCHES

Missing part of his hair, he couldn't do much.   <u>SAMSON</u>
1. OFFERINGS 2. SANCTUARY 3. REMOVE 4. SPOIL 5. MONTH 6. PORTION

She had Abraham's first son. Who was she?   <u>HAGAR</u>
1. BREADTH 2. ASSEMBLY 3. STRANGERS 4. NAME 5. DRANK

It took seven years of his life for Jacob to wed this girl. Who made him wait so long?   <u>LABAN</u>
1. DANIEL 2. BRASS 3. CUBIT 4. BABYLON 5. COUNSELLOR

What plant with purple or white flowers is used for medicines?   <u>MANDRAKE</u>
1. MASTER 2. BEASTS 3. SEVEN 4. KINGDOM 5. ROOTS 6. OCCASION 7. SPEAK
8. REIGN

It means "the house of God."   <u>BETHEL</u>
1. TROUBLE 2. GREATNESS 3. PETITION 4. HEAVEN 5. TREMBLE 6. LIVES

Who sold Joseph to Potiphar in Egypt?   the <u>MIDIANITES</u>
1. INFORM 2. FINISH 3. DESTROY 4. BUILT 5. DESOLATE 6. ABOMINATION 7. MIGHTY
8. AGAINST 9. LEASE 10. VISION

It's one of the longest waterways in the world.   the <u>NILE RIVER</u>
1. WICKEDNESS 2. EPHRAIM 3. BLIND 3. CORNET 4. HARVEST 5. DESIRE 6. LOVELY
7. REAPED 8. SISTER

"I'm up to my elbows in mud and straw. What am I making?"   <u>BRICKS</u>
1. BURNED 2. UTTERLY 3. ARISE 4. CHASTISE 5. KNOWLEDGE 6. CONSUME

This was found on the ground, but it was good for eating.   <u>MANNA</u>
1. TEMPLES 2. PASTURE 3. GARMENTS 4. NORTHERN 5. VALLEY

This meal helps Jewish families remember that God saved them when they were slaves in Egypt. the <u>PASSOVER</u>
1. PRUDENT 2. ALTAR 3. GARNERS 4. DESOLATE 5. ROTTEN 6. VERILY 7. HERDS
8. WITHDRAW

This is known as a message from God.   <u>ORACLE</u>
1. BEHOLD 2. DRINK 3. FOUNTAIN 4. CLEANSE 5. DWELLING 6. GENERATION

These were made of wood, straw, or metal and were worshiped by many.   <u>PAGAN IDOLS</u>
1. PLACE 2. WANDER 3. GARDENS 4. PROCLAIM 5. VINEYARDS 6. WITHER 7. ADVERSARY
8. IVORY 9. MULTIPLY 10. HARVEST

It smells sweet, but it is not for wearing.   <u>INCENSE</u>
1. NEIGHBOR 2. INIQUITY 3. BRANCH 4. RAIMENT 5. VINE 6. SCATTER 7. CATTLE

These were made of stone, with a whole new way of living chiseled on them.   <u>TABLETS</u>
1. TENTS 2. JUDAH 3. BRING 4. PEARL 5. KINDRED 6. THIRTY 7. ASSYRIA

As Jewish people left their homes, they would touch these boxes that hung on their door frames. **MESUZAH**
1. MOURN 2. JEWEL 3. WISE 4. YOUNG 5. BAPTIZE 6. VANITY 7. HEART

She was a woman with a "worldly profession." **RAHAB**
1. GREATER 2. BLASPHEMY 3. EARTH 4. MEASURE 5. SABBATH

A pile of stones would serve as a way to remember a special event. **MEMORIAL**
1. CONSUMED 2. MOCKED 3. MOUNT 4. ALLEGORY 5. TUTORS 6. MANIFEST 7. WEARY 8. FLESH

These were the tanks of ancient armies. What were they? **CHARIOTS**
1. COVERED 2. WEALTH 3. LAWFUL 4. DISHONOR 5. EDIFY 6. DISPOSED 7. PARTAKE
8. SHAME

They didn't have plastic bottles back then, but they did carry liquid with them. What did they use? **GOAT SKINS**
1. GLORIOUS 2. POWER 3. BRAWLERS 4. FIDELITY 5. SAVIOR 6. MEEKNESS 7. DESPISE
8. CRETIANS 9. HEIRS

In the Old Testament times, some men had one or more of these. **CONCUBINE**
1. PRECIOUS 2. FOUNTAIN 3. UNRULY 4. SCRIPTURE 5. IMPUTED 6. BRIDLE 7. FRIEND
8. WANTON 9. MEMBERS

This amount came to be equated with betrayal. **THIRTY PIECES**
1. COUNTRY 2. HEAL 3. SMITE 4. MINISTER 5. NAZARETH 6. PHYSICIAN 7. PUBLICAN
8. LIKEN 9. DANCED 10. COUNSEL 11. TOUCHED 12. BAPTIST

Many who had an important job to do for the Lord received this first. What was it? **ANOINTING**
1. SAILED 2. NATURE 3. SLOTH 4. GIVEN 5. SNARE 6. CONTEMPT 7. INTREAT 8. PRINCE
9. GRASS

He led a rebellion against his father. Who was he? **ABSALOM**
1. FLAME 2. STUMBLE 3. DISTRESS 4. STAGGER 5. SWALLOW 6. CROWN 7. STORM

To the Jews, this was the most important day of the week. **SABBATH**
1. SPOKEN 2. LAUGH 3. BEHOLD 4. BEFORE 5. WASTE 6. DAUGHTER 7. CHARIOTS

CROSSWORD PUZZLES

Puzzle #218

```
A R E   C O V E R   G E M
I I M   A W A K E   R T E
R E B U K E   E F F E C T
    A N E S T   R O C
F O L D S   A R A B I A N
A R M E   I L A I   A G O
U P   R I S K I N G   A B
L A W   W H E N   A R I L
T H E R E I S   S H I N E
    A I N   T R E A D
S E N A T E   A R M I E S
E V E   T H E S E   N R A
A I D   O I L E D   G E T
```

Puzzle #222

```
L A T E   B A L M   A H A
A V E N   A B I A   L A P
W A R D   B E E N   A T E
    R E B E L   N O S E S
P R I D E   R A M
R O B   G A T E   E D E R
I S L E   G E E   R I S E
M E E T   U N D O   V E T
    A R E   A L I K E
S H A M E   C A R E S
T E L   A T A D   A I D E
A R M   D I N E   V O I D
R E S   Y E A R   E N D S
```

Puzzle #220

```
P E E P   A H A B   S E M
E L S E   H O P E   A V A
N I T R E   E A S T E R
    H I R E   W E A R Y
F E E L I N G   I N N
E A R   D E A L T   O N
A S   W O U L D   P I
R E   T O W E L   D E N
    R A N   L O T H I N E
C H I L D   W E E D
R E D E E M   L I N U S
E N E   R E A D   R O S E
W A R   S T I R   S T E W
```

Puzzle #224

```
D A N   S A N E   S T E P
A R A   A M O S   E R N E
Y E T   R E B E L L I O N
    I R O N   O V E N
S W O O N   L I V E D
T E N D   M E D E S   S E
E S S   S E A L S   M E N
P T   C E A S E   S E E D
    G I A N T   S E A M S
D U E T   A C T S
H A I L S T O N E   U E L
E L L E   O N A N   R O E
N E E D   W E N T   E N D
```

Puzzle #226

```
            A S P S
      A B I   P E A C E
    S T I R   P E R I S H
  S T A T U T E     E T A
  L A D S     E A   G N A T
          E R R   A C T S
    A S A   A R E   T E E
  W E P T   R O D
  A N I M   R R   C O O S
  R E T     I S L A N D S
  N A T H A N   A G E D
    S L I N G   Y E S
        E N D S
```

Puzzle #232

```
      D A Y S   F A D E
    M A N E H   O W E S T
  T U R T L E   R E N T A L
  A S K   L A D E   S H U A
  S H E M   L A V A   E N D
  K I N A H   D E S E R T S
        R E I   R O C
  B E N A M M I   P H A S E
  E N E   S P I N   O B E Y
  L E E S   O M E R   A R E
  L A D I E S   S A L T E D
    S E R V E   T R I E D
      D E E D   S E E D
```

Puzzle #228

```
  H A H A   J O B   E B A L
  O M A R   A D O   N I N E
  P U N I S H E D   S T A G
  E N D O R     Y O U T H S
      C O R P   H E E
  W I S H   A I J A   R H O
  A R T   D I N E D   L U D
  G U R   I N C H   D Y E D
      A W E   H U G E
  S K I R T S   E N O C H
  N O T E   P A R T I C L E
  O R E S   A G O   E T A M
  W E N T   N E T   D O D O
```

Puzzle #234

```
  D R A V E   A L I E N
  C A E S A R   S I S T E R
  O G   K I R J A T H   E H
  A G E   L I E   I D D O
  S E N D   N U T S   O L D
  T R A I N   Z E A L   E A
    N E A R   D U E T
  S O   T I E D   L A I S H
  T W O   L I E D   D E L E
  A N N A   A R A   D A R
  L E   Z E A L O U S   Y D
  E R R O R S   S C A L E S
    S A R A H   S A C A R
```

Puzzle #230

```
  A N T S   T R A P   H E M
  C O R E   O A R S   O L D
  T R E E   E G O   A L M S
    A T E   E D I F Y
  R U S H E S   I R I   B C
  I R U   R E U   A S H U R
  O G R E   A S A   H E L I
  T E E N S   A L T   A G E
  S D   T E L   L E A V E D
    P E T E R   A R E
  S T A R   P E T   O N A N
  O W L   N E B O   O L I O
  W O E   T R A P   T Y R E
```

Puzzle #236

```
  P A N   B R I M   P A N T
  E V E   E A S E   A T E R
  N A A M A N   A M I   H A
    R A M   A T E   B U D
  D O E R   L B S   H O M E
  E A R   S O S   M A Y
  N T   A L T E R E D   B E
      D R Y   N O T   B E N
  A V I M   A C T   F O L D
  B E E   A W E   H I T
  A I   T R A   L A T T E R
  S L U R   R O O T   L A Y
  E S P Y   E N D S   E R E
```

Puzzle #238

R	E	D		S	L	I	P		D	A	L	E
I	R	U		W	O	V	E		A	V	E	R
P	A	S	S	O	V	E	R		V	E	I	N
E	N	T	I	R	E			G	I	N		
		A	D	D		L	E	D	G	E	S	
S	I	G	H	S		H	O	T		E	L	I
T	O	L	A		B	A	G		S	T	O	A
O	N	O		R	I	D		A	C	H	I	M
P	A	R	T	E	D		T	W	O			
		I	R	I		H	A	R	S	H	A	
T	H	E	E		D	A	R	K	E	N	E	D
W	I	S	E		O	G	E	E		O	R	E
A	N	T	S		R	E	E	D		W	A	R

Puzzle #244

C	O	R		C	R	E	T	E		S	E	A
A	R	E		O	I	L	E	D		H	A	D
B	E	C	A	L	M		L	E	P	E	R	S
		A	R	T		H	E	R	O	N		
P	A	L	M		R	E	M		R	I	B	S
A	L	L		S	E	R		S	C	R	I	P
P	I		S	E	V	E	N	T	H		T	O
E	V	E	N	T		A	N	Y		H	E	R
R	E	N	A		E	N	E		L	E	S	T
		T	R	E	A	D		B	O	W		
C	L	I	E	N	T		U	R	G	E	N	T
O	U	R		T	E	A	S	E		R	E	I
O	D	E		E	R	R	E	D		S	E	E

Puzzle #240

P	A	S	T		B	E	L	A		B	O	W
E	S	T	H		I	G	A	L		E	R	A
S	P	R	E	A	D		C	L	O	S	E	R
		A	R	M	S			O	N	I	O	N
A	B	N	E	R		S	A	T	E	D		
M	A	D		A	H	A	B		S	E	A	S
O	R		M	I	T	E	S			B	E	
S	E	T	H		D	A	L	E		T	I	E
		H	O	S	E	N		E	T	H	A	N
S	H	O	U	T		U	S	E	R			
T	E	R	R	O	R		S	T	R	E	A	M
A	I	N		P	U	R	E		S	A	L	E
Y	R	S		S	E	E	D		E	D	E	N

Puzzle #246

C	O	W		L	A	N	D	S		J	A	H
O	W	E		A	B	O	U	T		E	L	A
M	E		S	P	I	D	E	R	S		I	I
E	D	G	E	S				A	S	T	E	R
		L	E	E	S		P	I	E	R		
T	W	O		S	H	E	E	T		U	T	E
O	A	R			A	R	A			M	A	R
I	R	I		S	L	I	C	E		P	R	E
		F	E	L	T		E	L	S	E		
M	A	Y	B	E				D	O	T	E	D
U	R		B	E	C	O	M	E	S		Y	E
S	T	Y		P	A	N	E	S		B	E	E
E	S	E		S	P	E	N	T		A	D	D

Puzzle #242

H	U	R		T	R	A	P		S	H	O	D
E	S	E		H	A	T	S		H	O	L	E
M	E	N		I	C	E		B	I	R	D	S
	E	L	S	E		G	U	R				
S	O	W	E	R		H	I	T	T	I	T	E
I	N		V	O	W	E	D		S	N	A	G
G	I	N		D	I	B	O	N		C	R	Y
H	O	O	F		D	E	M	A	S		A	P
S	N	E	A	K	E	R		T	I	G	H	T
		T	E	N		P	U	R				
U	N	I	T	Y		B	A	R		P	A	W
S	A	T	E		D	U	R	A		O	W	E
E	Y	E	D		E	Z	E	L		D	E	N

Puzzle #248

S	T	A	Y		E	L	S	E		S	O	P
E	A	S	E		A	I	A	H		E	H	I
A	M		L	O	S	T			P	E	E	P
		S	L	A	Y		P	T	A		L	E
W	A	T	E	R		T	A	I	L	S		
A	L	A	D		S	W	I	M		O	D	D
Y	A	K		T	H	I	N	E		L	A	Y
S	S	E		R	A	G	S		H	E	R	E
		S	O	U	L	S		T	A	M	E	D
E	R		N	E	T		T	O	R	N		
L	O	V	E			B	R	E	D		Y	E
A	D	O		F	R	E	E		E	D	E	N
H	E	W		M	E	D	E		R	O	A	D

Puzzle #250

```
B E D   M O O N   A B E L
E R E   E A R I N G   D O
      R E A R   G I E R   S
L A B A N   S E T   A N T
O V E R   J A R   A H A
V A   B O Y   P R A Y S
E   S E A T   A R A B   H
D E C A Y   A D O   U R
  L E T   A R D   L U K E
G I N   H I T   M U S E D
A   T A I L   O O Z E
T O   S P E A R S   S A W
E N D S   D I E T   T H E
```

Puzzle #256

```
W A S   R U T H   S T A R
I R A   A R E A   H A R E
T A L C   I M P   A L A S
S H A R P   A P P L E
    E H I   I L L   O R
T E S T I M O N Y   A V A
E L S E   P R E   A M E N
N O W   R E A S O N I N G
T I   F O R   S A G
    T O W I T   R E B E L
O M A R   O I L   L O S E
W A R D   U R I M   W A N
E Y E S   S E E R   L U D
```

Puzzle #252

```
U S E S   R O T   P O E M
N O A H   E N E   E S A U
N O S E   S E E   R E T S
I N T E N T   T R I E S T
  T I E   H A S
R A I S E T H   W H E L P
E R I   H E M   W O E
D E M A S   N E P H E W S
    S U P   N A Y
P L A C E S   T I M B E R
L A D E   A H I   N O N E
A V E N   L E O   A N O N
Y A R D   M A N   L E N D
```

Puzzle #258

```
O H H   B A R E   S P E W
N A Y   A R E A   T R A M
T I M B R E L S   A E R O
O R N A N   Y E A R S
    A S A   D E E P S
S E E R   D O D O   N O T
A B D A   E N E   A C R E
L E O   I R O N   W E E P
A R M E D   S P A
    W R O N G   O R A T E
H E I R   A N S W E R E D
I S L E   M A T E   A L E
T O L D   E W E R   M E N
```

Puzzle #254

```
L A P   S L I P   H A R P
O W E   T I R E   E L O I
P E R   A N S W E R E S T
  S O R T   M E R E
S T O N E   R E M I T
P I N E   B A S O N   H A
A D S   S E V E R   R E T
N E   Z E L E K   B E R A
  W O M A N   W A V E D
  T A P E   R A T E
R U S H I N G O F   N O R
B E T A   E A S E   G E T
I S E R   E D E R   E R E
```

Puzzle #260

```
D A R T   M A D E   L E D
A H E R   A M I D   O N O
N A M E   R A N   L A D E
    E E L   L A B A N
D A M S E L   H A D   A D
E B B   G O D   G E R A R
D O E R   P I T   N E R I
A D R I A   G O T   P O E
N E   D I D   E R R A N D
    H E R O N   I I I
S E E R   T O O   G R O W
A L L   S E N D   H E R E
D I P   O D E D   T R O T
```

Puzzle #262

L	E	H	I		V	A	L	E	
H	E	R	O	N		E	N	E	A	S
S	E	A	S	O	N		S	T	A	R	T	S
O	D	D		K	E	Y	S		D	I	E	T
A	G	E	S		R	E	E	L		N	R	A
P	E	R	I	L		S	L	I	N	G	E	R
	D	U	E		S	E	A	
D	E	S	E	R	V	E		D	A	R	T	S
U	L	E		K	I	T	E		M	U	S	E
B	E	T	H		D	A	L	E		L	A	W
S	A	T	I	R	E		E	L	D	E	R	S
	D	E	D	A	N		P	O	U	T	S
	R	E	N	T		H	I	G	H

Puzzle #268

A	P	O	O	L		S	A	L	M	A
B	A	S	K	E	T		A	T	T	A	I	N
E	R	E		P	I	B	E		D	N	A
L	E		R	E	T	I	R	E	D		E	N
	J	E	R	U	S	A	L	E	M	
A	L	A	S		S	A	M		S	O	A	R
D	A	R	T			C	U	R	E
O	R	E	O		A	U	S		E	S	A	U
	B	R	I	M	S	T	O	N	E	
A	D		E	A	R	N	E	S	T		O	H
I	I	I		M	A		A	H		A	V	A
A	N	D	I	A	M		L	E	S	S	E	R
H	E	A	R	T		A	W	A	R	E

Puzzle #264

S	I	F	T		S	O	I	L	
S	A	R	A	H		O	R	N	O	N
A	L	L	U	R	E		L	O	N	D	O	N
B	A	T		F	R	O		G	I	E
L	I	E		I	T	E	M	S		E	S	E
E	N	D	O	W		S	O	U	N	D	E	D
	L	E	S		N	I	E	
N	E	E	D	E	T	H		T	W	I	G	S
I	N	N		P	R	I	E	S		N	I	P
L	E	V		E	T	A		T	A	O
E	M	I	L	I	E		S	I	L	E	N	T
	Y	E	A	S	T		E	V	E	N	T
	S	P	A	S		D	Y	E	D

Puzzle #270

H	A	D		A	S	H	A	S		C	O	R
U	R	I		S	C	A	L	P		O	N	O
R	E	D	S	E	A		T	E	R	M	E	D
	S	T	A	B	S		A	T	E	
A	B	I	E	L		L	I	K	E	T	H	E
L	A	T	E		L	A	C	E		H	E	X
A	T		P	R	A	Y	E	R	S		R	I
R	H	O		E	B	E	D		I	D	O	L
M	E	A	N	E	S	T		B	L	A	D	E
	T	E	D		H	E	L	A	H	
E	S	H	E	A	N		W	E	S	L	E	Y
T	O	O		N	O	S	E	S		I	R	E
A	L	F		D	R	O	S	S		A	R	A

Puzzle #266

S	P	A	N		F	R	E	T		C	A	B
E	A	S	E		L	E	V	I		A	G	E
A	N	S	E		E	N	A	M		L	U	D
	E	D	R	E	I		N	A	M	E	S
T	E	N	S	E		B	A	G	
R	A	T		D	A	R	A		A	N	A	B
I	S	E	T		D	I	D		G	E	B	A
M	E	D	E		A	B	E	L		I	L	L
	A	R	M		A	N	G	E	L	
S	T	A	R	E		I	M	N	A	H	
A	H	I		N	E	R	I		O	B	E	D
F	E	D		E	R	A	N		M	O	T	E
E	Y	E		W	E	N	T		I	R	O	N

Puzzle #272

G	E	T		L	I	S		N	O	T	E
O	A	R		S	I	N	E		O	P	A	L
G	R	E	A	T	E	S	T		T	E	L	L
	A	T	A	D		T	R	A	N	C	E
A	F	T	E	R		E	L	A	S	
L	A	I	R		F	R	E	C	K	L	E	D
A	S	S		A	R	O	S	E		E	L	I
S	T	E	D	F	A	S	T		B	A	S	E
	R	A	G	E		H	E	R	E	S
I	N	F	O	R	M		M	E	A	N
S	E	E	P		E	T	E	R	N	I	T	Y
L	E	E	S		N	O	N	E		N	O	E
E	D	D	Y		T	I	E		G	O	T

Puzzle #274

R	E	A	P	A	B	O	U	T	E	D

(Puzzle #274 grid)

Row 1: R E A P — A B O U T — E D
Row 2: A — T E N D — R E I — S O
Row 3: G O — N E A R — L E S T
Row 4: E V E — W R A P — D E A D
Row 5: E N E — R A W — A T E
Row 6: I R O N — M E L E A — E A
Row 7: M — S A M E — S T I R — L
Row 8: A S — M A D L Y — J E W S
Row 9: G A D — Y E A — A B I
Row 10: E W E S — S I G N — A S K
Row 11: E N O N — D R E W — H E
Row 12: A S — M A R — E T A M — P
Row 13: I T — E N D O W — S E N T

Puzzle #276

Row 1: P I T — P O S T — A R A H
Row 2: A R E — O A T H — R I S E
Row 3: W O N D E R — I M P O S E
Row 4: S N O U T — N E A T
Row 5: N E S T S — A D E L E
Row 6: L U S T — R E A L — D E W
Row 7: O R — M E A N S — N E
Row 8: S I T — I S L E — B A T S
Row 9: S M A R T — S M E L L
Row 10: B A R E — V O I C E
Row 11: R E L I E D — J E W E L S
Row 12: A V E N — E N O N — N A P
Row 13: M E S S — R O B S — S P Y

CryptoScripture Puzzles

1. I John 3:11—For this is the message that ye heard from the beginning, that we should love one another.

2. I Thessalonians 5:18—In every thing give thanks: for this is the will of God in Christ Jesus concerning you.

3. Isaiah 44:6—Thus saith the LORD the King of Israel, and his redeemer the LORD of hosts; I am the first, and I am the last, and beside me there is no God.

4. Jeremiah 9:23:—Thus saith the LORD, Let not the wise man glory in his wisdom, neither let the mighty man glory in his might, let not the rich man glory in his riches.

5. Psalm 9:10—And they that know thy name will put their trust in thee: for thou, LORD, hast not forsaken them that seek thee.

6. I Corinthians 1:18—For the preaching of the cross is to them that perish foolishness; but unto us which are saved it is the power of God.

7. Acts 5:29—Then Peter and the other apostles answered and said, We ought to obey God rather than men.

8. Matthew 6:1—Take heed that ye do not your alms before men, to be seen of them: otherwise ye have no reward of your Father which is in heaven.

9. Deuteronomy 31:8—And the LORD, he it is that doth go before thee; he will be with thee, he will not fail thee, neither forsake thee: fear not, neither be dismayed.

10. Leviticus 20:27—A man also or woman that hath a familiar spirit, or that is a wizard, shall surely be put to death: they shall stone them with stones: their blood shall be upon them.

11. Isaiah 66:23—And it shall come to pass, that from one new moon to another, and from one sabbath to another, shall all flesh come to worship before me, saith the LORD.

12. Matthew 11:29—Take my yoke upon you, and learn of me; for I am meek and lowly in heart: and ye shall find rest unto your souls.

13. Romans 5:8—But God commendeth his love toward us, in that, while we were yet sinners, Christ died for us.

14. 2 Timothy 3:16—All scripture is given by inspiration of God, and is profitable for doctrine, for reproof, for correction, for instruction in righteousness.

15. Ecclesiastes 3:14—I know that, whatsoever God doeth, it shall be for ever: nothing can be put to it, nor any thing taken from it: and God doeth it, that men should fear before him.

16. Psalm 143:10—Teach me to do thy will; for thou art my God: thy spirit is good; lead me into the land of uprightness.

17. Revelation 21:4—And God shall wipe away all tears from their eyes; and there shall be no more death, neither sorrow, nor crying, neither shall there be any more pain: for the former things are passed away.

18. Hebrews 9:28—So Christ was once offered to bear the sins of many; and unto them that look for him shall he appear the second time without sin unto salvation.

19. Matthew 15:11—Not that which goeth into the mouth defileth a man; but that which cometh out of the mouth, this defileth a man.

20. I Samuel 2:2—There is none holy as the LORD: for there is none beside thee: neither is there any rock like our God.

21. Psalm 56:4—In God I will praise his word, in God I have put my trust; I will not fear what flesh can do unto me.

22. Proverbs 31:30—Favour is deceitful, and beauty is vain: but a woman that feareth the LORD, she shall be praised.

23. Joel 2:27—And ye shall know that I am in the midst of Israel, and that I am the LORD your God, and none else: and my people shall never be ashamed.

24. John 6:35—And Jesus said unto them, I am the bread of life: he that cometh to me shall never hunger; and he that believeth on me shall never thirst.

25. Nahum 1:7—The Lord is good, a strong hold in the day of trouble; and he knoweth them that trust in him.

26. Ephesians 4:29—Let no corrupt communication proceed out of your mouth, but that which is good to the use of edifying, that it may minister grace unto the hearers.

27. John 14:26—But the Comforter, which is the Holy Ghost, whom the Father will send in my name, he shall teach you all things, and bring all things to your remembrance, whatsoever I have said unto you.

28. Isaiah 55:9—For as the heavens are higher than the earth, so are my ways higher than your ways, and my thoughts than your thoughts.

29. Joshua 1:5—There shall not any man be able to stand before thee all the days of thy life: as I was with Moses, so I will be with thee: I will not fail thee, nor forsake thee.

30. Jeremiah 31:3—The LORD hath appeared of old unto me, saying, Yea, I have loved thee with an everlasting love: therefore with lovingkindness have I drawn thee.

31. Romans 8:30—Moreover whom he did predestinate, them he also called: and whom he called, them he also justified: and whom he justified, them he also glorified.

32. Psalm 36:7—How excellent is thy lovingkindness, O God! therefore the children of men put their trust under the shadow of thy wings.

33. Luke 12:10—And whosoever shall speak a word against the Son of man, it shall be forgiven him: but unto him that blasphemeth against the Holy Ghost it shall not be forgiven.

34. Proverbs 13:7—There is that maketh himself rich, yet hath nothing: there is that maketh himself poor, yet hath great riches.

35. John 9:31—Now we know that God heareth not sinners: but if any man be a worshipper of God, and doeth his will, him he heareth.

36. 2 Corinthians 1:3—Blessed be God, even the Father of our Lord Jesus Christ, the Father of mercies, and the God of all comfort;

37. Psalm 63:1—O God, thou art my God; early will I seek thee: my soul thirsteth for thee, my flesh longeth for thee in a dry and thirsty land, where no water is.

38. Deuteronomy 22:5—The woman shall not wear that which pertaineth unto a man, neither shall a man put on a woman's garment: for all that do so are abomination unto the LORD thy God.

39. Exodus 33:17—And the LORD said unto Moses, I will do this thing also that thou hast spoken: for thou hast found grace in my sight, and I know thee by name.

40. Psalm 90:2—Before the mountains were brought forth, or ever thou hadst formed the earth and the world, even from everlasting to everlasting, thou art God.

41. Ecclesiastes 8:12—Though a sinner do evil an hundred times, and his days be prolonged, yet surely I know that it shall be well with them that fear God, which fear before him.

42. Colossians 3:17—And whatsoever ye do in word or deed, do all in the name of the Lord Jesus, giving thanks to God and the Father by him.

43. 2 Peter 2:9—The Lord knoweth how to deliver the godly out of temptations, and to reserve the unjust unto the day of judgment to be punished.

44. Jude 21—Keep yourselves in the love of God, looking for the mercy of our Lord Jesus Christ unto eternal life.

45. Mark 10:27—And Jesus looking upon them saith, With men it is impossible, but not with God: for with God all things are possible.

46. Lamentations 3:26—It is good that a man should both hope and quietly wait for the salvation of the Lord.

47. Obadiah 15—For the day of the LORD is near upon all the heathen: as thou hast done, it shall be done unto thee: thy reward shall return upon thine own head.

48. John 17:3—And this is life eternal, that they might know thee the only true God, and Jesus Christ, whom thou hast sent.

49. 1 Timothy 2:1—I exhort therefore, that, first of all, supplications, prayers, intercessions, and giving of thanks, be made for all men.

50. 3 John 11—Beloved, follow not that which is evil, but that which is good. He that doeth good is of God: but he that doeth evil hath not seen God.

51. Psalm 125:3—For the rod of the wicked shall not rest upon the lot of the righteous; lest the righteous put forth their hands unto iniquity.

52. Numbers 23:19—God is not a man, that he should lie; neither the son of man, that he should repent: hath he said, and shall he not do it? or hath he spoken, and shall he not make it good?

53. 1 Kings 8:61—Let your heart therefore be perfect with the Lord our God, to walk in his statutes, and to keep his commandments, as at this day.

54. Proverbs 25:21—If thine enemy be hungry, give him bread to eat; and if he be thirsty, give him water to drink.

55. Luke 15:10—Likewise, I say unto you, there is joy in the presence of the angels of God over one sinner that repenteth.

56. 1 Corinthians 1:27—But God hath chosen the foolish things of the world to confound the wise; and God hath chosen the weak things of the world to confound the things which are mighty.

57. 1 Timothy 6:10—For the love of money is the root of all evil: which while some coveted after, they have erred from the faith, and pierced themselves through with many sorrows.

58. Hebrews 12:28—Wherefore we receiving a kingdom which cannot be moved, let us have grace, whereby we may serve God acceptably with reverence and godly fear.

59. Deuteronomy 32:4—He is the Rock, his work is perfect: for all his ways are judgment: a God of truth and without iniquity, just and right is he.

60. Jeremiah 10:12—He hath made the earth by his power, he hath established the world by his wisdom, and hath stretched out the heavens by his discretion.

61. Psalm 27:5—For in the time of trouble he shall hide me in his pavilion: in the secret of his tabernacle shall he hide me; he shall set me up upon a rock.

62. Leviticus 27:30—And all the tithe of the land, whether of the seed of the land, or of the fruit of the tree, is the LORD'S: it is holy unto the LORD.

63. Genesis 2:18—And the LORD God said, It is not good that the man should be alone; I will make him an help meet for him.

64. Ecclesiastes 12:13—Let us hear the conclusion of the whole matter: Fear God, and keep his commandments: for this is the whole duty of man.

65. Mark 8:35—For whosoever will save his life shall lose it; but whosoever shall lose his life for my sake and the gospel's, the same shall save it.

66. Luke 11:13—If ye then, being evil, know how to give good gifts unto your children: how much more shall your heavenly Father give the Holy Spirit to them that ask him?

67. John 19:19—And Pilate wrote a title, and put it on the cross. And the writing was, JESUS OF NAZARETH THE KING OF THE JEWS.

68. Isaiah 1:18—Come now, and let us reason together, saith the LORD: though your sins be as scarlet, they shall be as white as snow; though they be red like crimson, they shall be as wool.

69. Psalm 51:1—Have mercy upon me, O God, according to thy lovingkindness: according unto the multitude of thy tender mercies blot out my transgressions.

70. 2 Corinthians 5:10—For we must all appear before the judgment seat of Christ; that every one may receive the things done in his body, according to that he hath done, whether it be good or bad.

71. 1 Timothy 6:17—Charge them that are rich in this world, that they be not highminded, nor trust in uncertain riches, but in the living God, who giveth us richly all things to enjoy.

72. Jeremiah 32:17—Ah Lord God! behold, thou hast made the heaven and the earth by thy great power and stretched out arm, and there is nothing too hard for thee.

73. Psalm 28:7—The LORD is my strength and my shield; my heart trusted in him, and I am helped: therefore my heart greatly rejoiceth; and with my song will I praise him.

74. Exodus 15:11—Who is like unto thee, O LORD, among the gods? who is like thee, glorious in holiness, fearful in praises, doing wonders?

75. Romans 3:12—They are all gone out of the way, they are together become unprofitable; there is none that doeth good, no, not one.

76. Colossians 2:8—Beware lest any man spoil you through philosophy and vain deceit, after the tradition of men, after the rudiments of the world, and not after Christ.

77. Ephesians 6:4—And, ye fathers, provoke not your children to wrath: but bring them up in the nurture and admonition of the Lord.

78. Ecclesiastes 5:10—He that loveth silver shall not be satisfied with silver; nor he that loveth abundance with increase: this is also vanity.

79. Deuteronomy 15:11—For the poor shall never cease out of the land: therefore I command thee, saying, Thou shalt open thine hand wide unto thy brother, to thy poor, and to thy needy, in thy land.

80. Amos 5:14—Seek good, and not evil, that ye may live: and so the LORD, the God of hosts, shall be with you, as ye have spoken.

81. Romans 1:16—For I am not ashamed of the gospel of Christ: for it is the power of God unto salvation to every one that believeth; to the Jew first, and also to the Greek.

82. I Peter 2:15—For so is the will of God, that with well doing ye may put to silence the ignorance of foolish men.

83. Job 5:17—Behold, happy is the man whom God correcteth: therefore despise not thou the chastening of the Almighty.

84. Jeremiah 17:5—Thus saith the LORD; Cursed be the man that trusteth in man, and maketh flesh his arm, and whose heart departeth from the LORD.

85. Mark 16:9—Now when Jesus was risen early the first day of the week, he appeared first to Mary Magdalene, out of whom he had cast seven devils.

86. Galatians 3:13—Christ hath redeemed us from the curse of the law, being made a curse for us: for it is written, cursed is every one that hangeth on a tree.

87. Ephesians 4:32—And be ye kind one to another, tenderhearted, forgiving one another, even as God for Christ's sake hath forgiven you.

88. Genesis 6:13—And God said unto Noah, The end of all flesh is come before me; for the earth is filled with violence through them; and, behold, I will destroy them with the earth.

89. Psalm 25:7—Remember not the sins of my youth, nor my transgressions: according to thy mercy remember thou me for thy goodness' sake, O LORD.

90. Jonah 3:10—And God saw their works, that they turned from their evil way; and God repented of the evil, that he had said that he would do unto them; and he did it not.

Spotty Headline Puzzles

	Missing Letters	Hidden Name		Missing Letters	Hidden Name
1.	NASOSM	Samson	31.	ARHSA	Sarah
2.	HONA	Noah	32.	SAICS	Issac
3.	IDVDA	David	33.	NHSMAEAS	Manasseh
4.	BARMAHA	Abraham	34.	ZLEEEJB	Jezebel
5.	SALU	Saul	35.	AAANNM	Naaman
6.	AEDLIN	Daniel	36.	AREOJHM	Jehoram
7.	MDAA	Adam	37.	MEOSS	Moses
8.	SEOMS	Moses	38.	OJB	Job
9.	JHAEIERM	Jeremiah	39.	MLESUETHHA	Methuselah
10.	ICNA	Cain	40.	ONJAH	Jonah
11.	OHPJSE	Joseph	41.	AHANHN	Hannah
12.	NOLOMOS	Solomon	42.	HEIARZACH	Zechariah
13.	HGAIGA	Haggai	43.	EDGION	Gideon
14.	RIZAEHHCA	Zechariah	44.	ZZNHUBECDARAEN	Nebuchadnezzar
15.	ABMHAAR	Abraham	45.	DIDAV	David
16.	RSETHE	Esther	46.	TNOHBA	Naboth
17.	OMANI	Naomi	47.	AALMBA	Balaam
18.	AJUSOH	Joshua	48.	ZREA	Ezra
19.	BAJCO	Jacob	49.	CEBLA	Caleb
20.	SUEA	Esau	50.	LDIALEH	Delilah
21.	OLT	Lot	51.	INGDOE	Gideon
22.	EKEAHRB	Rebekah	52.	EJLA	Jael
23.	EIADNL	Daniel	53.	EZZBSRHAAL	Belshazzar
24.	ZKHAEHEI	Hezekiah	54.	HPARHOA	Pharaoh
25.	MLOOSON	Solomon	55.	HIAASI	Isaiah
26.	EMSOS	Moses	56.	LARSEI	Israel
27.	DGO	God	57.	MHNAA	Haman
28.	JLEAIH	Elijah	58.	EEV	Eve
29.	JSOHAI	Josiah	59.	BJCAO	Jacob
30.	CJOAB	Jacob	60.	UEALMS	Samuel

BIBLE QUOTATION PUZZLES

JOHN 1:4—In him was life; and the life was the light of men.

ISAIAH 12:5—Sing unto the LORD; for he hath done excellent things: this is known in all the earth.

3 JOHN 4—I have no greater joy than to hear that my children walk in truth.

REVELATION 22:12—And, behold, I come quickly; and my reward is with me, to give every man according as his work shall be.

ECCLESIASTES 3:1—To every thing there is a season, and a time to every purpose under the heaven.

ISAIAH 59:1—Behold, the LORD'S hand is not shortened, that it cannot save; neither his ear heavy, that it cannot hear.

EXODUS 20:3—Thou shalt have no other gods before me.

PSALM 145:1—I will extol thee, my God, O king; and I will bless thy name for ever and ever.

JOHN 6:47—Verily, verily, I say unto you, He that believeth on me hath everlasting life.

HABAKKUK 3:18—Yet I will rejoice in the LORD, I will joy in the God of my salvation.

PROVERBS 15:1—A soft answer turneth away wrath: but grievous words stir up anger.

MATTHEW 11:29—Take my yoke upon you, and learn of me; for I am meek and lowly in heart: and ye shall find rest unto your souls.

PROVERBS 2:20—That thou mayest walk in the way of good men, and keep the paths of the righteous.

JUDE 2—Mercy unto you, and peace, and love, be multiplied.

PSALM 76:4—Thou art more glorious and excellent than the mountains of prey.

LUKE 14:11—For whosoever exalteth himself shall be abased; and he that humbleth himself shall be exalted.

HEBREWS 13:8—Jesus Christ the same yesterday, and to day, and for ever.

JAMES 1:8—A double minded man is unstable in all his ways.

JOB 23:10—But he knoweth the way that I take: when he hath tried me, I shall come forth as gold.

ROMANS 12:17—Recompense to no man evil for evil. Provide things honest in the sight of all men.

HEBREWS 3:15—While it is said, To day if ye will hear his voice, harden not your hearts, as in the provocation.

PSALM 133:1—Behold, how good and how pleasant it is for brethren to dwell together in unity!

LUKE 2:14—Glory to God in the highest, and on earth peace, good will toward men.

JONAH 2:7—When my soul fainted within me I remembered the LORD: and my prayer came in unto thee, into thine holy temple.

JOHN 1:5—And the light shineth in darkness; and the darkness comprehended it not.

PROVERBS 15:33—The fear of the LORD is the instruction of wisdom; and before honour is humility.

JAMES 5:8—Be ye also patient; stablish your hearts: for the coming of the Lord draweth nigh.

ISAIAH 60:1—Arise, shine; for thy light is come, and the glory of the LORD is risen upon thee.

PSALM 70:1—Make haste, O God, to deliver me; make haste to help me, O LORD.

PSALM 119:10—With my whole heart have I sought thee: O let me not wander from thy commandments.

PSALM 121:1—I will lift up mine eyes unto the hills, from whence cometh my help.

PROVERBS 9:10—The fear of the LORD is the beginning of wisdom: and the knowledge of the holy is understanding.

LUKE 2:11—For unto you is born this day in the city of David a Saviour, which is Christ the Lord.

I SAMUEL 12:24—Only fear the Lord, and serve him in truth with all your heart: for consider how great things he hath done for you.

JOEL 2:21—Fear not, O land; be glad and rejoice: for the LORD will do great things.

PSALM 145:9—The Lord is good to all: and his tender mercies are over all his works.

PROVERBS 16:7—When a man's ways please the LORD, he maketh even his enemies to be at peace with him.

PROVERBS 22:6—Train up a child in the way he should go: and when he is old, he will not depart from it.

I SAMUEL 2:2—There is none holy as the LORD: for there is none beside thee: neither is there any rock like our God.

GENESIS 27:8—Now therefore, my son, obey my voice according to that which I command thee.

EPHESIANS 6:11—Put on the whole armour of God, that ye may be able to stand against the wiles of the devil.

PSALM 91:1—He that dwelleth in the secret place of the most High shall abide under the shadow of the Almighty.

JOHN 10:11—I am the good shepherd: the good shepherd giveth his life for the sheep.

EPHESIANS 2:8—For by grace are ye saved through faith; and that not of yourselves: it is the gift of God.

Telephone Scramble Puzzles

ALLEGORIES
HAGAR
LIONESS
SARAH
VINE
VINEYARD

PRISONERS
HOSHEA
JOSEPH
PAUL
PETER
SAMSON
SILAS
SIMEON

GENEALOGIES
ABRAHAM
ESAU
ISAAC
JESUS
JOSEPH
MARY
SIMEON

MEASUREMENTS
BUSHEL
CUBIT
DENARIUS
DRACHMA
OMER
SHEKEL
TALENT

ANIMALS IN THE OLD TESTAMENT
ASP
CAMEL
DOVE
EAGLE
FISH
GOAT
LAMB

OFFERINGS
GOAT
GRAIN
LAMB
MEAL
MEAT
OIL
SON

CONVERSIONS IN THE OLD TESTAMENT
ABRAHAM
CYRUS
DARIUS
DAVID
JACOB
RUTH
SAMUEL

CITY WALLS
BETHSHAN
DAMASCUS
JERICHO
JERUSALEM
MOAB
RABBAH
SAMARIA

GOD KNOWS OUR...
DEEDS
FRAILTIES
NEEDS
SORROWS
THOUGHTS
WORDS

PRIESTS
AARON
ANANIAS
ANNAS
ELI
EZRA
JOSHUA
ZACHARIAS

JUDGES
ABDON
DEBORAH
EHUD
GIDEON
JAIR
OTHNIEL
TOLA

DEACONS
NICANOR
NICOLAS
PARMENAS
PHILIP
PROCHORUS
STEPHEN
TIMON

AUTHORS
  DAVID
  JOHN
  JOSHUA
  LUKE
  MATTHEW
  SAMUEL
  SOLOMON

BOOKS OF THE OLD TESTAMENT
  DANIEL
  ESTHER
  GENESIS
  JEREMIAH
  NUMBERS
  PROVERBS
  PSALMS

FOODS IN THE NEW TESTAMENT
  ANISE
  VEAL
  FISH
  MINT
  MUSTARD

MOUNTAINS
  ARARAT
  CARMEL
  HOR
  HOREB
  MORIAH
  OLIVE
  SINAI

PEOPLE IN THE OLD TESTAMENT
  AARON
  DAVID
  ELIJAH
  ELISHA
  JACOB
  MOSES
  SOLOMON

HEAVEN IS A PLACE OF...
  ANGELS
  BEAUTY
  ETERNITY
  HOLINESS
  JOY
  PERFECTION
  UNITY

CURSED
  CAIN
  CANAAN
  GROUND
  JEHOIACHIN
  NATURE
  SERPENT

ANAGRAM PUZZLES

Books of the Bible: Leviticus
Bible Cities: Bethany
Paul's Missionary Journeys: Antioch
Women of the Bible: Martha
Places: Golgotha
Rivers/Bodies of Water: Euphrates (Genesis 2:14)
More Books of the Bible: Exodus
New Testament People: Eutychus (Acts 20:9)
Bad Guys: Antichrist
Bible Cities: Sodom
Kings: Nebuchadnezzar
Events: Transfiguration
Books of the Bible: Revelation
Women of the Bible: Rebekah
Places: Macedonia

Even More Books of the Bible: Ecclesiastes
Bible Cities: Jerusalem
New Testament People: Sanhedrin (Acts 22:30)
Even More Books of the Bible: Ephesians
Events: Passover
Books of the Bible: Numbers
Bible Cities: Jericho
Bad Guys: Pontius Pilate
New Testament People: Onesimus
More Books of the Bible: Colossians
Women of the Bible: Delilah
Events: Last Supper
Even More Books of the Bible: Malachi
Women of the Bible: Elisabeth
Kings: Agrippa